PUT YOUR HEART ON PAPER

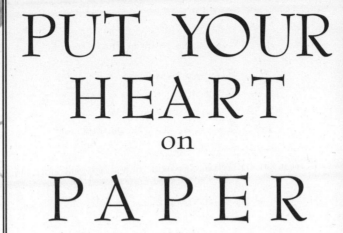

PUT YOUR HEART on PAPER

Staying Connected in a Loose-Ends World

Henriette Anne Klauser

BANTAM BOOKS
New York Toronto London Sydney Auckland

PUT YOUR HEART ON PAPER

A Bantam Book / September 1995

Grateful acknowledgment is made for permission to reprint from the following: Rabbi Jack Riemer,
Guides to Ethical Wills, Personal Growth. Originally produced for the United Jewish Appeal,
Young Leadership Cabinet, by the National Jewish Conference Center, New York.
Copyright © 1978 by National Jewish Conference Center.

Library of Congress Cataloging-in-Publication Data
Klauser, Henriette Anne.
Put your heart on paper : staying connected in a loose-ends world
/ Henriette Anne Klauser.
p.   cm.
ISBN 0-553-37446-X
1. Self-disclosure.   2. Self-disclosure—Case studies.   3. Letter
writing—Psychological aspects.   4. Interpersonal communication.
5. Interpersonal relations.   I. Title.
BF697.5.S427K57   1995
158—dc20   95-8739
CIP

Published simultaneously in the United States and Canada

PRINTED IN THE UNITED STATES OF AMERICA

FFG   10 9 8 7 6 5 4 3 2 1

An author dedicates a book to those who brought life to that project, those to whom the author can honestly say, Without you, there would be no book. I dedicate this book, with love and wonder, to my sons, James and Peter, to my daughters, Emily and Katherine. I owe you my life, not the other way around.

CONTENTS

Contents

AN INTRODUCTION
and *Thank You*

ONE GORGEOUS AUTUMN DAY, WITH THE BLUEST SKIES YOU ever saw glistening all around, I board the Bremerton ferry to escape and write. As I travel the sea lanes back and forth across Puget Sound, I notice a good-natured fellow pushing a broom and emptying the garbage each time we pull into port. He is whistling some tune. He stops to talk.

"You're working hard."

"So are you."

He tells me a little about himself. His name is John. He has three children, ages five to fourteen. In answer to his question, I say that I am working on a book about how anyone can use writing to get close and stay close to people they love. In it, I tell stories about people who have used writing to heal hurts, to celebrate joys, and to communicate with each other on a deep level—even if they've never written much of anything before.

He looks pensive for a moment, and then blurts out, "Hurry up and write your book. I don't know how to reach my teenage daughter. Hurry up and write your book. I need it."

So here it is, John—for you, and for all the people like you who sometimes feel disconnected in this fast-paced world of ours. Getting reconnected is as simple as a piece of paper and as near as your pen.

*   *   *

Every single story in this book is true. The people are all real, and most of them wanted me to use their real names. (A few names have been changed for privacy.) They come from normal families with ordinary lives, as rushed and chaotic as yours or mine. These families do not spend their nights sitting by the fire making corn-husk dolls. They do not spend every waking hour writing to each other. But writing has given each one a new sense of belonging.

Some of the stories, as you'll see, come from my family—you'll get to know all of us quite well—and many of them come from the people who over the years have taken my writing workshops or who wrote to me after reading my first book.

Once I started this book, I became a magnet attracting stories; I was radioactive, sending out signals, and the people I needed to meet and the stories I needed to hear came up and tapped me on the shoulder. My writing comes alive when I take it out of the house, out of the office, away from the desk; even now, as I write this, I am sitting in a café—it is almost midnight—and life is happening all around me. Often as I was struggling for just the right word or example, the conversation at an adjacent table would suddenly come into focus and gave me just what I needed.

The people I met not only gave me their stories, they blessed my work in daily, unexpected ways, sometimes without even realizing the boost they provided. Once when I was sitting in dark café, hunched over my Powerbook and notebooks, the espresso *barista,* who had been taking the trash out to the back lot, stopped by my table and grabbed my hand.

"C'mere. You've *got* to see this. You've been working hard enough. Come."

Startled, I left my computer, my coat, and all my paperwork on the table and followed his lead through the storeroom, out to the dumpster. Was it an animal curled up asleep that he wanted me to see?

Triumphant, he pointed to the sky with a sweep of his hand.

"*Look* at that sunset! You just had to see it. Now you can go back to work."

Moments like that were like a sign; they kept me believing.

This book about connections would not exist without the connections in my own life. First, my family:

- Jim, my husband, resourceful, creative, unstoppable, who has some of the same people skills that I notice in our children—the apple doesn't fall very far from the tree. He is also the behind-the-scenes genius, who spent hours and hours and uncounted hours on the computer, formatting and printing and making the manuscript workable.
- Our firstborn, James, imaginative, original, and adventurous, with uncompromising loyalty to family and friends, who will not accept the answer "Nothing" to the question "What's wrong?"
- Peter is the next in line, with a wit that keeps us all going. He is good-natured and gregarious; a good listener and a romantic, he teaches me how to listen and love.
- Vivacious Emily lights up a room with her energy and positive attitude ("Whatever it is, take it as a compliment.") She is self-confident with a natural grace that puts others at ease, adults and children alike. The other side of Emily is the thinker and the planner, the charger, the go-getter. She can negotiate anything.
- Sweet Katherine, with her smile and her hugs, is affectionate and loving and sticks up for her friends. Katherine is sensitive and sharp, keen to notice others' needs. She says the wisest things.

I thank my husband, my sons and daughters, for all their support, and for their willingness to let me tell their tales here in the generous hope that the telling might be of service to others.

I am grateful to Worldwide Marriage Encounter for showing me the power of communicating through writing and for bringing into my life people who have the integrity to live by their convictions. Thanks, too, to all those who promised to pray for me, especially Deanna Lucas and Gerrie Kasper, who kept it up, and each and every one of you who shared your stories—some funny, some sad, all courageous. You are my heroes.

A heartfelt thanks as well to those who cheered me on when I needed it most:

- To my young neighbor, Alicia Hovland, and her cousin Adam Hovland. When I came down to the last fourteen chapters, they made me a glorious construction-paper chain, one link more imaginative than the next, and assisted me gleefully in tearing them off one at a time as I neared completion.

• To Nancy Skinner Nordoff, who has created a place for women writers at Hedgebrook Farms on Whidbey Island. She taught me about the importance of pacing and in her nurturing of me allowed me time to nurture ideas.

• To Bob Barnes, M.D., for sharing the agony and the ecstasy, for running alongside me as I run alongside him. Your book is next, Bob.

• To Joey Johnson, whose own relentless dedication inspired mine.

• To Toni Burbank, my brilliant editor, who lived this book along with me and used its concepts with her own family.

• To Shelley Roth, my agent and now friend, who held my hand throughout this project and then asked the magic question, What will we do next?

• To Natalie Goldberg. Reflecting back her own haunting image in *Long Quiet Highway:* she is a burr now in my clothing ("Go on, take us with you, carry us to root in another place"), and I like to think she has a bit of me—and my family—in the hem of her garments as well.

And, finally, thanks and thanks and ever thanks to the *baristas* who "pull" the espresso and those who brew the tea, and the patient proprietors of all the places where I hang out and write, especially:

• Vivace Roasteria Cafe ("una bella tazza di caffe"). I especially love to be there on roasting days, drinking coffee that tastes as good as it smells, watching Daniel wave the temperature tester cone next to his cheek like a dance—the Zen of roasting. Mostly, I sit at the high windows with the view out to the reservoir and its fountain. Thanks to those who make the caffes lattes with the velvet foam and who make my day brighter with their news and friendliness: to Todd and Mary, Andy, Lisa, Amy, Katy—wiser than her years—and David Schomer, owner and writer himself, who designed the place to be hospitable to writers, with power outlets along the wide window ledges.

• The Big Moose, tucked in the corner of the campus at Seattle University, where the customers and servers alike challenge my mind with their intellect and thinking commentary, especially Don and Mira and Liz.

• Teahouse Kuan Yin, "a tea drinking establishment," where I can sit with a single pot of tea for three hours or more, and listen to the pockets of involved conversation around, and hear the sitar music and smell the rich Cameronian and ginger blend, and have Miranda's warm welcome in five different languages. Sometimes a "good fairy" hides a chocolate-dipped almond tea cake under the lid of my tea cup.

• Capons chicken place, across the street, where Aaron, Stacy, Sasha, Dave, John, and Britt always make me feel welcome and save my table in the corner by the brick wall, even when all I'm ordering is a diet Coke (with lemon).

• And thanks to the captains and crews of the Washington State ferries M. V. *Hyak* and the M. V. *Yakima,* where the background music is sea gulls and the giant heart throb of the mighty engines. Riding on the ferry puts both motion and steadiness in my writing, power as well as peace. And it lets me meet people like John.

I like to say this is not a "how-to" book but a "why bother" book. In every instance, I have tried to show why it was worthwhile for the people in the story to do what they did, and why it would be worth your time to follow their example—in your own way.

A newsletter I picked up while browsing at The Tattered Cover Bookstore in Denver gave me this provocative quote from Hanna More:

"The world does not require so much to be informed as to be reminded."

I am not here to give you something you don't yet have, but rather to encourage you to use what is already there.

This is not a passive, curl-up-by-the-fire book. I want these stories to take the top off your head—that's how I felt when I heard some of them for the first time. I want you to read one chapter, any chapter, and then put the book down because you are so excited you can't wait to put that plan in motion. Why, I could do that. You mean, it's that simple, that much fun?

And then stop reading, run and grab your pen, and *do* it.

PUT YOUR HEART ON PAPER

1
Writing for Relationship

WHY WRITE? WHY WRITE TO PEOPLE YOU CAN TALK TO, TO PEOple you see perhaps every day? My good friend Peter Scharf asked me this point-blank when I first told him about my plan for this book. I showed Peter a letter that a fourteen-year-old boy had written to his six-year-old sister on her birthday. The father of this boy, who took my workshop, had sent this letter to me after asking his son's permission to share it. That letter, and the stories in this book, are the answer to Peter Scharf's question.

What is the difference between writing something and just saying it? In the case of the boy's letter, the message might never have been spoken, because the opportunity might not have been there and because there is a certain embarrassment about speaking out loud in tender terms to your sister. Writing gives you privacy, a chance to be yourself; it is safe. When you write, you can express yourself freely without interruption, without second-guessing the meaning of a lifted eyebrow or another gesture from the person you are communicating with, a gesture that might make you change your conversational horse in midstream. You can be tender, you can be funny, you can use big words if you want.

So maybe it was because of writing that the boy was able to say to his sister,

> *I'd like to compliment you on being so bright and cheerful throughout your first five years on this confusing planet. I think you are the smartest little sister a kid like me could ever have. I am so glad you were born.*

Writing Helps Heal

Writing can be like the biblical scapegoat, the beast of burden who carried the sins of the people into the wilderness, or the Peruvian "worry dolls" of today—give each one a worry and put them under your pillow, and they will take care of your worries for you. Writing helps you tell the truth; you can't be phony. A woman in a workshop summed it up: "When you see it on paper, you want it to be true. It's too painful to see the lie in writing." And when you write something down and look at it, look at the truth, you can often say, "I can live with that." Once you get it down on paper, you no longer need to be consumed by it, no longer need to let it eat up both time and energy. Now that it is in writing, it is no longer a concern; let the worry dolls and scapegoat of pen and paper carry it away.

When you write, you can say things that stick in your throat.

So this fourteen-year-old boy was also able to say, toward the end of his letter,

> *I would also like to say sorry for a number of things. Please forgive me for all the times I've been mean, hit you, left you out, or just said a nasty word. I am sorry and am willing to begin again. O.K.? Let's be friends. I love you with all my heart, and will always be there at your side when you need help.*

When you write, you make it easier for the other person to listen; writing creates a bond of trust. Now that he had her attention, the boy added an extra plea to his sister,

> *P.S. If you want to play with my birds, just ask, all right?*

Writing Is a Legacy

As we talked, my friend Peter Scharf remembered something. He remembered how he had found his father's diary after his mother died; his father had passed away several years before. The diary was a chronicle of Peter up to age fifteen. He knew it existed, but he had forgotten about it. Reading it again, after his mother's funeral, recreated a bond with his parents. He smiled to see the kind of simple things his father noted about him.

That is another thing about writing. It is a legacy. A piece of writing can be a voice speaking to you across the years, a connection with people perhaps no longer with you.

A close friend of mine grew up without his dad because his father committed suicide when my friend was nine years old. Very recently, he came across a love letter his dad wrote to his mother before they were married. It stunned him.

"What a difference it's made in my relationship with my father; the fact that I could read his love letter gave me a different image of him."

A Powerful Way of Knowing

It happens often when we sit down to write—we do not know what to say. The trick is to let the writing help us say it. The fourteen-year-old writing to his sister describes the phenomenon neatly.

> *When Dad told me to write in this nice blue book I had no idea of what to say. But now as I pick up a pencil with the book in my lap, it all pours out.*

Isn't that what happens to us, too? When you sit down to write with an open heart, you often wind up sharing what you did not even know you had to say.

You do not need to know the ending before you begin. In fact, there are times when you do not even know the beginning before you begin. Just begin. If you do not know how to start, write, "I don't know how to start this"—and *keep on writing*. If you are terrified of the opening sentence, start with the second sentence, and go back and write the opening sentence later. Go to your writing empty-handed, with the questions, and let the writing answer. As you write, the act of writing itself will help you uncover your ideas, let you know where to begin and when to end.

The lesson for the day on the reader board I passed on Aurora Avenue said, "It's what you know after you know it all that counts." Writing is one of the best ways I know to get at that knowing beyond knowing. How? Let go of rules; forget about punctuation and spelling and correct form. Just write. Change your mental schooling, which dictates that writing is an expression of ideas and concepts already formulated, and instead look at writing as exploration of thought, helping the ideas to take shape.

As a workshop participant once said to me, "This is exciting. I never knew I could let my writing help me think."

Be willing to let go of another school-taught idea: that writing happens while sitting up straight in a chair behind a desk. You can write anyplace. In the park. On a rock. In a restaurant, on a bus.

Writing behind a desk is about schoolwork. The kind of writing I am talking about here is not about schoolwork, it's about mind work and self-work, and relationship.

The Initiator

The fourteen-year-old letter writer did not come up with the idea to write a birthday letter to his sister by himself. It was his father who asked him to do it, who, in fact, handed the boy the book to write in and the pen. That did not make the letter he wrote any less special.

Sometimes you will be the one to thrust the paper under another's nose and hand them the pen.

You provide a forum, an occasion to which the other rises. A friend has a phrase I like that fits here: Make it a difference rather than a wrongdoing. It does not mean that you are a better person since you were the one to throw the first pitch. The others are heroes too, who fielded the ball. It is a gift and a skill to be the initiator, and at different times in life the role changes.

A woman I interviewed told me about letters her father has written to her that would not have come easily to him and how dear those letters are to her. Because her mother writes and sometimes hands the stationery to the father, it makes it easier for him to write—it paves the way. The letters from him are still a treasure.

Living a Life of Connection

Speaking from years of experience, an organization that sponsors students traveling overseas and staying with host families tells the anxious parents left behind, "Write to your son or daughter abroad. A letter they can read and reread and keep you with them. With a phone call, when you hang up, it's over."

When my husband, Jim, was in the Navy, he wrote letters to me and counted on me to pass on any news to his parents. When he wrote a letter directly to his dad, his father carried that letter proudly in his pocket for six months, until it was worn.

Putting your heart on paper is about so much more than writing; it is about living a life that is connected with others.

In *Writing Down the Bones*, Natalie Goldberg tells a story about a landlady she had in Israel. Natalie's Israeli landlady had a repairman come four times to fix the TV set. Natalie says she told her he could have brought the correct tube and fixed it immediately. "She looked at me in astonishment. 'Yes, but then we couldn't have had a relationship, sat and drunk tea and discussed the progress of the repairs.' "

Natalie sums it up, "Of course, the goal is not to fix a machine but to have relationships."

Write from the heart. It's not about writing, it's about relationship.

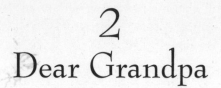

2
Dear Grandpa

MY FRIEND MATT TOLD ME HE WAS WORRIED ABOUT HIS GRAND-daughter, Rebecca. She was overweight, silent, lethargic. She watched TV all the time, and he thought she seemed so sad.

He filled me in on the family situation. Her mom, his daughter, and her dad were divorced; the dad rarely came to see her. The mom worked all the time, it seemed—two jobs—a daytime job and the night shift three times a week at the hospital. In between, she came home, fixed dinner, checked up on Rebecca, and headed out the door. Matt didn't blame his daughter. He knew what she was up against and how frantic she felt. It's just that he worried about Rebecca. She seemed distant and sullen, and he didn't know how to reach her.

One day Rebecca was visiting, and she typed little letters to him and to Grandma.

I want to work in the garden.

I'd like to take a walk with you.

Matt was astonished. Until she typed those plain little notes, he didn't know. He was delighted to walk with her, and soon they made it a regular routine. Grandma never realized that Rebecca thought gardening was anything but a chore. That plaintive note with its easy request opened up a whole world of working together in the garden, in the dirt, on their knees, side by side among the flowers that Grandma loved and the herbs she grew there.

Rebecca was able to type out what she could not bring herself to say out loud. Her world changed because of two simple notes.

Now You

Give a single piece of paper to someone in your life you are trying to reach. A message-cube piece of paper (three and a half inches square) is big enough. Tell him to type or write you a note with a single sentence, telling you something he would like to do with you. A single request: "I would like to . . ." or "I want to . . ."

This works both ways. If you can think of one small step that you wish a person you live with or love might take that would improve the quality of the life between you, write it on a scrap of paper to hand to her. "I want to . . ." "I would like you to . . ."

It might become a regular routine.

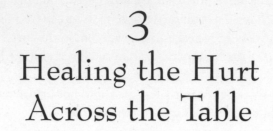

3
Healing the Hurt
Across the Table

W<small>E MET AT A COMMUNICATIONS WORKSHOP. SOMETIMES I WONDER</small> if Ken knows the impact that his story made on me. It crystallized a truth I had been elusively chasing for several years. The seeds of this book were planted in that conversation.

The story Ken told me was about his daughter Aria and him. They had not spoken for several days, maybe even a couple of weeks. Who knows what set them off? Maybe it was an argument about curfews or grades or hairstyles. The incident no longer mattered. It had become a matter of pride, of being right. They were at an impasse. Each one thought, "I'm not going to be the one to give in." There was a barricade between them, with the sandbags piling higher and deeper every day. Two good people were hurting each other, and neither one knew how to break through that hurt, let down that reserve, and get back in relationship again.

It was Ken who took the initiative to end the standoff. He wanted to take away the heaviness in his heart. He suggested that they go to McDonald's. When they got there, though, they were both still mad, and now hurt on top of the mad. Neither could speak, except perfunctory phrases about what to order and where to sit. Neither wanted to bring up the topic of the heavy feeling gnawing away inside them. Finally, Ken said, "If we can't talk, maybe we can write. Got any paper with you?" Aria reached inside her bag and pulled out a couple of pens and tore two sheets of lined paper from a school notebook. She shoved one sheet across the table to her dad. "You don't understand me!" she spat.

"You're right. I don't. Write me a letter to help me understand. Write down everything you're mad about. Fill the page. What's bugging you?"

Then he started to write too, and she wrote because he was writing. It was a struggle at first, and then it was like a runaway train. She let go of everything pent up inside. They sat across the table from each other, a daughter and her dad, two people who had not spoken to each other in days, and let it all come out on paper.

Ken said that what he first wrote was hostile, and then he started to soften. He remembered how they used to be such pals. She was "Daddy's girl" and would wait for him at the door, to run and give him a hug as soon as his car pulled into the driveway. Now she hid in her room, and if he asked her any questions, she answered with a monosyllable.

He looked up and said, "When you finish writing everything that's bugging you, write about what's going well." Again, they bent their heads over their papers and poured it out, oblivious to the other customers around.

Then they read each other's letters. Ken thought, "This is what it's like to walk in Aria's shoes."

The Big Macs got cold. The french fries got cold. They looked up at each other and smiled. Small smiles, but smiles nonetheless. Aria said, "Let's talk." They talked for two hours. Then they got up and went for a walk in the park and talked some more.

When Aria got home, she called her mom at work. She was crying.

Today, neither Ken nor Aria remembers what the fight was about; both of them remember "that time we were so mad we couldn't talk, and we went to McDonald's and wrote to each other." Both of them remember the healing.

One of the things that fascinates me about this story is the fact that they went to McDonald's to write. Because they changed the locale from home, they could be free, be true. They could let go of the dance, the familiar steps between them.

At home, the automatic, trained response kicks in. The "no daughter of mine will . . ." song, and the "my parents just don't understand" tune. A change of locale changes the music. It's okay to sing a different song.

Had Ken and Aria gone to a fancy restaurant, with tablecloths and candlelight, the father might still be superior; the daughter, one down, feeling like a little kid. McDonald's was the great equalizer. There they could both be kids.

And because they wrote out their hurt, they could suspend the "Oh, yeah? Well, *you* . . ." that escalates a verbal argument out of control. And because they wrote past the anger, what also came out was the part they now remember. She missed him. He missed her. There was a longing there to reconnect, a wanting to be close again, but not knowing quite how to do it without compromise, without giving in. A paper duel at McDonald's was how.

Now You

A change of locale can provide a change of dynamic. Think of someplace nonthreatening, like a fast-food place, where the distinctions of authority are blurred. Not one-up, one-down, but two human beings, ordering french fries, and writing, being true.

4
Landmark Birthdays

IT STARTED OUT AS A GIFT FOR HIM; IT TURNED OUT TO BE A GIFT for us. My uncle Dan was celebrating his eightieth birthday, and we wanted to do something special. We asked his wife of fifty-three years, my aunt Mary, to send us a list of neighbors, friends, cronies, and relatives. We also asked her to tell us, Who are his heroes alive today? His favorite columnist? What sports does he follow, and who are his favorite teams? Out went letters, asking each for a birthday greeting. We told the celebrities he was a fan of theirs and how much it would mean to him to hear from them; for those who knew him, we suggested two avenues of thought: Tell a funny story or adventure, and include the qualities they most admired in him. We asked people to write the letters to him, but send them care of us, to go in a scrapbook. The letters could be as long as they liked, but we asked them to keep them on one side of each page.

The letters poured in by every possible transmittal—fax, overnight express, priority mail, dictated by phone; stop the presses, stop the pasteup, here's one from the president. The styles spanned the ages; each presentation said something about the person who had penned it, from the spidery hand of the neighbor of forty-six years to the carefully printed note from a grandniece of ten; from the broken e's, the faint g's, and the wonderfully archaic Wite-Out on the typewritten tale from the fellow FBI agent, to the crisp computer-generated shadow boxes and modern fonts from the granddaughter in California. One letter smelled funny and faintly familiar. I sniffed again. No mistake—this stationery had been packed in mothballs. There was some formal language ("Dear Dan and to whom it may concern . . ."; "We want to be included among those expressing congratulations to you at this time . . .") and lots of funny stories. We wondered, was it true that he had climbed out onto a twenty-sixth-floor ledge of the Federal Building in New York City in a frantic attempt to recapture a top-secret teletype that had blown out an unscreened window and was floating down to Foley Square? And just while we were smiling at such an image, something sentimental and personal would make us cry. After teasing him for his long letters "measured by the pound, not the pages" and his expert opinion delivered on a wide range of topics, what it came down to was,

> *You and I have been friends and associates for nearly fifty years. Don't ever change, Dan, I like you just the way you are.*

The advice from fellow octogenarians was priceless: Become outrageous, because now you can get away with being an official eccentric:

> *Most are in awe of your achievement. While they are awed, hit 'em hard with your new authority. Proclaim early that you are now the Godfather and hence all powerful. Cultivate the posture and performance of an eccentric. The worst that can happen to you is that people will regard you as they do me. I wear old work clothes and skip a few days shaving to confirm my local standing.*

We laughed out loud at the sheer joy of receiving a personal postcard from William Safire. Who better than the master linguist himself could sum up, in two words, both the glory of the occasion and a prescription for life from this point on:

> *Embrace octogenarianism!*

As we opened each letter and pasted it into a big blank book, we smiled. We felt good all over. We were having as much fun with this as we knew Uncle Dan himself would. We took delight in the well-turned phrases, the elegant language of his contemporaries, the entertaining advice and amusing anecdotes. Mostly, we took delight in the picture that emerged of a man I have loved since I was a little girl. The same compliments, the same themes came up—the family man, the patriot, the Adonis on the beach, the young man playing touch football on East Twenty-eighth Street, and later, the man in his seventies, still going all out for a two-sewer pass. The grandpa riding his mountain bike with the grandkids to Rockaway Beach. The good neighbor who lends his tools and keeps his lawn immaculate. The good friend who drove four hours to upstate New York to rescue a new bride and groom when the groom got ill, a drop-everything kindness still cherished fifty-four years later.

The notes made me cry, because they brought back a flood of memories of my own, memories of an uncle who made wooden toys for us at Christmas, who formed the Camera Club for his own children and his nieces and nephews and took us for photo-opportunity outings at Prospect Park. He made us feel important as we set off jauntily with our Brownie box cameras and his light meter, and he showed us how to look for shadows and the play of sun on the squirrels standing still.

Uncle Dan was thrilled when we presented him with the collection. He wrote personal notes to thank each of those, including the six living presidents, who had written him. Then he wrote a thank you to us:

Being eighty is great; look at all the nice people I got out of it.

A Week's Worth of Good Wishes

The idea for Uncle Dan's scrapbook was a variation on an idea I got from Nancy, a friend who lives in Texas. Her father-in-law, Wilbur, lives in Ohio. When Wilbur turned eighty, Nancy and her husband, Eric, couldn't be there for the celebration. That made it even more important to do something that would join in the fun and let Wilbur know how much they cared. Nancy set her cap to let the mails bring Wilbur eighty letters or cards, starting with some from famous people. By the time you turn eighty or celebrate your fiftieth wedding anniversary, you have earned official recognition. Upon request, the White House Greeting Department will send a card from the president. Nancy had a neat extension of that.

She wrote to Mike Royko, Wilbur's favorite columnist; she wrote to Mike Ditka, the coach of the Chicago Bears. The letters Nancy sent to the celebrities were "slanted toward each one in terms of Wilbur's relationship with them." She told them something about Wilbur, about how he had read Mike Royko for years, rooted for the Cubs even when they were down. To Royko, she mentioned that Wilbur was a wonderful storyteller: "You would love to hear him spin a yarn, like the one about the family bulldog who took a bite from the mailman's pants."

She told the politicians he admired that Wilbur was an upstanding member of the community who had served in the armed forces in World War II and was a role model for his family of community involvement.

Next, Nancy sent a letter to each of her own and Eric's friends. She went down the whole Christmas list and asked their friends to send a birthday card to Eric's dad. I was one of the people asked and was happy to comply. Many of their friends had met Wilbur over the years of knowing Eric and Nancy. Those who hadn't, wrote and shared their relationship with Eric and the stories they had heard about his father. Nancy's goal was for Wilbur to get eighty cards; the fifty-five that came tickled him. The friends' cards flooded in during his birthday week, with the celebrity cards interspersed. Nancy had sent the celebrities cards already stamped and addressed to Wilbur; all they had to do was sign and mail. Several of them wrote personal notes as well. Mike Royko's began, "Here's looking at you, kid." Most of the cards from friends of the family had letters too; many referred to Eric. Wilbur told Nancy, "I got such a kick out of that, hearing those stories about my son and knowing what I had meant in his life."

Wilbur was delighted. He never knew what the day's mail would bring, and he walked around all morning with a smile on his face. He said gleefully, "This is the best birthday present I've ever had."

For the Next Generation

Celebrating a landmark birthday can be a legacy for the next generation, to remind them of their roots. One of Uncle Dan's sons, a grown man with children of his own, wrote in his birthday letter to his dad:

Some of my own earliest and happiest memories are of family summer vacations: the swimming hole, Monopoly, penny candy, Kool-Aid, the bugler blowing taps at Gardner's Bay.

He went on to affectionately describe the fishing, the evening softball games, the sound and smell of coal-fueled trains, and he said in conclusion:

These memories have caused me to make family vacations an important part of my children's lives.

I can still picture the look on my dad's face when he opened the gift of letters we gave him for his seventieth birthday, and then tenderly read each letter, turning the pages as tears fell, laughing out loud and smiling throughout. It was a book he returned to and reread many times before his death, and now it is something we treasure in his memory. I like to read the letters to my children, especially to Emily, who was too young to know him well, and to Katherine, who was born after he died. It is a joy to read about his exploits and the great love that people had for him.

Now You

Landmark birthdays. Occasions for celebrating not only the day but the life of the person. You can bet that the birthday person is stopping to take stock. It's something we do at every birthday but most especially at the biggies. These are the questions the celebrant is asking: What have I done with my life? How will I spend the years left ahead? Have I made a difference?

What better time for you to organize the troops, to help provide the answers? What better time to write, not only of your own caring, but to gather together the caring of others?

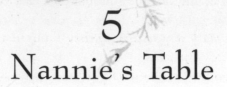

5
Nannie's Table

MARY ANN AND BILL BOYLAN ARE THE HEAD COUPLE FOR MAR-riage Encounter, a movement based on couples writing to each other. I wrote to them in Pennsylvania to ask if they could share with me the names of any families that had used this writing-and-sharing method with their children. Mary Ann wrote back with a story about their own family. It had to do with a beach house and with Mary Ann's mother, whom the children called Nannie.

"Let me tell you a little bit about my mother," said Mary Ann. "Dad died when I was eighteen, my mother was a widow at forty-seven. She had a lot of spirit, she was a spunky lady—she had to be. She had four kids to raise, one retarded. My mother was courageous. In those days, people kept retarded children under wraps. Not her. She had a little school to teach my brother and other kids like him."

Nannie wasn't at all the apple-pie-baking kind of grandma.

"The kids liked my mother 'cause she marched to a different drumbeat. She was their crusader. She'd wink at bad grades, always champion their good points."

Nannie had a beach place located in North Wildwood, New Jersey, southwest of Philadelphia, on the bay. Mary Ann and her brothers and sisters went there every year.

"We grew up there during the summer. We learned how to swim, to become comfortable with water."

After Bill and Mary Ann married, they brought their own children there. It was a relaxing place.

"It has a nautical feel to it—in fact, it used to be a boat house, an old boat house right on the water. No back door. You could jump out the window to the water, and at times we worried the kids would. It had horizontal wood strips in a very dark rich boaty look.

"It's not a fancy place, not the kind of place I would picture the Kennedys have. There was no dishwasher."

The Table

The kitchen was little, the dining room fairly small, but in the middle was a great big table, with five leaves, ten feet long. It was a huge table, toward which everybody gravitated. In many ways, the table was the center of the house.

"Everyone had a place around it. That was important: You knew there was room for you there. It could easily sit a dozen. Nannie bought it at an auction. Sometimes at dinner, we would play a little game, 'Say something nice about the person to your right,' and then each person, all around the table, would come up with a compliment for the person next to them."

Meals were noisy; everybody talked at once, and nobody was listening, yet they all felt heard and included and had a sense of belonging. After dinner, they would play cards to see who did the dishes. The two who lost did the dishes.

"We would play a cold hand of poker. Bill would spread out the cards and announce, 'Pot's right and the cards are coming.' The pot was the dishes."

The table was a place where the family gathered, not just for meals but for Scrabble, and Monopoly, and cards with Nannie—Rummy Royal and a little Old Maid. There was no TV and no radio, so long games were welcome.

So it seemed fitting that the table was where they came now, now that

Nannie had died and Mary Ann and Bill had decided to sell the place. She had been sick for a long time, and it had gotten run-down.

"During the long months of my mom's illness, who had time to think about the house at the beach? It was in bad shape."

They came to fix it up, to put it on the market, and to take one last time to sit around the table as a family. Bill, Mary Ann, and their four children, ages ten to fifteen, sat down, and Mary Ann passed out paper.

"Around my mother's table, we all wrote letters about how we felt."

Maybe it was some magic in the table itself, the scene of so many happy and boisterous times. Perhaps the children felt the presence of their grandma there in her old house. I do not know. What I do know is that the letters the Boylans shared with me were happy, not sad, filled with memories, of funny tales, of adventures that the house evoked.

What the Children Saw

The children saw something the parents had missed. To the adults, the place was run-down and in need of repair. The children saw beyond that, or maybe they saw back, back to the happy times they had spent there. They thought it was *fun playing cards to see who does the dishes;* they liked *swimming in the bay once your jobs were done* and the *chance to get out of our routine days.* They wrote about the fun on the boardwalk, and crabbing and catching minnows, and the *nice neighbor who gives me bait.* They wrote about the sea gulls and feeding the ducks, which Nannie had liked to feed also.

They dreamed of creating, with their own future children, the spirit and the fun of the place. They felt surrounded by love and security and comfort.

"The kids shared that they liked the sense of history Nannie's house stood for, and someday they would like to bring their children down. They saw beyond its obvious needs to the sense of family it did and still does stand for."

Mary Ann concluded, "I was touched that my mother's spirit had permeated the house, touched that the children saw the house as a rooted experience, not just a place to go. It was a place to be connected."

Chris, the youngest, wrote,

I wish Nannie were still here,

and then added,

It chost needs a little fixing up and it will be nice again.

They decided not to sell it.

Now You

When you are making a decision that will impact the whole family, bring your children in and provide them with the opportunity to write down their thoughts and feelings. Listen to the words between the lines when they read their letters out loud. In their innocence, they see what is real.

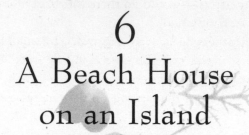

6
A Beach House
on an Island

JUDY, A STRANGER, SAT DOWN OPPOSITE ME AT THE SURROGATE Hostess on Capitol Hill, cleared a place for her morning coffee and bowl of granola, and looked over at my work, spread out on the long communal oak table. It's that kind of place—the long tables, the smell of herb bread baking, and the gunny-sacks of Centennial Crown flour stacked against the walls invite strangers to sit down together and start to talk.

"What are you working on?"

"A book about people communicating through writing. Sometimes people find it easier to say on paper things they can't say face to face."

"Give me an example," said Judy.

So I told her about Nannie's Table, because it is one of my favorite stories, and it has been a beacon to me in writing this book, kept me going when I might have lost heart.

Judy said, "Call my brother John. We have a story like that in our family."

This is the story John told.

The beach house was built on an island in 1953, the year that John was born. His father and his older brother built it. The house is on several acres, twenty feet above the beach, with one hundred and fifty feet of waterfront. Every year, the family—John and his mom and dad, his two brothers and four sisters—would go there for three months, from the end of school to the start of school.

"Until the bridge was built, Dad commuted by small boat. We grew up there in summers; it was one place we could be free. We were all close, running back and forth, running all around the beach. There are strong family ties, and we all feel that strong tie to house as well. It's part of our heritage."

Today, there are twenty-six grandchildren and lots and lots of cousins. And they all like to go to the island.

"It is an idyllic area, and we had a feeling of belonging. It was our house, part of our childhood, a very important core source of my life. It was a comforting place to be—dumpy old furniture and casual living. For us, it represented a coming of age, a growing-up thing—and we wanted that for our children, too, as well as recapturing it for ourselves. We liked going there."

Then something happened that changed all that.

John's mom died, and his father fell in love with Ingrid. Ingrid took good care of the house, and it always looked neat, but she posted rules and regulations to help keep the order she liked: "Come in the back door to collect all the sand in one place." "Don't leave towels on the floor." "Brush off feet."

"It was in my dad's handwriting, but it did not sound like him. The rules were reasonable enough, but it was more the attitude than the rules—'we expect' this place to be spotless; 'you shall,' etc. was the tone."

John and his brothers and sisters resented the rules.

"This is a beach house, not a city house," they thought. "Before, we could come in any door we wanted."

The list of rules and regulations changed how things operated. Some of the family liked the way Ingrid ran the place, some did not. They felt torn; the tension mounted. Unspoken, the enmity started to build; it began to extend to their interactions with her and with each other, even when they were not at the beach house.

"We would rather he sold the place than have this divisiveness."

None of them wanted animosity.

"Ingrid has been the best thing for my dad. He was pretty lost after

Mom died. I saw him come alive after he met Ingrid. A lifelong friend of his called to tell me, 'He's got it bad,' when he found Dad bouncing tennis balls off the side of the house—Ingrid had a tennis court. It was a happy thing to see my dad full of life—dancing, travels. She's been very good for him.

"We did not want anything to come between them, and I wanted the rumor and backstabbing to stop. We were in a bind."

Gathering Thoughts, and the Family, Together

It was John's idea to organize a campaign and have a family meeting—"I wanted to get these things resolved"—and he decided to do it in writing.

"I don't write a lot of things down myself, unless something is very important to me. I write it out first to gather my thoughts, then forget the paper. I thought that if each of the family had a chance to write out his and her thoughts ahead of time, it might be easier. It would give people a chance to think it through and give everybody a chance to have their views heard. Instead of each one talking to my father individually, this would focus things presented at one meeting."

John sent a letter to his brothers and sisters. Before writing it, he took time to get straight in his own mind what his own goals were: to bring about a resolution of some sort, to answer unanswered questions, to end the innuendo that was threatening to destroy his family. Those goals guided him as he wrote the letter.

> It's time to put an end to the bad feelings and misconceptions concerning the island property. To that end I am calling a family meeting to allow all members of the family to let their feelings be known.
>
> I've put together a few "fill in the blank" type questions for everyone to answer before they arrive. This will help us all to gather our thoughts and keep things moving and "on track" during the meeting. Please take the time to go over all these and bring the form with you to the potluck.
>
> I realize that some family members live far away and will not be able to attend, but please fill in any and all thoughts, feelings, and hopes and send the form back to me so that all concerned may have a voice.

His letter was neutral, noncommittal, simply saying, let's work this out via letters, followed up by a meeting.

Let's clear the air, have some fun and move forward. See you at the meeting.

"I wanted to keep it simple, so I asked everyone to answer just three questions."

1. *My feelings about the beach place in the past were . . .*
2. *My feelings about the beach place now are . . .*
3. *My feelings/hopes for the beach place for the future are . . .*

John asked for letters from both spouses and even their children: Since they were part of the place too, "their input could be valid." Everyone wrote. One sister from Ketchikan, Alaska, who could not be there, mailed her letter and asked to have it read at the meeting.

John asked Ingrid to write as well. "We didn't know what her feelings were, either."

A potluck barbecue at John's house seemed like a nonthreatening way to come together. After dinner, sitting around the table in the backyard, they all read their letters.

"We established some simple guidelines: The chief one was, everyone be quiet when somebody else is reading. Not Robert's Rules of Order exactly, but 'no butting in.' "

There were some surprises. The sister from Ketchikan wrote,

It was a wonderful place to grow up. I felt it was part mine.

But now,

This is Dad's beach house. And how he chooses to live there is not up to me.

John's oldest brother, the one who had helped build the place, similarly distanced himself.

I'd love to have the opportunity to use the house for a week or two during the summer, but I cannot quibble with his decisions. Whatever Dad chooses to do with his property is his prerogative.

What came out in all the letters was what the house represented: memories of childhood and images of freedom, a break out of the work-week stress and structure:

> *. . . a place to celebrate life with those we love—a place to gather around the hearth sharing time with family in harmony, simple joys, the warmth of a fire, the gathering of wood, passing a bowl of popcorn, a cup of hot cocoa, quietly reading, leisurely games of Monopoly, lightning quick double solitaire. Simple pleasures.*

> *I remember sitting around on rainy days playing cards, reading comic books, and keeping warm by the fire. On sunny days it was up for breakfast of bread toasted over the fire, smothered with butter and fresh blackberry jam. Mmmmmmmmm!! Out the door after chores and down to the beach, a combination playground and science lab. There were tidal pools to explore and sand castles to be built, firewood to collect and rocks to skip. Time to swim, scoot around in the boats. . . . In the evening Uncle Bill would tell war stories or signal to the occasional navy boat with his signal light.*

There were statements of sadness at what it had become, a symbol of "turmoil and unease":

> *I no longer feel welcome at the family beach house.*

> *I feel like a trespasser; it is no longer a family place.*

> *I feel displaced, walking on eggs.*

What also came through loud and clear was a willingness to work together.

> *We'd be happy to contribute to maintenance, repairs, etc., of the house if we were able to use it more.*

"The structured part of the meeting broke down after a while; the goal was achieved in everyone's mind. The letters, the meeting, were a means to an end. It accomplished what we wanted. The letters made a great difference; otherwise, there would have been a lot of bitterness."

It took gumption to ask everyone to write. John was sticking his neck out and taking a risk. He thinks the payoff was worth it.

"The payoff is a closer relationship all around. I have become a lot closer to both Dad and Ingrid. We all seem to get along better as a family. We understand my dad's point of view, and he understands where we are coming from. Dad realized how important the island was to us, and the dialogue was kept open. As for Ingrid, she responded very well—maybe a little defensively at first. Relations have been a lot more open with her since then. We were all pleased that she wrote a letter and that she listened to ours. All around, we feel more comfortable with her.

"Ingrid has the place looking better. Before, it was a cabin place. Now it has more of a house feel. She planted flowers, put up curtains, painted the place a lighter color—it used to be rust stain. We've all tried to work together with her to spruce the place up.

"The letters and the meeting brought her into the family."

My hopes for the future are that there would be more trust and more participation, a lessening of the hard feelings and more open hearts all around.

Now You

The story of Nannie's Table and the story of the beach house on the island have this in common: The house was more than a house. It was a metaphor. It stood for a doting grandma, for childhood freedom. By focusing on the house and what it meant to them, both families were able to come together in a new way.

Take an unresolved issue in your own family. Find the metaphor beneath the dissension. Target that as something to write about. Invite everyone concerned to write a letter, to be read at a meeting of all

25

members. Keep it simple, define three, maybe four, key points to address, and then set a date, with maybe a month's warning, to read the letters together. Make the meeting a neutral spot, doing something people enjoy doing, like John's backyard barbecue, where everyone will have a chance to relax, be with each other, and read their letters.

It takes less effort to hear another's point of view when you know that your turn is coming; it is easier to give your undivided attention to someone who has just extended the same courtesy to you. The discussion that follows the reading of the letters will come into a different space. It is the space of people listening to one another.

7
Great Expectations

IT IS A SUNNY SUMMER AFTERNOON, AND I AM RIDING THE FERRY, watching a young couple play with their baby. The baby is about nine months old, just beginning to be able to hold herself up by gripping the back of the ferry bench. She is dressed in a little sunsuit and is so happy; she keeps giggling, letting out little cries of delight. Her parents take such pleasure in her little shenanigans. She is trying to put the straw in the plastic glass of ice with the map of the San Juan Islands on the side, and she misses more often than she hits it. From where I sit, I cannot see the mom's face, but she takes her in her arms whenever she crawls across the table, turns her, and sends her back. Her bearded dad keeps one arm around her, holding her steady. He smiles a smile of sheer amazement whenever her straw hits the target and shakes his head in wonder. Everything about his look says, "Isn't she wonderful? Isn't she smart!"

Now the dad laughs out loud, and the baby laughs a sweet baby laugh in return, and I chuckle too—you can't help it, it is infectious—and I wonder, did my dad ever take such delight in me? I'd like to think so.

Children Need Cherishing

If you keep a baby journal before your children are born and as they are growing, they will know for sure of the delight you took in them.

This is not just about putting in the results of the sonogram and the dates of the first DPT shot. It is about noticing and recording your feelings, your hopes and fears and dreams, your inside view of the developing stages. Most of all, it is a permanent record of your sense of wonder.

Tracy, a new mom I know, had to go back to work soon after her daughter, Danielle, was born. Tracy sits at the computer during breaks at work and writes letters to three-month-old Danielle.

"I just hate being away from her," she told me, "so I type up little notes about how I love her, and my dreams for her, and how I am thinking about her and wish I was with her."

She seemed almost embarrassed to mention it, and her husband Kevin was amazed. "You never told me you were doing that," he exclaimed, and she answered quietly, "They are kind of private, just between me and her."

Katherine's baby book, called *Welcome to the Planet Earth,* has a special section called "Waiting for Baby," which invited me to mention physical and emotional changes, diets and cravings, favorite music, books read, and advice from doctors and midwives, among other suggestions. I am glad for the prompting, which inspired me to include details that today make me smile, looking back almost tenderly at that earnest young mom who was me, who worried about the protein she was giving the baby in utero, and was I drinking too many milkshakes.

I have been charting my protein intake and keeping a food diary for the last few months, because I want to make sure this little one has good brain-cell development (last trimester). This is not easy, but one day I managed to consume 120 grams of protein, I am eating so much tofu, Jim said the baby would be fluent in Japanese.

I have a great craving for chocolate milkshakes, which Jim kindly indulges, sometimes at midnight. One of the low points of my pregnancy came when the midwife told me during a prenatal visit that chocolate inhibits the absorption of calcium, so my milkshakes had absolutely no redeeming qualities.

I am also amused by my later "interpretation" of every anecdote of the baby's antics. A useful parenting principle I learned years ago is to ascribe motivation only to admirable actions. Never assume bad qualities, like selfishness or rudeness, but be quick to point out the good qualities behind positive behavior. So don't just tell the story of Jimmy doing this, or Sally doing that—add your "objective" judgment: "Wasn't he sharp?" "Isn't she clever?" Add a generous dollop of exclamation, of maternal or paternal pride to any story you tell. Here are some typical "editorial comments" from Katherine's book:

She astonishes me with her memory.
What a mind to put those two things together.
She has a great sense of humor.
Such strong maternal instincts.
(This from a four-year-old!)
Isn't that a picturesque phrase—a childish twist of language and logic.

A truth I learned from Dorothy Briggs a long time ago still stands: Children need to be cherished. In her classic work, *Your Child's Self-Esteem,* she notes,

"Children survive on acceptance but they do not blossom on it. They need something stronger. They need *cherishing.* They must feel valued and precious and *special* just because they exist. Then, deep down they can like who they are."

And later on in that same wonderful work, she tells us,

"Every effort you make toward enlarging your capacity to cherish is reflected in your child's self-esteem."

To my mind, that is exactly what keeping a baby book is all about: enlarging your capacity to cherish.

A Love That Is Fierce

Patti Payne, anchor/host at KIRO, has her own TV and radio shows and leads a glamorous life traveling around the country tracking down stories. In addition Patti is a professional musician and has appeared onstage as a singer, drummer, pianist, and guitarist. She has a wall full of awards, including an "award for the most awards on a wall." What is more precious to her than any and all of the above is her relationship with her two grown daughters, Jill and Lee.

I was interviewed on her show recently. Afterward she proudly showed me a letter Jill had written to her "out of the blue," extolling Patti's virtues—her compassion, her understanding, and her "weird incredible sense of humor." Mostly her daughter thanked her for her fierce devotion. She got that right; Patti Payne is passionate about her family.

This was not something that happened overnight. Patti has a woman-to-woman relationship with both of her daughters because she started at day one. From the time they were babies, she wrote them letters and read them to them as she rocked them in her arms.

Patti says, "I read everything the day I wrote it. I wanted them to hear, even before they understood the words, the awe and wonder I had surrounding them.

"When they were babies, while they were napping, I would spill out on paper all I was thinking or any little developmental things I noticed—rolling over and so forth—and then when she woke up, I would take the baby in my arms and say, 'Baby dear, this was my letter to you today.'

"It made *cement* out of us"—she emphasizes the word *cement* with her fist. "Nothing could ruffle that cement. It is there in *concrete*," she adds fiercely.

As the girls started to grow, Patti would note on index cards their latest exploits and achievements and the funny things they said. She kept a recipe box on the counter—"That's all it is, nothing fancy"—and when she caught the girls doing something clever or smart, she would write it down on a three-by-five card, date it, and throw it in the box. Not organized, no dividers, but all in that one box.

"Sometimes I would pull one out and read it, and the girls themselves liked reading them randomly when they got a little older."

"Now they are grown, and we do wonderful things together as women—'Let's go see *The Secret Garden.*' 'Let's go dancing.' We do things together that keep us close—we share everything—the deepest, darkest secrets of our lives. They come to me; I go to them.

"The letters I wrote to them when they were young cement it. You can look back on those things and feel the emotions, feel the love that went into them. When you start writing letters to your children as babies, the love you have in those letters will be the bond you share forever."

Patti has a hint for parents of teens.

"My advice to someone having trouble with a teenager: Draw on this original love, and recapture some of the miracle you felt when you first saw them. Think about the little hand on your shoulder, the dependency and bond—everything else falls by the wayside."

"I Forgot"

Sometimes, quite simply, we forget. We forget why we wanted this child; we forget our idealism—eating tofu, singing to the unborn baby—we forget our delight. A baby book helps us remember. A close friend of mine who is a father was going through a particularly rough period with his teenage son. He told me poignantly, "I was sorting out some old boxes in the garage, and I came across the book that Merissa and I kept when she was pregnant with Joel, our comments watching him grow during that first year of life. They were just jottings, mostly fill-in-the-blank stuff, one or two sentence notes, but I cried as I read it, remembering."

He opened his hand in a gesture of vulnerability and openness. That gesture was an invitation to understanding. He went on in a small voice, almost inaudible.

"You see, I forgot. I forgot those times, that unabashed joy and the fear and the fumbling.

"Reading it again helped me remember. Hey! This is the same kid. This is the boy I taught to read by carving letters deep in wood so he could tactually feel the J and the O, the E and the L. This is the boy we stayed up with all night when he had the chicken pox and his fever soared to a hundred and five; this is the baby I cradled to sleep when he woke up with a nightmare. *This is a relationship worth fighting for.* And it had all those years, all that solid foundation to call upon."

He started to think about their current impasse differently.

"It shifted my whole perspective. I wanted to reach him, to reach out to him, to heal the chasm between us."

So you young newlyweds out there, you young parents or parents-to-be, you may think keeping a baby book is a cute or clever or nice thing to do. I say, you are writing your history.

Giving Up a Baby for Adoption

Abigail Van Buren printed a letter from the adoptive mother of a little boy of seven, who had been abused and was going through a miserable time of tantrums, screaming and screeching. Then he received a present and a note from his biological mom. He tossed the gift and went straight for the note, printed in big letters. Bravely, he read out loud,

> *Dear Son, I am very, very proud of you and how well you are doing. I'm glad you have such wonderful people to take care of you, since I can't. I want you to know that even though we can't be together, I will always, always love you very much.*

The boy stopped reading and started to cry softly. Then he read on slowly and deliberately,

> *You will always be with me in my heart. I love you. Mom.*

At first he did not say anything, and then, according to his adoptive mom, he "crawled up on my lap and began to sob." Before this, he did not think "his mom wanted him or even missed him."

She rocked him while he cried for nearly an hour.

The letter to Abby ends with a plea to all parents who have given a child up for adoption to put aside their own pain and include a letter like that in a birthday or Christmas gift:

"Give your child one more gift—the gift that may well be the key to his or her ability to be healed and restored. These children must know that they were loved and therefore are now lovable. Please give them a tangible keepsake; it doesn't have to be fancy or grammatically correct. . . . But do tell them they were loved. The healing that this can bring is beyond measure."

The little seven-year-old boy took the letter from his biological mother and kept it in a special place. He would not let anyone tack it up on his bulletin board because he did not want it to have a hole in it.

"Embrace and Release All at Once"

Ever notice how it is in the kitchen where you find out major things in your life?

"There is something I have to tell you . . ." often comes after dinner as you do the dishes together, and the whole earth shifts.

Garrison Keillor says his mother told him only once, "Your father and I are proud of you." They were standing in the kitchen.

It was in the kitchen, standing by the sink, that a friend of mine recently found out that her son, who is now twenty-six, fathered a baby when he was nineteen, and that he and the mother, his teenage girlfriend, gave the baby up for adoption. Her mind is still trying to process this information, that she has a seven-year-old grandson somewhere that she did not know about, and that she had to, in her words, "embrace him and release him all at once."

Her first thought, after the shock, was to write the boy a letter to go in his file, that he could read when he was eighteen, if he chose to. She wanted him to know he had a grandmother who cared, and his great-great-grandfather was on his college crew team and his great-great-aunt was an attorney, back in the days before women went to college.

"I would like this child to know he is descended from a colonel who went to West Point and was a Civil War hero."

And her second thought was, did he get the shoes he wanted to start school this week?

She reflected that no one ever thinks of grandparents of adopted babies. She herself, as a woman who works with family issues, never thought of it.

"I turned to writing as a resource, to do something with these emotions, to take action, to handle the loss, and the gratefulness, and the grief.

"I want to put my heart on paper for this child, and stay connected—that's what it is all about.

"This boy needs to know that his parents talk to each other every year on his birthday, and that we think of him when school starts each fall."

Double Digit

Even if your son or daughter is already grown or growing, you can still write about his or her birth. A landmark birthday is as good an excuse as any to recall that momentous occasion.

Cathy Cornell's son, Michael, celebrated his birthday a few days after she took a workshop with me. Inspired by some of the stories I shared, she sent him this letter:

Dear Michael,

It is so hard for me to believe that you are ten years old today. I still remember when I carried you inside my tummy and all the changes my body went through while you grew. I loved feeling you move and watching Dad's face when you rolled over and my stomach looked like a wave. Dad would put his hand on my belly so he could feel you kick too. We would both talk to you and, when you were late, ask you to come out and play with us.

We didn't know whether we were having a boy or a girl baby, although my dreams told me I was having a blond blue-eyed boy just like you. How delighted we were when you were born on that bright sunny April day. A wonderful, cuddly, beautiful, child—our firstborn!

Michael, we have enjoyed watching you grow, develop your sense of humor, your sense of identity, your sense of caring. We love you very much and are proud of you and proud to be your parents.

Happy double digits!
Love, Mom

Later she told me, "I gave it to him first thing on the morning of his birthday. I watched him read it, and I could tell from his expression that he was moved. When he was done, he gave me a big hug and was teary-eyed. He said, 'Thanks, Mom.'

"We're a very verbal and openly affectionate family (my husband included), so what I said to him about being proud and loving him was no surprise or new, but putting it in a letter made him feel very special. I know it made me feel good to do it. To give him a gift no one else could."

Reading Them Back

Anytime you choose is the right time to read back whatever you write about your children. Patti Payne read her babies what she wrote about them the day she wrote it. Some parents like to present the book or the letters on a special birthday, like sixteen or twenty-one. Or maybe when the child is going through a tough time at any age. An eight-year-old feeling blue, for example, would know he was important as he laughed at the stories his parents wrote about him as a baby.

Julie kept a diary of her daughter's birth in an appointment book and read it to her one Mother's Day. She wrote to tell me of the bonding effect of reading it together.

"Reading my feelings and thoughts of her birth to her on Mother's Day was a time of intimate sharing. I was remembering her six-pound-ten-ounce form emerging while I looked into her beautiful young adult face. She is now nearly seventeen. I was twenty at the time of her birth. To me it was evident that I was reading the thoughts of someone very young and naive, but to her they were the thoughts of me as I am now, her mother. She wasn't judging, just absorbing.

"Reading this book on Mother's Day could turn into a tradition with us."

"No Longer an Orphan"

In a short piece in the "Neighbors" section of *Woman's Day*, Hazel McKinley of Orlando, Florida, tells how meaningful a journal she kept for an infant daughter became in later years. Soon after the baby's birth the father died, and as a way to work through her own grief as well as to create a gift for her baby, Hazel started to record memories.

"I wrote down all the little things that showed her how her father had loved her. I put down how much her father had looked forward to her birth, how he had carried her picture in his wallet and asked everyone in the office, 'Want to see my pretty baby?' How he danced with her in his arms, singing, 'I could have danced all night.' "

Hazel says keeping a memory book was therapy for her and invaluable later, "when my daughter felt that her father had abandoned her," and she brought out the book to share with her.

And Claire, whose mother died when she was a teenager, tells a tender story. When Claire was expecting her own daughter, she wondered what it had been like for her mom, but her mom was not there to ask.

"When I was pregnant with Erika, I visited my grandma in Texas. She gave me a packet of letters, saying, 'You might like to see these.' They were letters my mother had written to her own mother, my grandma, about being pregnant and bringing home a new baby from the hospital. That new baby was me. It stunned me to read those letters. My mother died when I was fifteen, and I always thought of myself as an orphan. My father was in law school when I was born and was not too involved at home or paying much attention to what was going on. When I asked him what was it like when I was born, what was I like as a baby, he'd say, 'I don't remember.' Now here were these documents.

"I read them, and thought, 'Wow, that was my mom, her handwriting is so much like mine'; and she was feeling a lot like I was feeling being pregnant. I felt like a discoverer of rare documents. As I read them, I cried. My first thought was, 'I'm not an orphan.' "

Claire offered to send me copies of the correspondence. Read these excerpts as though it were your mom or your dad speaking about you.

Keep in mind her reaction, how much these everyday words meant to her.

The first letter was written from the hospital, soon after the baby was born.

I'm writing this lying down, I hope you can read it. Do you like the name?
I was early, and the baby came quickly.

36

Her mom describes the delivery with the kind of factual detail that every new mother thinks is unique and special.

> *I began to get funny little cramps in my tummy. I thought it was just a few too many onions.*
>
> *We timed the cramps and they were coming every 15 minutes. And the doctor said to come in when they were 8–10 minutes apart. So Hank and I didn't know what to do, but he decided he'd better call work, and I straightened up the house and got dressed, and we called the doctor about a quarter of ten and left the house by ten.*
>
> *We got to the hospital by 10:30, and Hank rushed me upstairs. They had me in the labor room by 11:00 and the doctor there at 11:45, just in time, and the baby was born at 12:02. It was really a rush at the end. I'm sure glad Hank was there with me. He is so level-headed and at the same time sympathetic. He held my hand until they took me into the delivery room. . . . Were your babies born very much differently from this?*

The next letter describes the baby's features to her mom and tells what it's like to nurse her.

> *I feel just fine now except of course for the stitches. Claire is adorable—of course. I'm nursing her, and she has an appetite like her father's. She is a little carbon copy of her brother except for more hair, a little fatter face, and, Mom, she's finer toned. She has long thin fingers and feet—oh, she weighed 7 pounds and was 21 inches. She's so precious. She just nuzzles around until she finds her supper, and she sucks so hard she almost chokes herself at first. It's so much fun nursing a baby again.*

Thirty-five years ago, new mothers stayed in the hospital longer, so Claire's mom is still at the hospital a week later as she writes the details that only her own mother would care about.

> *We are going to have diaper service for a little while. That will make things awfully nice. Hank spent the morning cleaning my stove for me. That was the only thing I hadn't thoroughly cleaned before I left cause*

I couldn't get it apart myself, but I sure didn't expect him to do it. It really was sweet of him. It sure will be nice going home to a clean house.

And the details a new grandmother devours—the kind of detail that gets lost today because we share it on the phone instead of writing—

The girl across the street gave her the sweetest little blue check flannel three-piece outfit. They're real popular around here. And one of Hank's buddies at work gave her an adorable little pink dress—size one—I suppose she can wear it this summer. Anyway it's so nice to have something frilly, and they're all so tiny. There are too many adorable clothes to get for little girls. Barons had a sale the other day of Carter's things and they had some of these sleeping bags of cotton jersey—you know what I mean. The little mittened sleeves and with drawstring at the bottom, but I didn't get a chance to get any.

Between the lines of these ordinary daily life sharings, Claire's mother expresses tenderly her feelings about her own mom.

I guess I am just rambling now.

I hate to stop writing to you. I keep thinking how nice it would be to see your sweet face peek around the corner of the door.

It sure would be nice to talk to you, Mom, just for a little.

I hope you are happy about our having a girl, and the name we picked.

When I read these letters and remember their impact, their simplicity touches me. It makes me think of the wise words of a dear friend who summed it up:

"You don't have to make it fancy to make it work."

Now You

"This child was loved in the womb," said a psychic at a writers' conference when she saw me with the bright-eyed six-week-old Emily. I wasn't quite sure what she meant by it, but it went straight to my heart and gave me a glow that started at my toes and moved upward. How did she know that about us?

Now if you write even one letter to your unborn baby about your longing and how you felt after he or she was born, about your dreams and your fears and your caring, then your child won't need a psychic to tell that.

A line I am fond of from Crescent Dragonwagon's *Wind Rose* says it all:

"For nine months we wondered, but you were so much more than we could ever wonder."

Let your child know your wonder, before and after.

And by the way, remember the axiom, "It is never too late to have a happy childhood." No matter how old your children are, write down for them what it was like for you in the nine months before they came into the world, and what it was like afterward, watching them grow.

It's a tale that only you can tell.

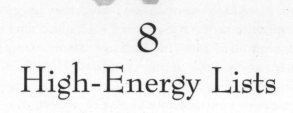

8
High-Energy Lists

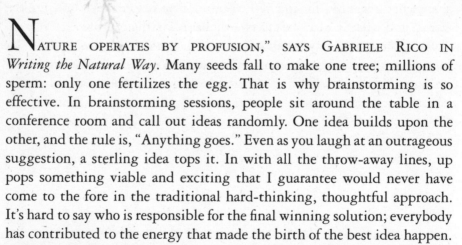

NATURE OPERATES BY PROFUSION," SAYS GABRIELE RICO IN *Writing the Natural Way*. Many seeds fall to make one tree; millions of sperm: only one fertilizes the egg. That is why brainstorming is so effective. In brainstorming sessions, people sit around the table in a conference room and call out ideas randomly. One idea builds upon the other, and the rule is, "Anything goes." Even as you laugh at an outrageous suggestion, a sterling idea tops it. In with all the throw-away lines, up pops something viable and exciting that I guarantee would never have come to the fore in the traditional hard-thinking, thoughtful approach. It's hard to say who is responsible for the final winning solution; everybody has contributed to the energy that made the birth of the best idea happen.

List-making is brainstorming on paper, a high-energy way to generate ideas and stimulate surprises. Like brainstorming, list-making has one cardinal rule: *Suspend judgment.* Dump out every idea as it occurs to you, the faster you write the better, without evaluating or considering what you write. Often the idea the head says to dismiss is the clue to the heart's desire, and in it is the seed of a brilliant solution.

There is something psychologically invigorating and expansive about setting out to think things up within the structure of a numbered frame. "Come up with ideas" leads to two or three suggestions. "List twenty-five ways" leads to twenty-five: some silly, of course, but that's part of the fun.

Lists give the writer a healthy sense of abundance, a sense of plenty and power. You needn't be stingy—there are so many more where those came from. When I was teaching at the university, I had a student named Margot Denke who brought me homemade cookies. Not just a couple of cookies, but three or four dozen cookies at a time. I had such a sense of largess; I gave them out all over campus. It was like the loaves and the fishes. I felt so happy to have such bounty. I could afford to have a few crumble or even to give one to a fellow who had been rude to me. List-making is like that. Ideas? Take a few. There's more than enough to go around!

100 Ways to Have Fun in Hawaii

It's easy to generate "should" and "ought" lists; sometimes a "play" list is harder. Cancer specialist Carl Simonton has his patients write a list of forty ways to have a good time, half of which cost under five dollars. He considers "play" to be part of our essential creative energy, vital for healing, and the challenge of writing a long list is bound to produce some workable ideas.

My sister and her husband were going to Hawaii for the first time. Jim and I and the kids were excited for them and wanted to come up with a special card for their bon voyage party. We talked with a neighbor who had been to Maui, and we picked up brochures at a travel agency to get ideas about fun things to do there, and then we just imagined what it might be like. We each wrote a list of twenty-five ways to have fun there, then crossed off the duplicates and combined the best ones. Together, we came up with "a hundred ways to have fun in Hawaii."

Later, I read in Kathleen Adam's book, *Journal to the Self,* that in lists of a hundred, the first thirty-three items are predictable; the next thirty-three are silly; the last thirty-four are off the wall—and your best. It's as though the brain were saying, "Trust me on this one, and I'll give you another." Numbered lists are a contest, the glove thrown in challenge, and the brain rises to the occasion.

Tandem Lists: Two Heads Are Better Than One

My sister Mary and I planned to video some old family photos in celebration of our mom's seventy-fifth birthday. We gathered all the old albums together and dug through the drawers of memorabilia that every household has, coming up with a wonderful assortment that chronicled our mother's three-quarters of a century of life. Hundreds of pictures and old mementos lay spread out before us. Now what? What controlling principle, what organizing scheme could gather these myriad memories into a coherent whole? We needed a frame, some images to flash on the screen between sections to give a historical sense, a sense of the passage of time. We knew that once we had the framework, the rest would fall into place. Then we would have a sorting principle for that pile of old pictures and scraps of paper.

Mary and I took a break from the photos and went to the Mill Town Espresso Shop in Woodinville. We talked and talked yet couldn't seem to come up with a single organizing idea. We each ordered a second latte (tall vanilla single skinny with two percent foam) in hopes that either the caffeine would jolt our brains or the steamed milk soothe our frazzled nerves. Then I shoved a piece of paper across the table and suggested that we each list ten possible frames. Mary's first response was incredulous. "We can't even think of *one* idea, and now you're saying the solution is to come up with *ten*?"

"Ten absurd ones are okay," I answered. "Anything goes. Write even stupid stuff. Just keep on writing without judging. Come up with ten. Fast. Now go."

So we sat across the table from each other and wrote without stopping and came up with two lists that looked like this:

HENRIETTE'S LIST	MARY'S LIST
Famous women in American history	New York's changing skyline
Historical events	Car ads
	Cigarettes

Popes	Presidents
Books she's read	Products
Parallel events	Clothes
Changing ads for Hershey's	Architecture
Passages	Food fads
Trips and travels	Hospitals
Campbell's Soup ads	Furnishings
N.Y. Historical	

"Great!" I said. "Now another list."

"Groan," said Mary.

I redeemed myself quickly.

"This time, write down ten things you think of when you think about Mom. Fast. Without pondering, just off the top of your head. What comes to mind? Go."

Five minutes later, we exchanged lists. Many of the items matched. My mother is a painter; we both had listed "artist." She is a deeply spiritual person; where Mary put "nun," I had "saint." We both had "great cook" and "party giver." Both had listed our mother's sense of tradition and family values. Now we had two lists, one a personal and the other a historical reference. We put the two together and saw that what fit the many talents of our mom was the Famous Women in American History frame.

So the best idea turned out to be based on the first one, but it needed the others around it to show that it was best, and until we teamed up the two lists, it hadn't occurred to us to directly parallel a famous personage with a quality or talent of my mom's.

The best part of this planning meeting was that it was fun. There wasn't the stress that can come up in such sessions. Both of us had a chance to get our ideas out, examine them together. Both of us felt listened to, and the final product was definitely a combination of two heads being better than one. Looking through old magazines, we located a picture of a famous woman to match each of our mother's strongest traits, including Julia Child for the great cook, Dolley Madison for the "hostess with the mostest," Mother Seton for the native American saint, Amelia Earhart for the great adventurer. Using those famous pictures to set off the sections, we lined up all the family pictures behind the appropriate category. It was a nice compliment to our mom as well as an organizing principle, because the juxtaposition said, "You are as remarkable as these women, and just as talented in so many ways." And it was a tandem list-making session that got the ball rolling.

Saturday Listing

Two lists, side by side, can help a couple prioritize their plans, whether for a simple Saturday or for an elaborate holiday. Bud and Marion Trebon, friends of ours who were parents of a large family, often experienced tension on Saturdays. Each had hidden agendas and expectations for how they wanted to spend the day, and they often wound up at cross-purposes. Then they started making lists together. Saturday morning after breakfast, they would pour a second cup of coffee, sit across the table from each other, and answer in writing the questions, "What are my goals for this weekend? Which things do I hope to accomplish today, which tomorrow? What is the number-one item on that list?"

MARION WOULD COME UP WITH A LIST LIKE THIS:	BUD'S LIST MIGHT READ:
finish photo albums	clean garage
fix leaky faucet	fertilize lawn
picnic in the park	repair car
laundry	pay bills
plan week's menus	remodel kitchen
new headlight on car	

Then they would exchange lists, laugh at the grandiose ideas ("remodel the kitchen" and "finish photo albums"), combine the items that matched, talk over the ones that did not, and make up a new single list—to follow not slavishly but as a guideline.

Marion smiled broadly when she told me, "It made a difference in Saturdays. We were together as a team."

Tandem list-making helped them spend the weekend meeting both their needs; it also reminded them to put some fun in with all the chores.

Tandem List-Making as a Business Breakthrough

My friend Dorothy used tandem list-making for a business breakthrough. She needed some creative ideas on marketing. When she heard what Mary and I had done, she decided to try tandem list-making herself.

Dorothy runs a business of home care for new mothers called MotherCare. She has a staff of "doulas" working for her, trained to mother the new mother and make easier the transition of bringing the new little one into the everyday life of the family. In Europe, new mothers have used doulas for centuries, but here in the United States the concept is fairly new. Once people learn of MotherCare, they are eager to hire Dorothy and are thrilled with the peace and contentment she provides. Dorothy's chief marketing problem was how to get the word around that such a service was available. She asked her husband, Bill, to write a list of marketing plans at the same time that she was writing them. They sat at the kitchen table after dinner; each of them with a pencil and a piece of paper. Here's what they came up with:

DOROTHY	BILL
distribute brochures at OB/GYN's offices	write a best-selling book
have booth in shopping mall	offer 10 tips for nursing mothers, free
word of mouth	10 tips for siblings of new baby, free
article for *Woman's Day*	

DOROTHY (*cont.*)	BILL (*cont.*)
coupons for discount	address Kiwanis Clubs
radio shows	offer service as charity auction item
balloons (helium)	tie in with La Leche
newspaper ads and classified	reach grandmas—to give as a gift
advertise with diaper service	talk to pregnant moms in park
tie in campaign with diaper service	referral bonus
give presentations at birthing classes	baby stores/big department stores
	riders/ads with some benefit to store

Before dinner Dorothy had had no ideas; now she had twenty-two. Several of them she expanded and worked on successfully. Even more remarkably, some of them started to happen without any additional effort on her part. She believed in herself and in her business, and Bill did too, enough to write their lists; they were willing to suspend all questions of "Yeah, but how?" and the reward for that was that some of the items took care of themselves in magical, unpredictable ways. Is it that her antennae were out? Don't ask me how these things happen. Two weeks after writing this list with Bill, not *Woman's Day* but *Family Circle* called her. They were doing an article on woman-owned businesses and wanted to interview her. The item "Write a best-selling book" sounds pretty far-fetched, right? How about the next best thing? Within a month of this tandem listing, Dorothy met a well-known author at a luncheon. This woman had written a popular book about babies years before. She was in the process of revising it to reflect some of the modern changes in mothering. Delighted to meet Dorothy and to hear about doulas, she promised to put a section about MotherCare in her new edition.

Now You

Tandem list-making. All it takes is at least one other person who is willing to sit opposite you and write while you write.

Or make up a list of one hundred ways to have fun in Hawaii, or at home.

The glove is thrown in challenge. Are you equal to it?

9

Letting Someone Know You Care—After Forty-Six Years

It was such a simple thing, but it made a difference. He was a doctor, and she was his wife. They had been married for forty-six years. He was working on a book, and I was helping him, and one day when we met at the Incredible Edible, over almond latte, he told me with great warmth and affection how much he appreciated his wife's support. Not only now as he wrote this book, but throughout their life together. The older he got, the more he was able to look back and realize that he had sometimes let his "doctor mask," as he called it, interfere with his home life. He expected nurses to hand him the scalpel; he expected his wife to hand him the evening paper.

"It hit me," he said, "how her whole life was devoted to getting me out the door for surgery in the morning."

Now of course he told her that he loved her, and he said thanks when she made his coffee, or ironed his shirt, or made some special thing for dinner that was his favorite, and of course he brought her flowers on her birthday, but I wondered if he had ever put his thanks in writing and what a difference that might make. So I encouraged him, "Bob, put your heart on paper. Tell June in writing how you feel about her." This is what he wrote:

Dearest June,

I want to thank you for who and what you are, and for being my wife. Thank you for all the little things you do to make my life work. Thank you for washing my cup and putting food on my plate. Thank you for keeping the checkbook and telling me how to get where I'm going. Thank you for keeping me warm at night. I especially thank you for believing in me, and for the values you have and your willingness to serve others. And I thank you for your high arches, and your feminine pear shape, and your hairdo. You wouldn't be you without them. Please stay as you are, and know that I love you, and that I'm sure we were led by God to be beside each other.

Love forever
your most grateful husband,
Bob

June's response? First, she cried. She wanted to read it over and over. She put it someplace where she would keep finding it, to read it again and again and let it sink in.

She kept on doing all the things she did so well, but it seemed to go easier. It was nice to know someone cared, after forty-six years.

Now You

Do you have someone in your life you take for granted? Someone who has been there for you in such simple everyday ways that you can hardly remember life before this someone came into it? Maybe it is time to say—in writing—how much you care, how much that person means to you, how empty your life would be without him or her.

Pay attention to some of those small contributions to your comfort that you have come to expect. Spell them out specifically, and write an overdue, lifelong thank you.

10
The Three Be's

THE BEAUTY OF HEART WRITING IS THAT ANYONE CAN DO IT. You don't need to be a writer. You just need to be a human being. You don't need to be eloquent or poetic or have a way with words. You don't need to do, just to be, the three be's: Be kind. Be brave. Be you.

"Be kind" means be loving. Think of the other person as you write. "Be brave" applies to courage and vulnerability and a willingness to risk. "Be you" means tell about what you saw, how you felt; share a bit of you—that's what it means to put your heart on paper.

BE KIND

Virginia, a New England mother, sent me an interactive journal that she and her daughter, Tina, had written back and forth to each other when Tina was eight. Across the front, in a childish script, Tina had written, "Be kind." I never knew if Tina meant that pleading injunction as a message to herself or her mom, but the words burned into my mind and haunt me. They are a reminder to me to be gentle when I write.

The purpose of putting your heart on paper is to get closer to another. Raining insults on someone's head is not a good way to make that happen. A downpour of criticisms and judgments will make your reader defensive. If it helps, picture what it feels like for you to be on the receiving end of an insult shower; it has a dampening effect that you wouldn't wish on anybody.

"Be kind" means be other-centered. Think kindly of the person or people you are writing to.

Angry and Kind

Can you be angry and also be kind? Yes, you can. It has to do with telling the good parts too.

We are not kind when we are angry and just tell the anger or the facts masquerading as "constructive criticism"—a phrase that always amused me: Who are you trying to construct? We are not kind when we leave out the love and appreciation. Sending anger and hurt alone is emotional dumping: The *communication is incomplete.*

But we are also lacking in kindness and communicating incompletely when we just tell the love part and stuff down the anger and the regrets.

Suppressing anger is not kind.

When a relationship is in trouble, sometimes it feels like a bolt that has been rusted in place. Why even bother to disturb it, why attempt to dislodge it; what's underneath might be more gunk to face and to clean. I contend that people in a relationship with you, even one that is hurting, maybe *especially* one that is hurting, *know the truth anyway.* You think, "I wouldn't want to hurt her feelings by telling her this," or, "She might get mad and blow up and yell and scream at me." So instead of risking hurting her feelings outright, you take tiny pieces of her heart, bit by bit, like a carrion bird pecking away. A wall goes up here, a glance withers there.

When I was young, my motto was "Least said, soonest mended." Can't you just see that primly done in counted cross-stitch on a tapestry pillow? "Least said, soonest mended." It made stuffing it down a virtue.

William Blake had a different idea in "A Poison Tree." Holding back a hurt killed the person he was mad at, and telling it kept a friendship alive.

> I was angry with my friend:
> I told my wrath, my wrath did end.
> I was angry with my foe:
> I told it not, my wrath did grow.

Because he kept watering it and fertilizing it, the anger he held back grew into a shiny, poisoned apple, and one day he went out to his garden to find his foe "outstretch'd beneath the tree."

If you don't want to kill the friendship, maybe you need to share the anger.

Put the anger and your judgment first, and move through it fast. Follow it up with what you love and value in the other.

As you write your anger and your love, your words will unlodge that rusty screw, and after the first few arduous wrenchings, it will give way to something smooth. Just keep writing; the fluency will follow. And you might even feel, when you finish, as though you have put down a heavy pack that you did not realize you were carrying, did not even know until you put it down, and felt the relief, how heavy the burden had become.

Own Your Own Feelings and Watch Your Language

Can you honor your own reality and still be kind?

Yes. You do it by being *responsible* for your communication and your own feelings—not blaming the other, not making the other wrong. Take responsibility for your own *response.* That's all it is—a response. Given who you are and your view of life, given your own filters and perceptions, given your baggage and upbringing, this is your interpretation of the facts as you see them. Own your own feelings.

Kindness also comes in your choice of language. Words like *should, ought,* and *must* and phrases like "I can't believe you . . ." are ways of making your reader wrong. They are not kind. Substitute more life-giving vocabulary when these weed words crop up. Use words like *wish, prefer,* and *choose,* and *choice.*

Go back and take out the absolutes: "You *always . . . ,*" "You *never . . .*" Think of one exception to the absolute that pleased you.

Watch out for the *but. But* is a verbal barrier that often negates whatever went before it. Change the *but* to *and* as a bridge between ideas that coexist rather than cancel each other out.

Resolution and Response

Being kind also offers a solution and includes a request. What is your purpose in writing to begin with; what do you hope to gain? what is the result you are hoping for? what are you asking? Spell it out. Even if the solution is only a single-sentence suggestion, kindness includes that, and a request for a response as well, providing an opportunity for the other to respond and implying your willingness to listen in return.

Be clear with yourself about your reasons for writing. If you write because you care about the relationship with the person you are writing to, then your words will be kind.

BE BRAVE

When you are writing for relationship, there will be times when you feel afraid or reluctant. What will I say? How do I say it? I feel foolish. Even when what you plan to write is "nice"—a compliment or a cheery thought—you might feel inhibited and shy, and an inside voice might try to talk you out of it.

It is okay to be scared, to feel fluttery; in fact, I think it is healthy. The important things in life always scare us, and that activates our adrenaline and wakes up our brain to pay attention. Scared says, Be alert: something significant is going on here. Give it your best. No sloppy work, no half-dazed effort. Pay attention.

But how do you handle the voice inside trying to talk you out of it?

Chatter in the Box

When your brain starts hammering on you, "This won't work," "It might backfire," "She'll laugh," "He'll reject me," train yourself to talk back, to say to your carping brain, "Thank you for sharing that." And then write anyway.

Thank you for sharing that. Write anyway.

The Olympic runner Gail Devers almost had her feet amputated as a result of Grave's disease, yet she won the women's one-hundred-meter gold medal.

Reporters asked her, "How do you handle the chatter in the box?" (The box is the running position; the chatter is the Critic.) She said, "I don't even hear it; it doesn't exist." She kept her focus by paying no attention to the fear, by giving it no energy: "It doesn't exist." Giovanna, a workshop participant, said she uses windshield wipers in her head when her brain starts chattering. Swish, swish. Wipe it away. Don't give it power by letting it run you.

Joseph Vasquez, who teaches fire-walking classes, knows a lot about handling fear. Joseph says, "What do you want to accomplish? When you go in that direction, you will continue to have openings. As soon as you listen to the voice that says, 'Oh, this isn't working,' you stop dead. When you follow fear, you stop, shut down. When your choice is 'Go!' it leads to possibilities."

The Rocking Chair Test

My father was a master of the pithy aphorism. One of his favorites was, "I don't mind getting older, when I consider the alternative."

That is another way to get past the fear of writing something scary. Consider the alternative.

The motivational speaker Anthony Robbins suggests a Rocking Chair Test. Picture yourself twenty, thirty, or forty years from now, creaking away up there on the porch, reflecting back on the life you have lived. Robbins is speaking of lost goals and uncompleted dreams; the RCT is just as effective for lost relationships. So here you are, rocking back and forth, watching the sun set in a luminescent burst of color. Pale pinks, soft lavender, and you go back and forth, back and forth, in rhythm, reflecting on the good times and the bad. Project forward through that stretch of years a continuance of the relationships you value most *as they stand now*. Put yourself in that chair, rocking and thinking, rocking and thinking. Is there a sadness there, a regret? A sense of "If only . . ." or "What might have been . . ."

Imagine a youngster sitting at your knee, and listen to the tales you tell. What are your regrets? What would you have done differently? Now take the same scene, and experience your reflections on a life with relationships lived to their fullest. Lean into it. Stay with it. Does it feel different?

When you come back to the present, you may realize that some of your relationships could be stronger, some are worth fighting for, and some may need healing or a spark of renewal. And writing, putting your heart on paper, may well be the way to do it.

"This Night Stands on its Own Merits"

What if you write a difficult letter and the person you write to doesn't answer? It can happen to you. It has happened to me. In fact, once or twice, I myself have been on the receiving end of a letter, where the person writing to me put his or her heart on paper, and I chose not to respond. Your assessment of your decision to write cannot be based on results. For one thing, you often do not know the results or may not be aware of them for many years. Perhaps your written words made a difference you do not know about, or maybe not. You cannot let that consideration interfere with your decision to write.

Years ago fellow Fordham graduate student Bob Kleehammer gave me a valuable insight, when I gave up a night of studying to talk with a friend in crisis. I told Bob, "Well, if I pass that test tomorrow, it was worth it." He answered, "No, whether you pass or not, this night stands on its own merits."

That moment of wisdom stayed with me long past the pages of whatever book I might have read that night.

Joseph Vasquez tells his fire-walkers, "Stay detached from the outcome."

You cannot judge the prudence of an action by the results. What a hard truth and a profound awareness. It will give you great power when you are at peace with that.

Your writing, your being brave, and true, stands on its own merits. Let go of the outcome.

Another's Response

What if you write and the recipient gets angry? It is a useful thing to know that you cannot dictate another's response—and you are not responsible for it. You only have to answer for your own.

A friend of mine wrote a strong letter to his sister; she was so mad, she didn't talk to him for two years. Yes, that can happen. For a long time, my friend regretted writing the letter to his sister; then he realized that her response was a "reality check," a current evaluation of what was real. For her to have that kind of response, their relationship was already in trouble. Reality is something you can move with; otherwise, you are stuck.

Consider the alternative, let go of the outcome, remember that you are not responsible for another's response—and face the risk.

"To walk on fire," says Joseph, "accept the fact that you could burn yourself."

You do not eliminate the risk; you take that risk.

There is a risk involved in putting your heart on paper; relationship always implies risk. It is, in fact, that very willingness to risk, with its implied trust in the other, that is the foundation of relationship. The degree to which we are willing to be vulnerable determines the depth of the relationship.

I do not know at what point you sit up straight and say, "This is not working, and I have got to take some action to change it or spend the rest of my life like this." I do know that when that moment comes, writing it out, as the examples in this book show, can clarify your thinking and get your thoughts across to another.

Maybe she will reject you. Maybe he will laugh. Maybe you will look like a fool. Write anyway. Maybe your words, now more permanent in ink, will come back to haunt you. Write anyway.

Is it worth the risk? Only you can answer that.

But consider the alternative.

BE YOU

Who you are—the thoughts and emotions that shape you, move through you—is different from anyone else. Only you can express that voice which is you. When you put your heart on paper, your writing doesn't have to be as good as or better than anybody else's. It just has to be you. Being you is all about *connection,* about being *real.* When you are you, you *connect* with others.

Becky treasures the poem her father wrote the night she was born, wants to reproduce it in calligraphy, mount it, frame it, give it out to her sisters and brothers, her children—because it's his voice and he's dead now, and because he shared a bit of himself on paper the night that she was born. It does not matter if it is good poetry or not. What matters is that he froze in a time capsule a piece of himself for a daughter who would never know him but would always know this piece of what he was the day she was born.

Share yourself in your writing. That's what relationship is all about. Relationship is not just telling the other about events in your life, not just thinking up nice things to say about the other person. Closeness that you can count on comes from sharing yourself.

Are you putting your heart or your logic on paper? Are you sharing just the facts, or the feelings?

Share your response to the things that occur; how do they make you feel inside? Share your ideas and your dreams and your fears. What's it like, right now, to walk in your shoes? Only you can tell. The gift of what makes you tick is a gift that only you can give. Even your best friend, even someone who knows you well, can at best only guess at what is going through your mind.

When you put your heart on paper, you let another person in on the conversation inside your head.

Walk in Truth

"Write hard and clear about what hurts," said Ernest Hemingway.

Sondra Ray put it, "Tell the truth sooner." Get to the truth without rambling on about it and around it, without apologizing or defending. "Be you" means be honest. You cannot be fully you if you are worrying about what you write as you write it. You are editing yourself, and sometimes when you edit yourself self-consciously, you take out the you. You are expressing only a portion of yourself.

Write what is in your heart without regard to the right word or the correct way. When you put your heart on paper, you are tracking your mind. If a word pops into your head that expresses what you are thinking, then that's the word to use; don't change it to a word that's easier to spell or sounds more elegant. Don't stop to contrive a fancier way of expressing it. This is not a writing contest. It's a chance to share what is on your mind out loud with someone you care about.

Be true to yourself, without holding back, without wondering, "Will he like me? What will she think of me?" Holding back is not you, it's who you think the other wants you to be.

And when you write true, the truth will let you walk tall in the sunshine with your head held high. When you walk in truth, your step is lighter, you have a bounce. Your stride says confidence. The knot in your stomach unravels. Your eyes are clear and bright, you feel satisfied and content. The smile that plays on the corners of your mouth suffuses your whole body with a surge of well-being.

Give It Your All

Erich Parce is an opera singer and my friend. He has enormous presence onstage, whether he is singing in the intimate theater-in-the-round of

Opera Colorado in Denver or at the mighty Met in New York. Even when he is simply standing in front of an orchestra and chorus for the baritone solo at a church-held oratorio, he plants both feet firmly, and you can feel his commitment in the last row of the balcony or in the back pew of the cathedral. "I will not be blown away," his stance seems to say, and, "I am here for you, to give my all."

Writing from the heart is like that. Plant your feet in the middle of the page, and give it your all.

Be kind. Be brave. Be you.

11
Family Crisis Brings a Couple Close

Martha and I met in the old Pioneer section of town, at Elliott Bay Bookstore Café with its wooden stairs, old brick walls, and ceiling-to-floor bookcases. It was like being in the living room of an old well-read friend, and Martha had tears in her eyes as she handed me the folded sheets of paper.

It was these two pages, written in pencil on lined looseleaf, torn from a pad, ripped at the top in her haste to put down what was racing inside her head, it was these two pages that changed the tide.

These were the words, written out and shared with her husband John, that let out all the pent-up emotions they had been feeling ever since sixteen-year-old Theresa told them the news.

For three days they had said nothing. Their minds were like computers that had shut down, could not function. The situation was too painful even to think about.

Martha is down to earth, in a comforting, nurturing way. She has that soft southern sibilant way of speech that makes you feel as though you are being taken care of. She has a manner about her that says security and safety and sends a signal that it would be okay to let go of whatever you have been holding back. You have a sense that she would not let you fall, that she would be there to catch you.

Her grandson is almost two, and she beams and takes out pictures when you ask about him. Yet even after two years, the remembrance of the pregnancy makes her voice catch, and tears come into the corners of her eyes. Her daughter was sixteen, and the father of the baby was the same age.

Martha and John were devastated when Theresa told them the news. "All we could do was cry and hug her. And cry.

"What can you do when the words stick in your throat—just stick?" Here she starts to cry again, remembering the pain.

"Hearing the news was like a death—I'm ashamed now to say it—it was as though both my mom and my dad had died on the same day. It was like a death, but a death so great I could not even comprehend it, could not take it in.

"It was like LSD, reality warped and shattered, I didn't want John to touch me or hold me. I wasn't in a place to receive it."

They were in a stupor, mechanically going about their life's necessities without registering any vital signs; they were on automatic pilot, functioning, not feeling, hurting so deeply there were no words for their hurt.

"My first thoughts were for Theresa," Martha told me, wiping her eyes with the knuckle of her index finger. "I thought her life was over. She was only a child herself, just starting her junior year in high school, and now, I thought, she would never go to her senior prom, never finish school, never go to college. She had so much promise, so much intelligence, John and I had such high expectations, especially because she was our only girl, our miracle-baby. I was sick before she was born; we thought I could not conceive again. Theresa was a miracle-baby, and that played into our dreams for her. Now what we had hoped and dreamed for her could not be.

"And we wondered, what would people think, of us? of Theresa? She's such a good girl, a fine girl."

Here she bit her bottom lip and started to cry again, then checked herself.

"They might judge her forever after."

John was angry, very angry at first, and Martha says, "I didn't want to open that up; I didn't want to deal with his anger. Then I realized the anger was only a cover for the hurt. This was his little girl, his only little girl, and this changed her."

Martha's Fear

There was a cloud of gloom they could not penetrate. Martha told me she was afraid. She thought it was best not to say anything but to move forward. "I would think to myself, 'There's no sense in going into all this—you can't unspill milk—what's done is done, and we need to look at what's next, not dwell on the past.' "

Underneath that rationale was a fear and a judgment—the judgment that her true feelings were wrong, and a fear that she could not handle anything more.

Quite candidly, Martha shared with me that there was a history of mental illness in her family, and she was terrified of going over the brink. It was better to sweep it under the rug, to deny her feelings, than to dredge up feelings that she was afraid she could not handle.

Also, she wanted to protect John, and maybe to protect Theresa from John's anger. To bring it up, to discuss it with him, might only remind him of how angry he was. She wanted to put the pain behind them and do whatever they needed to do to support Theresa.

"We were blocking each other out; it's awfully hard to talk about something with somebody or to share with somebody when you know that it is going to be, at least at first, more painful for them. And I had this thing, this fear, about my breaking point. My mother is schizophrenic, she's been institutionalized; a younger brother has taken his own life; how much do I talk about, how much is too much, what will break me? Am I going to end up a babbling idiot? The storm was already raging, could our boat stand any more rocking? Am I going to cross the point of no return?"

The Letter on the Bureau

When John is angry, he responds with silence. When Martha is hurt, she responds with silence.

They had not talked for three days when she wrote the letter and put it on the bureau. At first it hurt too much for her to hand it to him.

"It's not that I didn't want John to read it. I just didn't know how to show it to him.

"When someone you love is hurting so bad, you have to step aside. I couldn't even write to him about it directly. The way I stepped aside was by a narrative. I told it like a story. And although it is written to John, I wrote about him in the third person, as though I were telling someone else the story.

"I wrote it out and left it on the bureau. Writing it out helped me get rational. What I wrote was not even meant to be a letter; it was an effort to clear my head."

Sometimes when you are hurting, you have to do something perfunctory, like clean the house, until it is the right time to talk. You have to find the right moment. Meantime, dig in the yard. Dirt is the only sane thing. The only sane thing is dirt, because dirt does not involve feeling. Something has got to be normal for a moment.

Martha told me she wrote this letter like a robot, "the way you clean the oven or get out on your knees in the garden, when you are in such pain you cannot think. It was a mechanical thing. I was on autopilot."

In the story, she went back to the things that had happened the day of Theresa's announcement, to get her bearings.

"I was trying to put the whole thing in context again."

Martha described a day filled with happiness and life and feeling close, holding hands and feeling like newlyweds.

It had been a beautiful weekend. J. and I had gone out on a date Saturday night. What a special night it was. I felt alive and in love with life.

Saturday morning we got up and spent the day working in the yard and catching up on paper work. We cleaned up and went out.

The whole world seemed bright that day, and Martha and John found themselves smiling at everyone, stopping to speak and reach out to others. They felt full of life; everything seemed "so real and alive to us." Then it was on to dinner and a movie.

63

It was such a sweet evening. One of those that we have just too infrequently and afterward we say we must repeat again soon.

We got home. Our children were out on dates, except our daughter. She was home and sitting at the kitchen table, the "family place" in our home. J. sat down in the living room as one of our sons came home, and they watched the news together. I was in the kitchen. I could tell from the moment I had walked in that something wasn't right. Theresa was too quiet. And she wouldn't lift her eyes to me. I went to the kitchen table and sat down across from her. I said, "Theresa, what is the matter?" She just stared at the wall, and her lip and chin began to quiver. I went to her— stooped down to her sitting level, took her hands in mine, and said, "What is it, Theresa?" The tears came quietly—my heart raced as I held her hands and waited for her to speak. I said, "Tell me, Theresa—it's O.K. Tell me what it is." Then the words came. "Momma, I'm pregnant." I took her in my arms and held her to me. The only words that came from me were, "Oh Jesus, oh Jesus." Our tears fell together as we held on to each other.

Opening Up

Looking at her feelings objectively, telling them to a third party in story-form, was like self-protection for Martha.

"Until then, I was not being honest with John. I had to reach a point where I could share with him that I was afraid I was going to have a nervous breakdown. I knew better in my head, but it didn't take away the fear any less to know it. Because in my own family I had experienced just too much, and it took over the intellectual understanding.

"After I wrote this, John and I were able to talk about my fear. There is something about saying a fear out loud. It doesn't run you anymore."

Martha's narrative unveiled the second pain, underneath the initial concern for Theresa. It was the realization that their lives, John's and Martha's, would never be the same again. Because of her story, they were able to identify what hurt the most. The contrast in the letter made it crystal clear.

"I hate to say this, because it sounds so damn selfish. John and I, after our kids were out of high school, we began to dream and talk about the things we wanted to do when the kids had left and gone their separate ways and all.

"The thought I had was for us. Our lives were ruined. We were at a stage where we wanted to spend more time with each other alone, without the kids, and now that our kids were getting older, it was our time. A baby in the house would change everything.

"John and I had been so looking forward to being able to take weekend trips, go places and do things, and have people over to our house—John loves to cook, gourmet stuff, and I love to cook desserts. We had looked forward to the times when we could have three or four couples over and just have a real bang-up meal and a fun evening—and the times when you can, you know, make love on your living-room floor, if that's what you want to do. Those crazy dreams of having the freedom, just the two of you. Our first son was born nine months and three days after we were married, and John was out to sea the first two years, so we really didn't have a lot of time without kids. We were looking forward to it.

"All of a sudden I pictured myself as a mama, a brand-new mama all over again, when Theresa couldn't handle it. A newborn. Could I be the mother to a newborn?

"My life. To me, she had taken away my life. We'd be sixty by the time that child was an adult, eighteen; was this what we had bargained for? We'd be too old to enjoy much of anything ourselves. 'Mama, will you baby-sit?' 'Mama, will you get the diapers out of the dryer?' I didn't want to be folding diapers now. And my plants would have to go. I love plants; now they would have to go; the baby would eat them or tip them over. A baby in the house would change everything."

The letter on the bureau was a breakthrough. After that, John and Martha were able to stop and acknowledge the feelings they were ashamed of; when they were able to be honest, able to address the reality of their feelings and their negative judgments, then they could move on. Before that, they were stuck.

Martha and John had learned through Marriage Encounter to share feelings with each other through writing letters. Over the next few months, they continued writing, staying connected, keeping the lines of communication open.

If you looked back over the letters of that time, you would not find one that dealt directly with the pregnancy.

"After that 'letter which wasn't a letter,' we could begin to write about questions like, 'What was my strongest feeling today?' We still couldn't say, 'How do I feel about my daughter being pregnant'—that was just too blunt. We couldn't bring ourselves to even ask the question.

"We might write about something else, to break it down into manageable pieces, so by the time we went through it, it didn't look like we'd done anything with the issue, but we had."

According to Martha, any couple could do this, even if they had not been on a Marriage Encounter weekend.

"The key thing is to keep communicating. Marriage Encounter has a tool; it's like going into the garden shed and getting a tool. Whatever works best for you; this tool works for us. I won't put down anyone else's way, but I would encourage this. This has worked for us.

"As long as we're communicating, as long as things are coming out, we're okay. It's when things get silent, that's the terriblest thing, when there is no communication, when communication breaks down."

New Directions and Lessons Learned

Martha had an attractive radiance and sureness about her as she told me that both she and John were going back to school in the fall. They were not waiting anymore for the right time—they had decided to "just do it!" One of her letters to John describes her feelings about this step:

It's scary for me, but now, besides that fear, I can experience also the excitement and adventure of trying something new and different. I have a new appreciation for the phrase, "It's never too late," as I try and envision myself in a classroom with people younger than our children!

I do love you,
Martha

Even though it still feels strange, John and Martha like being grandparents.

"Now I ask, what was in our heads to even say, 'Make the best of a bad situation. . . .' Now I am ashamed that at first we weren't even thinking about the miracle of life. Now I look at that baby and wonder, what was in my head, to 'make the best of a bad situation' instead of welcoming the miracle of life? And what was in our head to say, 'Theresa's life is ruined' and all those things you say? Her life is not ruined. Changed maybe, not ruined."

Martha says that what it comes down to is expectations, the expectations that you have for your children.

"What came out of it was the awareness that we were wrong in having expectations for any of our children. Frustration comes from your children not living up to your expectations; let go of the expectations in the first place, and let them live their own lives, not what you expect."

Shortly after the baby turned two, Martha wrote to John,

How does it feel being a grandparent? Some days it's a numbing feeling, like waking up in the middle of the night and getting dressed, thinking it's morning already. But for the most part, lately, it has been a pleasurable, satisfying, and rewarding feeling. Pleasurable that our grandson will let us comfort him when he needs it; we aren't strangers to him, and he enjoys being with us. This satisfying feeling smells like home cooking when you're hungry. It reminds me of the Little House on the Prairie mentality, the way things should be, simple and wholesome. I have the same feeling about our grandson as I do for our own children, as I see them growing up and becoming responsible adults. I don't want to keep them here, I know that in time they will leave and start their own families, but until then I'm (at the moment at least) happy and enriched by their presence.

It crosses my mind that we are truly fortunate to have the opportunity to be so close to our grandchild: my own parents didn't have this opportunity.

I love you,
Martha

Because of this crisis and their ability to write their way through it, John and Martha are closer today.

"Our family has grown, not just in size but in our caring for each other.

"Theresa knows that no matter what, we'll always stand by her. I know she has learned that. She feels safe, and she knows that we love her.

"For John and me, it's definitely made us stronger."

Martha confesses she found out something about John that she did not know before.

"My daddy didn't sexually abuse me, but I was physically abused; I was beaten, and food withheld, and that kind of thing. It was his background, he was a Southern Baptist, where he was coming from. I had known a father like a judge or a policeman. You know how you relate to God as you do your own father? Before this, I had pictured God as the Lincoln Memorial. After reading my story, John and I were able to talk, and John was able to—to go in to Theresa and hold her and tell her that he loved her. And he started crying, and he told her that we would stand by her, no matter what. He wanted her to know, 'We're behind you a hundred percent, and we'll see you through this thing.'

"I was standing in doorway, but I didn't want to intrude on that moment, and it was like something came over me."

Here Martha started to cry softly.

"And this may sound weird, but . . ."

Her voice got very soft, almost a whisper,

"I was able to experience a father's love, the way it should be, just by watching it. Something came over me: This is the way it was meant to be; the way a father shows love. I didn't participate in what happened to John and Theresa, I only saw it, but it made sense of something. It was a tremendous experience. It was one of those humbling experiences where you want the moment to stay there, you don't want it to pass, you want to make this moment last and last and last. I was seeing something like I took off sunglasses and could see something that I couldn't see before.

"What that did was create such an intimacy between John and me, even though the moment was between him and our daughter. Witnessing it filled me with love and affection for him. It changed my way of thinking, my whole perception of the way things could be between a father and a daughter.

"After that, my picture of God began to change, I began to see him as though we were walking beside a river, with green grass, and he had on white robes, and he had his arm around me."

Martha discovered something about herself as well.

"As for me, well, I guess I don't have to be afraid of breaking. I don't have to be afraid anymore. I'm not going to crack, I'm not going to break. I am stronger than I think I am."

Now You

When the words stick in your throat, know that writing is a way to give a voice to your pain.

12
Leaving a Legacy for Your Descendants
The Story of Your Life

To celebrate her eleventh birthday, I took Katherine to see a traveling exhibit on display at the Seattle Art Museum. The show included paintings of Picasso, Monet, Renoir, and Matisse, among other great masters. We do not see classic artists of that caliber in any permanent exhibit in Seattle, so I was excited for Katherine to experience it. I had seen this same exhibit at New York's Museum of Modern Art on a business trip and bought the catalogue. Before going to the Seattle show, I sat down with Katherine and went over the pictures, talking in an art critic's voice about line and color and negative space.

Then, early on a Sunday morning, to avoid the rush, we went. Katherine was stunned. She stood frozen in front of Degas's *Two Dancers* and said, incredulously, almost impatiently, "Now wait a minute. You mean, Day-gah actually used that sheet of paper!"

No reprint could duplicate the power of that moment, that awareness; all the art books in the world could not give her that. To stand where Degas stood in relationship to the very canvas he had used to create the original work, to see what his eyes saw—it was a magical moment of connection.

When you write your life story for your descendants, you give them a gift of that same kind of personal immediacy. No history book, no other account, can duplicate the story that you alone can tell of your own life to your own children and grandchildren.

At Nordstrom's Department Store I spotted a fill-in-the-blanks hard-cover book called *Legacy: The Story of Your Life*. I liked the way Nordstrom's showcased the book at their gift counter. A large-format book called *Quotes of Famous Women* sat on the glasstop counter near a similar-size *Quotes of Famous People*. Between them both was the *Legacy* book. The positioning said, "Your story is important too, your words might inspire more than you know."

You can buy a book like that as a guide, or you can sign up for a course. Being in a class provides the discipline of a deadline and the support and camaraderie of like-minded people; best of all, hearing the stories of others can unleash your recollections and validate the little things of your life that you might tend to dismiss as trivial.

One such course, taught at Highline Community College by Janine Shinkoskey-Brodine, is called "Remembering and Writing about Your Past." Janine's course is popular; she only planned to offer it once, and it has been running for four years now. Some of her students have enrolled all four years. What sets her course apart from other writing classes is that she teaches not only writing skills and editing skills but ways of remembering.

Janine says that people take the class for reasons as varied as the backgrounds and writing abilities of all the people signing up. Some come because their adult children or their grandchildren have encouraged them to record the family history; sometimes the children who signed them up come to class with them, and before they know what is happening, they are part of the class themselves, writing their own story for their own children. A historian came to observe and write her master's thesis, then got hooked herself. One man is now writing an "Old Timer" column for a Federal Way newspaper; another man is writing a novel about World War II.

Janine's own great-grandfather came from Germany to eastern Washington with seventeen cents in his pocket. In 1948, he wrote "The Story of Julius." It was a story about himself, Julius C. Johnson, written in the third person. Janine admits "The Story of Julius" is slow reading, probably only interesting to family members, yet "it does have some historical interest because it describes life in the wheat town of Almira in the 1880s. And my grandpa, his son, was pretty proud of it. He used to pull it out and show it to us."

Janine believes that long-term memory is like the hard drive on a computer; the information is in there, all you need is a way to get at it in order to use it. One technique Janine uses to help her students relax and remember is guided visualization. She asks them to bring an old photograph to class. She lowers the lights, then asks them to take a deep breath and concentrate on the picture while being absolutely, deeply quiet. She has them put themselves back into that picture.

The room is very still. They are alone with their memories as surely as though they had traveled back in a time capsule. Some wipe away tears, the moment is so real to them.

Then, with lights still lowered, they write what they remember.

The response is tremendous, especially from those who come to class saying that they have forgotten everything about growing up. Says Janine, "You've never seen pens write so fast, without stopping, for ten minutes or more."

Laura Esquivel, in her sensational book, *Like Water for Chocolate,* describes how her heroine, Tita, enjoyed smelling the sausage frying for the traditional Christmas rolls, mixed with onions, chopped chilies, ground oregano, and sardines.

> *. . . it was very pleasant to savor its aroma, for smells have the power to evoke the past, bringing back sounds and even other smells that have no match in the present. Tita liked to take a deep breath and let the characteristic smoke and smell transport her through the recesses of her memory.*

Janine brings pungent vials to class, some with wadded soaked cotton, others harboring the piquant item itself. She has a list of smells particularly associated with childhood: Noxzema, pickling spice, mothballs, yeast, "the stuff you live with," she says. Rose petals, lilacs, Ivory soap, wintergreen, calamine lotion, campho-phenique. She puts all the vials in a basket, and each student selects one, grab-bag style. Then they open it, smell it for a few minutes, and write without stopping for at least ten minutes. Tremendous memories open up.

By serendipity, a few days after she did this exercise recently, one student was delivering food to an elderly person. When she walked into the house, her nostrils were assaulted with the smell of musty old wallpaper. The impact was instantaneous; she started to cry. It smelled exactly like her grandmother's house.

As soon as she got back to the car, she wrote and wrote and wrote—so many memories of her grandmother came flooding back.

A Glimmer in the Eye

Frank Thomas, the author of *How to Write the Story of Your Life,* says that he had been teaching memoir-writing for six weeks before it hit him that writing about their lives was having an effect on the student writers themselves. He noticed, after the first few weeks, that they were dressing up to come to class, that they had a different rhythm in their walks. They were arriving earlier to class, eager to be there and to share their work. He noticed a glimmer in their eyes that had not been there when the class began. By writing their memoirs, they were getting a sense of self-worth. Writing put their youth and some of the actions of their lives for which they judged themselves harshly into perspective. For many, telling the tales locked up inside them was a relief. For several, it was the first time they had shared a particular part of their lives with others. And that was freeing.

Janine found a similar pattern and a sense of friendship building up in the class, where it was safe to share things. One woman, now age sixty-eight, lost twins when she was twenty. In her professional life as a singer as well as in her personal life, control was paramount. For her, that meant she could not let out her grief. For forty-eight years, this large part of her had been bottled up. She could not bring herself to tell anyone about the death of her babies. Janine's class was the first time she had ever shared her story.

"Those kinds of stories hit you in the heart," says Janine.

A sixty-year-old woman in the class at Highline is writing about Pepita, her monkey who died after being her pet for twenty-two years. She read bits of her story every week; three people were in tears when she finally read how the monkey died. That story elicited lost pet stories from others in the class. Pepita's story had given a dignity to their sorrow.

Living History

This is a story that gave me a smile and a shiver from my scalp to my toes. One of Janine's students, Catherine Rankin, is in her eighties. She left high school in 1929 for financial reasons and never finished. After taking Janine's course, she got up her nerve and wrote to her old high school in Duluth, asking what she could do to rectify that.

"Being eighty-one years of age, I have lived through two world wars. I think it would be nice to have a high school diploma. What are the requirements to receive a diploma at this late date?"

In the return mail, the principal sent her a cap, a tassel—and a diploma.

"You have lived more history than most people study," he wrote, then added, "You might want to organize a graduation party." He signed it, "Respectfully yours."

Catherine brought the cap and diploma to class, and the class cheered when she put the mortarboard on.

It took her over sixty-two years to write that letter. Writing her memoirs gave her the courage to do it. Until she took the class, Catherine said, "I didn't know how much I knew."

Now You

You need not wait for your senior citizen days to write your family history. Consider having your whole family come together periodically to write an ongoing family history. The saleswoman at Nordstrom's told me that that very morning a young mother with a baby in her arms bought a copy of *Legacy*. She told the clerk with a laugh, "I want to start now while I am living it."

13
Persuasion
The Art of the Deal

WHEN EMILY WAS TEN, SHE AND I WENT TO BRUSSEAU'S, A POPU-lar café and an Edmonds landmark. They have homemade bread and blueberry cobbler, and serve salads with garden herbs and fresh-picked greens. Their cheese comes from a local farm. Jerilyn Brusseau, the owner and my friend, has given the restaurant a decidedly European feel along with the distinctly Northwest flavor, and her place is a favorite meeting place. The café was celebrating the anniversary of its opening with a weekend of festivities, including a coloring contest (the prize was a year's supply of giant cinnamon buns), a live band, and discount prices on the quiche.

We sat at one of the sidewalk tables, biting into giant chocolate chip cookies, drinking fresh-squeezed apple cider, tapping our feet to the band music, and picking up on the vibes, happy to help celebrate a place that we are fond of. Emily's eye fell on a sweatshirt honoring the occasion, dis-played for sale on an inside wall. It was a black sweatshirt with ten candles in different colors across the front.

Right away, Emily said, "Buy me that!"

I balked. I thought it was expensive and an impulse buy. I only wanted a cookie and some cider, not a piece of clothing. I resisted. She kept pleading. Finally, I said, "Come up with a list of fifteen reasons why I should buy you a black sweatshirt." She grabbed a bright pink flier advertising the coloring contest and wrote this list on the back:

1. it has a nice design
2. out of the kindness of your heart
3. to be in the spirit of Brusseau's
4. black is a spirit color of Lynnwood Elementary
5. machine washable
6. soft sweater
7. it is warm
8. I like it
9. the money will go to Jerilyn's crew
10. good for the beach
11. nice material
12. Peter likes it
13. my friend Chris likes it
14. Katherine likes it
15. Jerilyn likes it

You can see that she cheated a little on the last four. She was laughing when she handed the list to me. I said, "I'm not convinced. I want concrete reasons. Why should I spend that kind of money on a black sweatshirt? Give me five more reasons." She went back to the list, and added:

16. easy to care for
17. black won't get dirty
18. black looks good on you
19. black looks good on me
20. XL will fit us both

She got the sweatshirt.

What I learned from this incident is that writing it down is a good negotiating tool. It is good for the person being persuaded, who can see the points laid out. It is good for the person trying to justify a position because it alerts you, as you write, to items you might not have thought to include. When Emily was negotiating verbally, she had come up with only one reason, and that a lame one: "Because I want it." Writing it down forced her to crystallize her thoughts and defend her position. She started thinking about some of the features of the sweatshirt that were attractive to her: It was warm, the color matched one of her school colors. The second round was more of a stretch. Having run out of features, she gravitated to benefits, and as any good advertising person knows, it is benefits, not features, that sell. "Machine washable" is a feature; "easy to care for" is a benefit. The best benefit of all was that we could get it in a size to fit us both.

When I am writing brochures for my writing workshop, I think this way. I put myself in the position of the person reading the pitch, and I ask, as they might well ask, "So what's it to me?" Then I go beyond the benefit to the benefit of the benefit. This is a trick I learned from Chuck Custer, master proposal writer.

> *This workshop teaches branching, a high-powered way to organize your material* (a feature; so what's it to me?)
>   *. . . and that will help you write faster* (a benefit; what's it to me?)
>   *. . . making your work more productive and your workday less stressful*
> (ah, the benefit of the benefit; now we're getting somewhere).

Above all, have a sense of playfulness about any negotiation, no matter how high the stakes. Herb Cohen wrote a fantastic book, *You Can Negotiate Anything*. Emily, at an early age, learned a lesson for life just by reading the title. At age nine, to the chagrin of her older brothers, she negotiated down the price of cotton candy at the circus, then sauntered into Pay 'n Save and negotiated last week's sale price on a school lunchbox.

Cohen says, "Train yourself to ask, no matter what the deal, 'If I lose this deal, will it cost me my life?' And if the answer is no, train yourself to say, 'Big deal.' Be willing to walk away from the table."

Emily and I were laughing during our negotiation. A large part of why she convinced me to buy her the sweatshirt was because I was enjoying myself so much. She made it fun to say yes.

Now You

Elaboration is a higher thinking skill. When we were in school, I remember learning that "marshaling evidence" is the cornerstone of rhetoric. What is the best way to marshal evidence? Write it down.

14
Write It Down
Make It Happen

Aᴛ ᴛʜᴇ ᴀɢᴇ ᴏꜰ ꜰɪꜰᴛᴇᴇɴ, ᴀ ʏᴏᴜɴɢ ᴍᴀɴ ɴᴀᴍᴇᴅ Jᴏʜɴ Gᴏᴅᴅᴀʀᴅ wrote a list of his lifetime goals. Although he was a teenager living in Los Angeles, his dreams were global: climb Mount Kilimanjaro, ride an ostrich, retrace the travels of Marco Polo. Land on an aircraft carrier. Appear in a Tarzan movie. Explore the Nile River. His life list, as he called it, numbered 127 goals, each one more fantastic than the one before. By the time he was fifty, he had accomplished almost all of them. Writing them down, he says, made them a kind of blueprint, and he was ready for any opportunity that came along. But the first step was to write them down, to conceive of them as a possibility, to see them as real in words before him.

Barry Green, principal bassist with the Cincinnati Symphony Orchestra and co-author with Tim Gallwey of *The Inner Game of Music,* had his music students keep a goal journal. He asked them to write out daily goals as well as list their plans for the next five or ten years. Green was astonished at the results.

After they had been using a goal journal for eighteen months, I found my students were improving dramatically. They were more confident about

*their ability to solve problems than ever before and found that looking back
over their journal notes gave them a sense of accomplishment.*

The process of writing their goals gave each of them a focus and, as Green
puts it, "a new sense of responsibility for their own futures."

I like that phrase, "sense of responsibility for their own futures." I like
the way it captures what writing it down is all about: taking responsibility
for the things that happen in your life and the things you want to make
happen.

"It was pretty scary at first," one of Green's students said, "to see my
goals written down in black and white—but it made them real." Making
goals real is claiming ownership of them and the first step toward making
them happen.

It is in the writing out that the responsibility becomes clear and that
the resolution or new direction presents itself.

The Winning Edge

Writing it down gave a winning edge to Green's conservatory students:

"Over a period of time," he says, "they became so good at focusing in on
their learning goals that they often eliminated them before they came to
class. . . . When they were clear on their goals, they'd allow them to settle
into the subconscious and begin to practice."

The students were able to move on and just practice, because by writing
goals down, they could "forget" about them and let their subconscious go
to work for them.

My son Peter came to me one day in wonderment and handed me a list
of goals he had written down two years before. He seemed pleased and at
the same time perplexed. He hadn't quite figured out the "why" of it.

"I found this list when I was cleaning my room," he said. "I thought
you'd like to see how many of these things came true."

Two years before, when he wrote the goals "build a new deck" and
"get a hot tub," those were not things our family was even talking about.
Now we had both in our back yard, and Peter had worked hard side by
side with his dad building and installing them. When I bought him a

parakeet for his birthday, I hadn't realized that "get a bird" was on his goal list, and even more significantly, as with the hot tub and the deck, he himself had forgotten he wrote it. He had also taken karate lessons, tried out for a play, gone to the park for dinner, spent an overnight at the beach—all without being conscious of checking off items on the forgotten list.

Please understand what I am saying here: Written goals often happen without any effort on your part. It is enough to write a goal down. Writing it down brings it out into the open from the dark recesses of your mind; it takes what was a shadow and makes it real. It is like a seed in a packet: While it is all closed up in that dark envelope, it cannot grow. You need to believe in it enough to open up the packet and plant the seed.

One of the happiest weeks of my life was spent in New York City after the publication of my first book. I signed books at Shakespeare & Company, a famous bookstore on Broadway, and one of the people who came by to congratulate me was Erich Parce, Seattle baritone, who was making his own debut at the Metropolitan Opera the following night. Erich invited me to come backstage after the performance, and then he said I could come as his guest to a dress rehearsal of *Turandot,* with Placido Domingo as the lead. I thought I'd died and gone to Opera Heaven, but it wasn't until I got back home that I found, like Peter before me, an old goals list. Wonder of wonders! Years before I wrote that book, my list included:

- write a book
- sign autographs on Broadway
- go backstage at the Met
- hear Domingo live in a full-length opera

I want you to understand that on the West Coast in Edmonds, Washington, where I wrote those goals, they were just as far-fetched and unlikely as one of the other items:

- have tea with Princess Di

Don't laugh. Maybe someday that too will come to pass.

Now You

Goals come in all shapes and sizes. They might be as simple as wanting to get up earlier in the morning, or longing to have a better relationship with a teenage son, all the way up to making a major life change or adventure.

Write down a "want," and it becomes a goal. Funny part of it is, we don't always know what we want. Many times, our life ambitions, our yearnings to be all that we could be, are so deep down inside of us that we have not verbalized them. Remember the seeds in the packet? We need to open the packet before we can plant the seeds. Write down your wants, your goals, and open up the packet. Do it as a group project with family and friends; and don't wait for January 1—these are not New Year's resolutions.

15
The Shoeless Joe Principle

*F*IELD OF DREAMS IS A MAGICAL MOVIE ABOUT BELIEF AND WHAT happens when you keep on believing in spite of setbacks. It is about acting on your dreams, dreams that to others seem far-fetched and unattainable. The hero, Ray Kinsella, a new farmer, is standing in the middle of his cornfield in the middle of Iowa, when he hears a deep-throated yet feather of a voice tell him, "If you build it, he will come."

Ray is startled: Is it the wind through the stalks, his mind playing tricks? Is he going crazy, hearing voices? It comes again, firm and uncompromising, "If you build it, he will come." Over the next few days, the voice keeps coming back. Finally the auditory imperative coincides with a visual one: A picture of a full-size baseball diamond appears in the north cornfield, then melts away. Straightforward, no-nonsense—and no instruction on how-to. Just do.

Despite the odds, despite all practical considerations that argue against it, Ray plows down his cornfield and builds his baseball diamond, complete with night lights, in the middle of a farm in Iowa. And he does come: first the great baseball hero, Shoeless Joe, who left the game in disgrace in the midst of a scandal in 1924, and then, in a wonderful twist, Ray's own dad, as a young man, returns to heal the hurt between them.

It's a corny movie, but it tugs at your heartstrings, and nearly everyone who sees it is moved because it touches a deep part of us—that part of us that knows that when we step forward in faith, in the face of monumental opposition, in the face of whatever weighty evidence to the contrary, when we believe enough to begin, the support will appear, the magic will take over.

This is not some modern notion limited to baseball diamonds. More than two hundred years ago, Johann Wolfgang von Goethe, in an oft-quoted couplet, summed up the same principle:

> *Whatever you can do, or dream you can, begin it.*
> *Boldness has genius, power, and magic in it.*

In the twentieth century, W. H. Murray added, speaking of his own experience in *The Scottish Himalayan Expedition:*

> *Until one is committed, there is hesitancy. . . . The moment one definitely commits oneself, then Providence moves, too. All sorts of things occur to help one that would never otherwise have occurred. A whole stream of events raising in one's favor . . . unforeseen incidents and meetings and material assistance which no man could have dreamed would have come his way.*

Ready to Receive: A Clear Sense of Intent

The Shoeless Joe Principle is about delineating dreams, becoming clear about your *conditions of satisfaction.* Ray knew exactly what his ballpark looked like before he built it. When you have a clear sense of intent, then the world can cooperate with you because it knows what you are asking of it. The bottom line becomes *how,* not *if.*

A friend of mine told me a classic story. He and his wife were ready to buy their first house. Before they went to the real estate office, they sat down together and wrote out a portrait of what the perfect house would

84

look like. Their description included the ideal price, the number of bathrooms, the best kind of neighborhood for them, the proximity to schools and shopping, and their hope for an extra room for an art studio for her. They also included that they would like this dream house to have a view.

Since they were so clear on what they wanted, it was not too long after this that the realtor located for them an amazing match. It had everything—except the view. The price was right and everything else was right, so they bought it and moved in. They were happy as clams even without the view.

Then one day my friend looked out and saw the garage next door through the side window and laughed out loud.

"We have a view," he told his wife. "We just forgot to specify we wanted *a mountain and water view.*"

When I went to buy my first car, I read *Consumer Reports, Car Buyers Guide,* and *Road and Track* magazine. I consulted the Blue Book, talked with satisfied owners of different cars, and test-drove various models. Then I wrote a list of the five things I wanted in a car:

1. reliable
2. burgundy
3. 4-door sedan
4. sunroof
5. no more than 5 yrs old; mileage under 50,000
6. price under $6,000

The day I wrote the list, I found an ad in the classifieds for a four-door burgundy Camry with a sunroof. By that afternoon, I had my car with all criteria satisfied. I have had many happy reliable years with this car.

Writing a description of what you want is a way of saying you believe that it's attainable and you are ready to receive it.

Napoleon Hill, in his well-known book *Think and Grow Rich*—still in print after more than forty years—states firmly, "There is a difference between wishing for a thing and being ready to receive it. No one is *ready* for a thing until he *believes* he can acquire it. The state of mind must be *belief,* not mere hope or wish."

Trust enough to step out in faith, based not on evidence but on belief. Build an image of what your dream would look like; the more specific you are, the more ready you are to have that dream come true.

Now You

When you write down a full description of something, you make a commitment to its possibility, and you show your readiness to receive it. On some unseen level, you set wheels in motion, sending a signal out to whatever gremlins are in care of the dreams department to come help. It's like running a cosmic classified ad. The calls start coming in.

If you build it, he will come.

16
Walls Are Doors

THE CANADIAN IRON MAN TRIATHLON IN CALGARY ONE YEAR had the theme "Walls are doors." Sponsors and athletes alike walked around town with T-shirts proclaiming it: "Walls are doors." At first, some people not part of the event were confused by the enigmatic slogan. Walls are doors? What did that mean? And then slowly, it would dawn: That which seems to stop us can actually be an opening. When you are writing for relationship and hit the wall—that is, when you think you have expended all you want to say, or when you judge that what you have written so far is not worth continuing—it is a challenge, an invitation, to keep on writing, past the point of wanting to quit, and to discover the door opening onto something unforeseen.

Walls are doors: What seems to block you actually asks you for some commitment, some willingness to risk; what stops you, then, is a challenge, and what waits on the other side is often worth pushing forward past the resistance.

Writing Through to Resolution:
The Lid Is Off the Box

Writing past the wall sometimes gives us a clue into what caused the breakdown in the first place. To understand our actions and reactions, we need to know what drives us, what is underneath our response. When you keep writing past all the obvious surface thoughts, there is often a "burp," and right past it, you uncover what was causing the block.

Perhaps you have heard of an experiment done with fleas. They put the fleas in a box and then put a lid on the box. As the fleas jumped, they kept hitting their little flea heads on the roof of the box. Ouch. Within a short space of time, every flea inside that box was jumping just below the level of the lid. The experimenters waited a little while longer, and then they took the lid off the box. Can you guess what happened? The fleas continued to jump—*just below the level of the lid.* Oh, maybe one smart flea jumped high, over the top—and out. Wheeee. Hey, guys, the lid is off the box! But the others would not listen. They were not going to risk hitting their heads again.

That is just like us, sometimes. Our actions, our responses, are based on rules we set up a long time ago that are no longer operative. I am here to tell you the good news: *The lid is off the box.* You no longer have to operate by principles that helped you survive when you were in the third grade. You are grown up now and have resources and experiences that were not available to you then.

Dr. James W. Pennebaker of Southern Methodist University did an interesting study with college students. Students who spent twenty minutes a day writing down things that troubled them showed "an increase in germ-fighting lymphocytes in their blood" and paid fewer visits to the infirmary. The key was that the students wrote long enough to get a new perspective about each problem. That is what I call "writing through to resolution."

To write through to resolution, get out the whine, go past the "useless questions," and uncover the upset underneath it, the imaginary lid on your box.

Writing beyond the wall presents us with the unexpected. If you quit, you might miss it. When you write through to resolution, there is a release of endorphins inside your head. You feel turned on, "lightheaded" about it. That "high" often comes when you persevere past wanting to stop writing.

When writing for relationship, as with other moments in life, the point of most resistance is the point of highest potential. Be willing to go beyond it.

Now You

When you want to quit writing, train yourself to follow this simple formula: three small words—*keep on writing*. Keep on writing, past the point of discouragement, of thinking you have run out of ideas, of judging you have said it poorly, of wondering if it sounds dumb and whiny. Keep on writing. Write through to resolution, write through to the surprise.

Walls are doors: It gets easier on the other side. Once you show that you are willing to go past the wall, the resistance yields and becomes a door, often opening onto something grand and unpredictable.

A wall stops you; a door gives way. Gives way to what? That's yours to discover as you go through the wall.

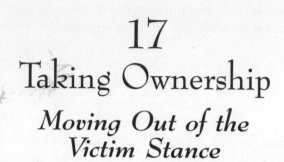

17
Taking Ownership
Moving Out of the Victim Stance

JIM AND I WENT TO A LECTURE GIVEN BY A HIGH SCHOOL COUNselor, Larry LaPorte. The title of the talk was "Why Some Students Go to Harvard and Others Drop Out at the Tenth Grade." That's a title that would intrigue any parent. One point he made that night stuck with me and has implications far beyond academics. He said you can tell the difference between sharp students and poor students by the way they speak about their grades. A good student says, "I almost got an A. I came this close and I missed the last question. Rats. I got a B plus instead. I came so close."

The poor student says, "He gave me a D. I can't believe it. He doesn't like me. I worked so hard on that report, and all he gives me is a lousy D."

The difference is not the B plus or the D. The difference is the ownership of the grade: "*I* came this close to an A" versus "*He* gave me a D." Smart people take responsibility for the things that happen in their lives.

Writing through to resolution is a good way around the "it's not my fault" syndrome. Writing is all about possibilities. Writing is an expansive, high-energy way to explore options. As soon as you start to write something down, what comes up is alternatives to staying stuck. It's the difference between seeing yourself as the brunt of outside forces, or noticing that you have a say in an awful lot that happens to you—and a lesson to learn from everything else.

For example, I have long believed that your car is a metaphor for your life: If you are having a brake problem, look at your life to see what that mirrors. Do you need to slow down? I know a driver who takes turns too sharply and sometimes winds up bouncing over the edge of the curb. Turns out, she's cutting corners in other areas of her life too—not getting enough sleep, low on funds. "What is the lesson life wants to teach me here?" is a useful question, and writing can help us get at the answer.

The Roommate from Hell

James's friend Lisa had a problem. A young woman she had gone to school with called her up one day and said she was going through a crisis; could she move in with Lisa without paying for a few days, to tide her over? Lisa is a good sort and felt sorry for her, so she agreed. She had no idea what she was leaving herself open to. Not only did her new roommate not leave in a few days as promised, but Lisa got a hint that she planned to stay even longer when mail started arriving in her name. "This spells trouble," thought Lisa. "A person who plans to stay for only a few days doesn't change her address."

Lisa said nothing. She wanted to be nice, to help out a friend. They kept pretty different schedules, so at first, Lisa figured it was live and let live. Then little things started to add up. One night, Lisa was having a snack attack and went to the cupboard to find that the roommate had eaten all of Lisa's Ding Dongs and her Chocolate Dip Granola Bars. Lisa went to do a laundry; the uninvited roommate had used up all her laundry detergent and left the laundry room a mess. Then Lisa got her phone bill. The roommate had used her phone to call France. To compound the horrors, she started playing loud music late at night.

Lisa was miserable. It got so she dreaded going home to her own apartment. She didn't want a confrontation. She would come over to our house and outrage us with one new story after another. The Ding Dongs and the laundry detergent were bad enough, but the call to France! and the change of address! This was truly the roommate from Hell.

91

Unless you've ever been in a similar situation with a pushy person, you might find it hard to understand Lisa's feeling of helplessness. Lisa was clearly the wronged person. Yet she could not bring herself to say anything. She kept hoping that maybe the problem would resolve itself, that one day she would come home from work and find the woman had moved out.

Not likely. As long as Lisa kept seeing herself as a victim, the roommate from Hell would continue to take advantage. One night, Lisa came over to our house, sat on the edge of our sofa, and almost cried.

"It's not my fault. I was only trying to be nice, and now I don't know how to get rid of her."

As soon as you hear yourself or someone else say, "It's really not my fault," hand them a piece of paper and a pen.

"It really *is* your fault," I say cheerfully. It is not a put-down; it is an acknowledgment of power, the power you have over the events in your life. The first step in clear problem solving is taking responsibility for the problem. It really *is* your fault, and there is a freedom in that, a freedom to make choices and to recognize that you have been making choices all along that got you where you are. Knowing that, you can now make new and healthier ones.

I asked Lisa to start with that premise, the premise that it was her fault, and write out what she could have done differently. I told her to write through to resolution and uncover the options of what to do now. She wrote:

It's hard to see this as anything I had a hand in, but I guess there are some things I could do now to get back in charge with a situation that seems to be running away with me.

Her first thoughts were of revenge:

I could change the locks on the door and mark her mail "return to sender." I could hide the granola bars and put a lock on the phone.

None of these options sounded attractive. Since she was still feeling powerless, a helpless victim, Lisa went on to answer the question, "What are some things I could have done differently?"

Well, I could have spelled out the rules early on; I could have questioned her about the change of address. What could I do now? I could ask for money to help with food and phone bills; I could establish limits—and deadlines. I could ask for consideration where music volume is concerned.

The next thing she wrote summed it all up and provided the solution Lisa was looking for:

"Why not write her a letter to tell her how I feel since it's hard to say it in person and we are on different schedules?"

Within two weeks of receiving Lisa's written requests, the friend moved out. Before she left, she paid part of the phone bill.

Writing it out helped Lisa take ownership of the problem and presented possibilities for improving the situation. People think they don't have options. Writing it out shows them they do.

Keeping the Curfew

Tom took my workshop with his wife, Lynn, and his teenage son, Jason. They are a close-knit family, and accountability ranks high as a value for them. When Jason came home late one Saturday night, his parents were upset. He protested that it wasn't his fault: The fellow who promised to drive wouldn't leave the party. Tom knew that it didn't help to yell or punish, so instead he told Jason to draw up a list of thirty-five ways he could have kept his word and gotten home on time.

Of the thirty-five, some were absurd ("skateboard home," "hijack a train"); some were feasible ("ask a different friend," "take the bus"). The best one of all was the one that came out at the top of the list: "call home."

Workable or far-fetched, all brought home the message—Jason took responsibility for being late instead of blaming someone else.

Taking Charge of Your Life

Sandra is a talented engineering supervisor who was unhappy in her job. She took my Planning and Problem-Solving workshop and later arranged to meet with me for consultation.

"I love the work I do, but I have a fundamental problem with my job," she said—"a boss who should not be in management."

Sandra was upset that assignments she could handle were passed over her head to someone else. This is what she wrote when I asked her to define her problem in writing:

Do I want to stay in this job and make it work, which means changing my attitude and working harder, or am I going to continue to whine as I have been doing lately, or am I going to actively seek another position? If I seek another position, will it be within this company, or will it be outside?

All I know is that I am not happy now—and that includes not being happy with my whiny, weepy attitude that I've had lately. My self-esteem right now is about as low as a mare's belly, and I have allowed that to happen.

When you start to take responsibility in writing, it often flows right into an action plan:

I need to update my résumé. It will make me feel better knowing that it is ready to send out whenever an opportunity presents itself.

I need to apply myself at work to make things more tolerable. This job might be an opportunity, a turning point.

I will start asking for additional tasks to perform. It bothers me that everything that comes into the group from within comes to my boss. I guess I can start by letting people know that I can handle the nonhardware-related questions and they should direct those to me. I have been feeling sorry for myself lately when they've been doing that.

After writing this, Sandra realized that putting together her résumé was a good idea; not only would it prepare her for other openings, it would also help her self-esteem by reminding her of her marketable skills and strengths. Also, she thought it was a good idea to ask for the work she knew she could handle.

"It's amazing how much better you feel when you begin to take charge of your life again," she told me.

When you own the life you live, you open the way to claim the life you want. Two weeks after she wrote the above, Sandra's boss was transferred to another division.

Now You

Make a decision to put yourself in the driver's seat, at the wheel of a clean and fully functioning vehicle. Whenever you hear yourself saying, "It's really not my fault," write through to resolution and responsibility; once you have the options laid out in front of you, you can choose not to act on them, but it's your choice. You are not a hapless victim but full-fledged owner and master.

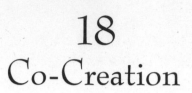

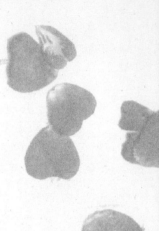

18
Co-Creation

EVEN NOW, YEARS LATER, WHEN I THINK OF THE PLAY PETER and I wrote together, a warmth comes up from my toes and a smile hugs my ears. It was a one-act comedy based on an incident that had actually happened to me while I was riding on the Command Bus in New York City.

When I came back from my trip, I told Peter about an outrageous conversation I had had with the woman who sat next to me on the bus. I said, "New York is a series of one-act plays. Every person you meet there has a story to tell." Peter, who was fourteen at the time and taking a drama class at school, said, "Let's write it up then."

We sat down together in the den, at the old workhorse, Epson QX-10, and cranked that thing out, amid much laughter and good-natured kibitzing. Peter typed, as we both said out loud what would come next. Sometimes we cut each other off, the words were tumbling out so fast. At first we sat side by side, then I started pacing and hovering over him.

It was like that high-energy scene in the old musical comedy routines, where one character throws out an idea, and another builds on it:

"I'll get the band—"

"I'll get the beer—"

"I have a barn—" and then in unison, usually followed by a tap dance, "*Let's* have a party!"

The Command Bus has two characters. One is me ("the writer"), and the other is an outspoken Orthodox Jewish woman, talking to the writer, telling her life history and that of her adult live-at-home son ("I almost DIED giving birth to him").

Peter razzed me for developing the part of "the writer" with elaborate stage directions and internal dialogue, which of course, I was privy to, having experienced it.

> *The writer, not wanting to offend, but realizing the value of direct speech, and wanting to meet her fellow passenger on her own blunt level, answers, "And you?"*

Peter was in hysterics.

"You can't do that! It's not balanced," he would holler. And, "The dialogue has to show what you feel by itself."

We argued good-naturedly over the right word, capped each other left and right. The fur was flying, and we were laughing hard. It was the kind of laughter that becomes a glue and sticks you together, the kind of connection that you do not want to end. You know, even as you experience it, that memories are being made here.

It took us four hours. Those four hours were a peak experience, what Joseph Campbell calls a "bliss hit" in life. I rewind that scene with sentiment through the VCR of my mind and flash-freeze that afternoon to get good vibes.

Then we produced the play. One of my favorite jobs was casting the part of the writer.

Naturally I steered Peter toward a leggy, tall, graceful student to play the part of me. We had auditions and call-backs. Then we set up a rehearsal schedule, directed it, and entered it in a high school competition. The props were simple. We borrowed two bus seats from Metro and sent to

New York for Bloomingdale's, Macy's, and Dean & DeLuca shopping bags. *The Command Bus* won two awards, one of which was Best One-Act Play in the District. I will never forget the feeling of pride and sheer joy as Peter and I walked up together to receive those awards.

It was a highlight of my life.

What I Discovered About Peter

What was most precious about this time spent with Peter was that I took such delight in him. I was astonished by his wit, and his comments about my contributions were right on target.

It was a chance for him to show off, and a chance for me to burst my buttons with proverbial pride. My heart grew ten sizes that day and has not yet returned to its original dimension.

Writing together. What a hoot.

Stars and Dragons

It reminded me of an earlier time with Peter's older brother, James.

James loved the stars, but I could find no books about the mythology of the constellations that were appropriate to his then-first-grade level. So I decided to write one for him. Now I know that if you are writing a book for children of a certain age, the best editors are children of that age. They will be blunt and honest and true. It pays to listen to them.

I would write a chapter a day, and in the afternoon, when James came home, I would ask him to read and respond to what I wrote. I still remember where we sat, side by side in the stairwell between narrow walls, close together on the carpeted tread. I expected James, at the age of six, to give me feedback on phrases that were "too big" or passages that did not make sense. He took his job much more seriously than that. I can see him now, still in his school clothes, with the pencil poised above the manuscript pages, tongue tucked in the corner of his mouth, "Hmm," and "Hmmmmmm." And then reading aloud the opening line of a new chapter, with his brow furrowed, thinking hard.

"Next day, the boy . . ." He took his pencil and with a deft stroke added a caret and inserted the word *The.* Then he read it aloud again.

" '*The* next day . . .' There. That sounds better. It reads more smoothly."

Then he corrected my mythology—"Mom, Diana had *two* horses"—and rewrote whole sections.

All these years later, I remember that scene, sitting in the cubbyhole below the landing, and how I looked forward to James coming home from school.

Ed Yourdon spoke with similar enthusiasm. When he concocted an epic dragon adventure with his then-eight-year-old son, they talked about it all the time, then wrote it together, a little bit each day, at the computer.

Ed paints a lively picture of going to the bus stop on West Eighty-sixth Street in Manhattan to walk his son home from school in the afternoon, or walking him there in the morning, all the while animated at what would come next. Ed himself looked forward to this break in his workday, and his son was eager to come home and get working on their tale together. That must have been a nice reception for him, rather than coming home to a preoccupied parent.

Pulling It Off, Together

Writing together brings laughter, and closeness, and a shared sense of mission and accomplishment.

When author/speaker Terry Paulson was asked to write a book, *Secrets of Life Every Teen Needs to Know,* he knew the book would be more authentic if he wrote it with a teen. He invited his son Sean to co-author it with him.

When his dad confronted him with the idea, Sean was ambivalent. His first reaction, he told me, was, "If I write this with my dad, I'll have to talk to him."

Terry kept encouraging him to do it.

"Dad was totally jazzed, I was apprehensive. At the time I didn't know what it meant, because I was only sixteen. I wasn't sure it would work out. Generally, if you go to a sixteen-year-old and say, 'Let's write a book,' they'd say, 'Whaddya mean, I got enough homework as it is.'

"At first it was a chore, and then second, it became interesting, and then third, exciting and fun."

Terry, for his part, liked the way Sean opened up to him and made honest comments. According to Terry, Sean would say, "Dad, I have to tell you this . . . ," because he was committed to the project. Otherwise, he might have been afraid to critique his father. Normally, if he thought his dad was doing something wrong, he would swallow it, keep it inside. The commitment to the project let him say things he would not otherwise have said.

Sean adds, "There were things my dad wanted to put in there, and I said, 'Nah, it ain't gonna happen.' For example, the chapter on sex. He wanted to say only, 'Save sex for marriage'; I told him, 'That's unrealistic—you have to include both aspects.' I was more realistic, because I saw those things that were going on around me in high school. And he listened to me."

For the final push they went to a hotel in Oxnard.

"The hotel room was to make me feel more serious about it. I was still a teenager, and everything that goes with that. Taking me to the hotel room meant, 'We're gonna do this, we're gonna cram.' "

Bringing the work to completion and publishing it was a source of great satisfaction for Sean.

"When I saw the completed copy and what was made of it, I was really happy. I got to see a finished product, as opposed to just a term paper; you write a paper, and it disappears. There's gratification in knowing you wrote something that matters and that makes money. Six years ago, and it's still selling. That's a good feeling."

Both Sean and his dad agree that the best part about writing together was learning about each other.

Says Terry, "There were things Sean told me that he would not have told me without this book. We had conversations we would never have had."

Sean felt his father had more respect for him after they finished the book.

"I think he learned a lot about me. Even though I've never been the classic student per se, he learned that I was capable of doing things. He learned to trust me more. Because even though I might not have been pulling it in school, I was pulling it with the book."

I Never Knew He Knew So Much

When Peter was a toddler, I published in a Baptist magazine a story called "A Day at Peter's Pace," where I talked about slowing down and seeing the world at a child's speed. The ending was a twist. I went on walks with Peter feeling magnanimous, thinking I was the teacher. The fun of it and the lesson came from the pleased surprise: He was teaching me.

I never knew he knew so much, until I bent down to listen to his running commentary on every house and car and tree we passed.

"I never knew he knew so much": an echo of that phrase seems to be a common thread in co-creation. The mutual respect, and the delight on the part of the adult, is what makes it so special.

That was the surprise that awaited Greg Palmer, when he and his son Ned wrote a play together for Ned's fifth-grade class.

I spoke with Marcy Wynhoff, teacher at Wedgwood Elementary, where Ned goes to school and where the play was performed. She said it was a good experience for all the kids, and especially for Ned, who has Down's syndrome. Since it was his story, the others looked to him to check things out, not just the kids in his own class but the honor students from the Horizon advanced learning program, who were also in the show.

They do a lot of writing at Wedgwood, she said. But this project was different because it was also about relationship, the relationship between Ned and his dad, Ned and his classmates, Ned and the other kids in the school.

Greg gives me the background of how the play came about.

"I like to lie down with Ned at night before he goes to sleep, and he tells me about his day. One night he told me about a play that they were doing in school called *The Magic Apple*. He described the plot of the play and recited his lines. This went on for over a month."

"I sent to his classroom teacher, Marcy, asking for a copy of the full script. That's when I found out that *The Magic Apple* was strictly a fantasy that he talked about at home, a game he was playing with me."

Greg decided to make *The Magic Apple* real.

"We went to my office on a Saturday morning, and Ned and I sat down at my computer. I said, 'Okay, Ned, tell me the story.' With very little prompting, the whole plot and dialogue poured out."

Ned and Greg had written together before. Often, to give his wife a break, Greg would take Ned to the office on a Saturday and sit down at his computer while Ned dictated a story, which they printed up and took home to Mom.

"Most of the stories centered around Chips Ahoy cookies, because they are Ned's favorite. The stories sounded pretty much the same; they were about someone who steals the cookies, someone who finds them, and then Mick Jagger appears, because Ned is taken with Mick Jagger. So we are used to writing stories together like this. I transcribe as he dictates."

In the beginning the stories were simple. This one was different.

"The first stories we wrote were three sentences: 'Boy gets cookies,' etc. *The Magic Apple* was by far the longest story he had ever written, 985 words long. And he had all the details worked out. He was *solid* on the details and on his lines in the play.

"I guess I underestimated Ned, not believing that he could imagine something that complex. He didn't change his lines once. I never thought he could do that."

In addition to having the plot all worked out, Ned had already mentally cast it: "Heidi plays the queen." There is one fellow in his class in a wheelchair named Dana, and so the Famous Fearless Four-Wheeled Fairy part was written for a kid in a wheelchair. Ned had already decided that that was Dana's part. He cast himself as Prince Gallant, and his very favorite line was early on in the story, when Prince Gallant says the name of his horse, calling his horse to come to him. He holds his sword aloft and calls dramatically, "Destiny!"

Greg adapted Ned's story as a play. He had to make what he called certain "school changes"—for example, less violence, and having the sister who marries her brother a step-sister. But most of the play is "pure Ned." Says Greg, shaking his head in wonder, "The elements Ned put in the story are priceless. I don't have the imagination to make an American king, King Albert, married to a Hawaiian queen named Rosaquilla. The main reason that Ned did that is because it gave everyone an opportunity to hula at the end."

The Magic Apple was produced in the school lunchroom. Ned told everyone he met—at the grocery store, the post office, at school—about his play. He invited them all to come, and many did, including the grocery clerk and two of the grocery store customers. His invited guests numbered twenty-seven.

The children who saw the play from the other classes wrote thank-you notes to Ned. They particularly liked the hula dance, and Dana playing the part of the Famous Four-Wheeled Fairy. They wished it were even longer, and they want to see more plays from Ned.

"I hope you can do another play for us," one fellow fifth-grader said. "Someday you may want to do *The Magic Apple II.*"

Writing the play with his dad and successfully presenting it had an impact on the eleven-year-old.

"It empowered him," says Marcy. "Now he is moving on to other things, emboldened by his little triumph."

Not only was Ned proud that it was his play, the kids who were in it and who watched it were proud of him. Says his dad, with delight, "He was not a 'DD kid' but one of their fellow kids who wrote a play, and they laughed and enjoyed it, and that made them proud; one of their own had done this play."

Now You

Writing together erases the distinction between writer and nonwriter, adult and youngster, expert and nonexpert.

When you agree to co-author, you change the rules. A joint project between adult and child provides an area of your lives where it is safe to be honest. There is a mutual respect and honoring of each other's ideas. The project is bigger than either ego.

It is not about writing, it is about relationship.

19
Passing Notes Without Getting Caught
The Art of Small Greetings

REMEMBER THE FUN OF PASSING NOTES IN SCHOOL—THE ADVEN-
ture, the risk, the clever ways we surreptitiously passed them? (My own
favorite method was inside the barrel of a ball-point pen.) Remember the
brazen ways we made them into airplanes to launch when the teacher's
back was turned? They were short comments, or jokes, or pleas for help
with homework. Some were plans:

Meet me after school.

or confidences:

Jason likes you.

or complaints:

This class is driving me crazy.

Notes like that were fun because they relieved the routine, because they were a way of staying connected and showing friendship, of sending secret smiles and support, and because they were a way of talking to each other without saying anything out loud. Everyday notes in life outside school are all that and more. Notes to the people we live with and love renew our bond with them. They are fun to write and fun to receive. They give the reader a sense of security, a warm feeling of being loved. They let someone know you care.

Lunchbox Notes

There are some time-honored places to leave notes, of course. A lunchbox note is a day-brightener and pick-me-up that often nourishes as much as the soup or sandwich. Peter used to forget his lunch all the time when he was in second grade. Jim and I took turns dashing off quick notes to include with the food to help him remember. Peter would grab the note and forget the lunch. He liked the notes better than the sandwich.

Rubber stamps and stickers make lunchbox note-writing easy. We keep a basket of different rubber stamps on top of the refrigerator so any member of the household can dash off corny notes. With the stamp of a dragon belching flames, "You're a ball of fire!" With a bear stamped upside down, "I do a flip when I think of you." With a musical note stamp, "Just a note to say, 'I love you.' "

Like every other kind of heart-writing, lunch notes go both ways. The older children went off to school very early in the morning when Katherine was a baby. She missed them when she woke up. They started leaving her little notes to be opened at noon. It made her happy.

Lunchbox notes are not only for the younger members of the family. When I was giving a workshop in Wisconsin, a man came to me at the break and told me tenderly of the love notes he received regularly in with his salad and Thermos of soup.

"For years, my wife has written me notes whenever I brown-bag it. I value the notes so much, I dump out whatever's edible"—he demonstrated with a shaking motion of a down-turned hand—"to get to the note. I can tell her moods by her handwriting and by what she says.

"What she doesn't know is that I have saved all of her notes in a big shoebox. I'm afraid it would intimidate her or make her self-conscious to know how much I treasure them. Occasionally I pull the box out and leaf through them. It makes me feel good all over again."

Hiding Notes

Post-it Notes are a great invention: those wonderful little sticky-at-the-top sheets that people use to flag important spots in documents, hang on the edge of file cabinets, and record phone messages at home and at work. The beauty of Post-it Notes for keeping in touch is first, they are tiny, so you do not have to write a lot, and second, you can stick them anywhere, so they are fun to hide. Thanks to Post-its, the art of small greetings is no longer relegated to lunchboxes. Now you can stick a note on the steering wheel of your wife's car or right on the dashboard of your son's truck. You can stick one to the side of your roommate's shoe, or slap it on the bedpost while your daughter is sleeping.

Think of the routine of the person you want to surprise with a note, and plan your attack to coordinate with some action he or she will be doing at the time you want your message to hit. If you want a member of your household to find a morning message, plant it in the coffeepot or a favorite mug, inside the medicine cabinet next to the toothpaste, stuck to the side of the shaving-cream can. One time I boarded a bus two stops before my friend's daily entry point, gave a note for him to the bus driver to deliver, and got off at the next stop, one before my friend boarded. This was an elaborate effort for a special occasion, but it shows the possibilities when you put your mind to it.

If you want them to find the note during the day, hide a message of cheer inside a schoolbook on the pages of last night's assignment, or put several inside your husband's or wife's attaché case. If you are the one in charge of making the beds that morning, put a Post-it Note where your spouse or your children will find it that night, or roll it up inside their pajamas.

People often put Post-it Notes on the refrigerator; why not stick some *inside* as well? For example, warnings:

Who touches a slice of this cinnamon bread
Dies like a dog. March on! (he said).

or diet aphorisms:

Nothing tastes as good as thin feels.

or love notes:

Drink plenty of milk. I love you.

You can hide notes on desktop calendars, putting them where they will be found a week or a month from when you wrote them, perhaps on an anniversary or birthday. On a rainy day put a surprise note in a furled umbrella; when the umbrella is opened against the elements, out floats a love note from you. It makes me smile just to think of it.

When you start hiding notes, you never know where it will lead. Once I had a typist who typed in buried notes to me, right in the middle of the chapter, praising a passage she liked or a phrase that caught her fancy. I did not know until I started to edit the printout that there were messages of support buried there.

My Pocket Friend

One September I went into Marshall's Cleaners with some of my favorite fall clothes, wanting to spruce them up for the new season. There was a nip in the air, so I took them out of mothballs.

"Empty your pockets," said the cleaning lady, strict as a policewoman.

I followed her command, and there on the counter were prized possessions that had been lost all spring and summer: some Canadian currency, a card from someone I was supposed to call last year, a small Hershey's chocolate bar with the wrapper written in Korean. Some paper clips. A rubber band. And a bunch of notes. The notes were all from my friend Marilyn. I call Marilyn "my pocket friend." Marilyn and I do not get to see each other as often as we would like, but whenever I do see her, she slips a note of cheer into my pocket before we part. I usually do not even know she has done it, until I reach in later for my keys or a hanky (or a Hershey's kiss). I stand in the parking lot and read it, or I find it as I hang the coat in the closet at home, and then I get to savor our meeting and our friendship all over again. Instead of tossing the note, I put it back in my pocket, to rediscover another day—or another season.

I know a grandpa who puts notes in his own pockets, maybe wrapped around a piece of gum or a small toy, and then tells his grandchildren, "There's something in my pocket for you." Think about coming home from work with a note in your jacket pocket for one of your own children, maybe taped to a magazine or newspaper clip or a clever cartoon that caught your eye. It makes it seem more like a gift when they have to scramble through your pockets to retrieve it. The note could be simple: "I thought of you when I saw this." That's what it is all about. *I thought of you.* In my busy workday, in my hectic travel schedule, you were there with me. I liked knowing I had you to come home to; I looked forward to seeing you and giving you this. What an ego-booster.

Thanks for the Intangibles

The other day, Emily left a note for Grandma on the ironing board, thanking her for ironing her clothes. When I saw it, it set me thinking: Saying thank you out loud is fine, but putting your thanks in writing is even better; the recipient gets to think about it and let it sink in. Somehow the glow stays longer. Lynn Lively, president of Pioneer Sonar, took my writing workshop. In appreciation, she baked me a loaf of bread and put a note in with it, thanking me for opening doors for her. The bread was delicious, but the note fed my soul long after the bread was gone.

Now You

Scatter notes everywhere; hide them anywhere. Shuffle them into things: in with tax forms, tucked in drawers. It makes you feel mischievous as you plot where to plant them. Before you know it, someone just might start hiding notes for you to find.

20
Mirror Messages, E-Mail, Refrigerator Writing

Wʜᴇɴ ᴡᴇ ᴡᴇʀᴇ ɢʀᴏᴡɪɴɢ ᴜᴘ, ᴍʏ ꜰᴀᴛʜᴇʀ ᴜꜱᴇᴅ ᴛᴏ ʟᴇᴀᴠᴇ ᴜꜱ messages that he wrote with soap on the bathroom mirror. Sometimes the soap scrawl was a reminder, a single word or two, like ɢᴀʀʙᴀɢᴇ ᴅᴀʏ or ᴄʟᴇᴀɴᴇʀꜱ. More often it was a soap smile face with "You're beautiful!" or "Knock 'em dead in math today." We would wash off his message and leave one in return for him to read that night. A bonus was that we had very clean mirrors.

Susan Jurgensen, a workshop participant from Newton, Massachusetts, wrote me this story:

> At one time my "significant other" was a chef while I taught during the day. We sometimes did not see each other for days. One way we communicated was to scribble notes on the bathroom mirror, written in eyeliner pencil or lipstick. Very often the messages were quotes, i.e.:
>
> "You do to me what spring does to a cherry tree"   —Erica Jong
> One day following an argument and pressed for time, all I could think of was "Out, out damned spot."

It really made getting out of bed fun and still gave a personal touch to the days when we didn't see each other.

When you want to get someone's attention, a message in the mirror gets the notice you want. Adrienne, of the University of Washington Escort Service, walks me across campus at midnight and tells me that when she went to visit her grandma, she left a little note for her tucked in the mirror.

"She kept it up there for three months. It got almost embarrassing," Adrienne said, but she sounded pleased.

Shaun, the other half of the escort team, says, "I swear, my mom and dad wouldn't have a marriage if it weren't for Post-it Notes and mirrors. They have a very erratic schedule and are hardly ever home at the same time. They leave notes for each other on every mirror in the house."

Many people are visual learners—that means they take in information best by seeing it or seeing some picture to represent it. If you find yourself saying to a member of your household, "I've *told* you a hundred times . . ." or "Why don't you *listen* to me?" maybe your child, your spouse, or your roommate learns better through his eyes than through his ears. Don't just tell him to do things—write them down, especially in colors. And when you want to make sure she gets that big thank you, that compliment, that notice that you caught him in the act of doing something good, when you want to make sure your cheerleading registers, write it down and post it in a place where she will see it, a place where it will catch his eye—the mirror.

Electronic Mail

My friend Ed is a computer nut. He and his wife each have a computer, as do their sons, ages seven and eleven. The computers are connected by a network, and so the family is able to communicate back and forth electronically. While the dad is working in his home office, for example, his computer bleeps to tell him he has a message waiting. When he checks it out, it is his seven-year-old saying, "I need help on math. Can you come when you're finished?"

The eleven-year-old is playing a computer game; he stops to send a message to his mom: "Will you take me shopping tomorrow? PUL-LEEZE. I need new shoes."

When Ed is on the road, he calls in from his laptop and finds daily messages from his family—telling him what they are doing while he is gone, and how they miss him. One time, when he got back, there was a message waiting on his home terminal. It said, "Welcome home. What did you bring us?"

My cousin Mary Frances is a graduate student at a university where all the students have been "on line" for years. Recently, I joined the revolution and now have my own electronic mailbox. Right away I got a message from Mary Frances, "Welcome to cyberspace!"

Mary Frances and I communicate frequently now and it keeps me up on the trivia you miss out on when a member of the family is far away. I helped her through her German exam; she supported me in a decision I was making. I was the first one to know when she was asked to deliver a professional paper at the University of Montana in Missoula (who else could she call at midnight?) and then—in the next breath—the text of her address showed up on my screen. With one tap on the Print key, I had a copy in hand.

This is far more fun than the old two juice cans and a string.

Refrigerator Writing

The refrigerator is the ultimate bulletin board of a household. I often think I know a family well after reading their refrigerator. Here's where the trophies are posted: who won an award, who's on a diet and needs a nudge. This is where the favorite pictures go—of a dream vacation spot, or a family member far away. Here are the clips from Abby about how to discipline, the sayings and aphorisms that struck us, and of course, the prized drawings and A papers, the compliments from teachers and coaches, held fast by funny magnets. The refrigerator also posts emergency phone numbers—police, fire, and pizza home delivery.

Over the years, whenever anyone asked us to pray for them or to send positive thoughts their way when they were going through a crisis or preparing for some test, we put their names up on our refrigerator. That way we knew we would remember them and wing a prayer their way, since the refrigerator is the most frequented spot in the house, the first place anyone goes when they walk in the door. All our friends know we do this; after a while a shorthand way to ask for support became, "Say, put us up on your refrigerator, will ya?"

So what better place than the old icebox for notes—messages of support and love, and chore reminders, especially for those chores that need to be done in the afternoon or early evening. Naturally you can use magnets and small squares of paper, but it was a happy day for us when we realized that dry-erase markers work on the refrigerator surface. Now the messages are big and splashy and colorful, and as far as chores are concerned, a quick swipe signals completion of each one. Then the kids wrote back messages and pictures for us. We dubbed it The Metropolitan Refrigerator of Art.

Peter is a highly visual learner. He responded most enthusiastically to our refrigerator billboard. One day we came home to find the written-down chores done and erased, and a four-color picture of Michael Jackson moon-walking across the side-by-side doors of both refrigerator and freezer. Underneath the lavish drawing, Peter had written, "Way to go!"

We got the message.

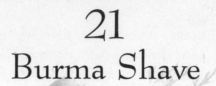

21
Burma Shave

Does your husband rant and rave
Grunt and grumble
Misbehave?
Shoot the brute
Some Burma Shave!

Before the interstates arrived with their fast-speed high-ways, the old Burma Shave ads placed along country roads would break up the monotony of a long car trip, provide diversion, and bring a smile, even if the ending was predictable. The spacing of the signs paced the reading of the verse, and each pause was an anticipation of what would come next. It was a message that made us work along with it.

No-Nag Reminders

The old Burma Shave campaign provides a model for a message with a zing, particularly helpful as a gentle nudge.

Peter often forgot his lunch. To help him remember, we hung a note inside his bedroom door:

We want you to know . . .

The next note was on the bathroom door:

We love you a bunch . . .

Can you hear it coming?

Please don't forget . . . (at the bottom of the stairs)
To bring your lunch!!! (on the counter with his brown bag)

It wasn't until he got to school and opened it that he found the final note,

Burma Shave! (couldn't resist that one)

Trail notes do not have to rhyme, but if you do decide to rhyme them, construct them backward. Katherine needed a reminder to feed her fish. Fish. Fish. What rhymes with *fish*? I got it—*wish!* Here goes:

(first note) *Go out and play*
(next) *Whenever you wish*
(and then) *But please be sure*
(here it comes) *You feed your fish.*

As you see, this is not deathless poetry, but it is not meant to be. It's throwaway verse, and it can be as bad as you want. The meter does not matter; the message is what counts.

When the string of notes are chore reminders, let the succession of notes lead directly to the job.

Peter Peter Pumpkin Eater, says the first sign. Intrigued, his brother James follows to the next one, which he can just spot at the top of the stairs.

Likes his room a little neater—now he's really curious. He moves on, and on the bedroom door is another: *So here's the word to brother James.*

And now, landing in the room itself, *PLEASE PICK UP YOUR MESS OF GAMES.* Too late to escape; he might as well pick up the games.

Physically, trail notes take the reader along the path to the completion of the task, and they take a lot of the drudgery out of the assignment. They engage the whole body and put the person in motion, not to mention in smiles along the way.

It was not long before our kids caught on that trail notes work both ways. One night Jim and I went out to the movies. As soon as we walked back in the door, we noticed the series of signs on the walls. They led from the front door, up the stairwell, and down the hallway, one page for each word. *TOOTH FAIRY,* the first two signs read. The 0's of *TOOTH* were big eyes with eyelashes, and underneath these sparkling orbs was a gap-toothed grin, with arrows pointing to the missing molar. Laughing, we followed the rest of the signs.

You know how it is. The Tooth Fairy gets busy on her rounds or sometimes falls asleep on the job. Try explaining that to a six-year-old, who has faithfully wrapped her tooth and put it under her pillow for four nights running, with no results. Emily decided the good fairy needed some direction.

This way to Emily's tooth.
Hint: the tooth is wrapped in tolit paper.

More arrows, more signs, and finally, on the door, *In Here!—Open door!— It's under the pillow.*

Maybe the Tooth Fairy was redfaced or added an amusement tax, but the fee was paid that very night, and the amount was double the usual tooth tariff.

A Sign of Caring

The most important message of trail notes is not the content at all but the message underneath, the message that somebody cares.

It's no fun to come home to an empty house. A note on the counter is nice, but a series of notes hung around is even better. A note on the counter just sits there; trail notes play with you. Following them along takes only about sixty seconds, but somehow when you finish, the place seems friendlier. Your friend, your mom or dad, has been here before you and was thinking of you. You think, "Somebody went to all this trouble to make it creative, to make it rhyme, to find the tape and hang it up, and that somebody loves me."

One young boy whose father left him a trail of notes regularly told me, "It's like a quick game that my dad is playing with me. He played his half before he left the house."

Quest: A Treasure Hunt

Welcome to the Quest
Are you in a good mood?
You'll find your first clue waiting
In a place we warm our food.

Emily and Peter devised a game they played over and over with some neighbor friends. They called it Quest, and it was a kind of treasure hunt. They took turns at being treasure-mapper and treasure-seekers. The treasure-mapper wrote clues that led the seekers, say, first to the microwave oven, where a new note directed them to the bookshelf. And so on. The mapper wrote and then hid ten poems. Each poem was a clue to where the next poem—and clue—was hiding. The final one led to some prize, some object the mapper was willing to give away, or the promise of a foot massage.

Peter says the rhymes were "fairly dumb, but we wanted them to rhyme because it was more fun; the rhyme was so poor, it was offbeat. The stranger the poem, the funnier it was. You got a good laugh over how stupid the poem was."

I asked him, "Why did you do it?" He answered thoughtfully, "We were recreating birthday feelings. Treasure hunts with a gift at the end were something you had done for us on our birthdays, and we wanted to create that birthday feeling in the middle of the year on an ordinary day."

Several times we turned the Quest game into a celebration of appreciation for Grandma Klauser. She is a hard worker, and when she comes to visit, she pitches right in. In thanks for the things she has done and as a reminder of all the good times shared, we buy her a bunch of little gifts and, with a series of rhymed notes, send her back to the ironing board, the dishwasher, the flower bed, the dustpan, the mop and pail, and the cribbage board to find each gift. Each gift has the next clue wrapped inside it, and the final one leads to the "real" gift. The grandchildren nip at her heels like eager puppies running alongside, as the clues take her up and down stairs, out to the yard, and back. Grandma always says, "Oh, you shouldn't have," then smiles all the way through it.

The Ultimate Quest

You do not have to limit Quest to your own back yard. One time we took a friend all the way to the Caribbean on a treasure hunt.

Our friend Shannon was celebrating his fiftieth birthday; with his wife we planned a holiday in the Caribbean to celebrate. Shannon knew only that the four of us were going on a trip together; he didn't know where. We left messages for him all along the trail—on board the plane, when we landed and changed planes in Chicago, at the baggage claim in Puerto Rico, at the airport bar in Tobago—before going on to Grenada, where we were to meet a sailing ship. We had the stewardess hand him the first note with a bottle of champagne. Once we had his name announced over the airport loudspeaker to come pick up a message at the United desk.

"When I heard my name announced, I was flabbergasted," said Shannon, recounting the story later, with a smile in his voice. "Who knew I was there? How did they know to page me?"

He never knew where the next clue was coming from; it kept him off-balance. At one point, he was expecting one and did not get it. At one stopover we had a couple of hours between planes, and we took him below to the baggage pickup area and stood in line watching the carousel spill out the luggage. Shannon was the only one who did not know there were no bags there for us, because our bags were on their way to the final destination. Meantime we gave a note to a beautiful Puerto Rican woman who went up to him with a smile and asked, "Are you Shannon? Happy Birthday!" and handed him the next clue. At each location we had him convinced that that was the place we were going—giving him pictures of the Sears Tower, brochures of the hotel we were supposedly staying at in San Juan, advertisements for scuba-diving in Tobago and Trinidad.

The poems were bad, very bad, but once again, the meter did not matter; part of the fun, as with Peter and Emily's Quest game, was the groan factor. The ending refrain on each and every clue-note was, "What a way / To celebrate a birthday!"

Shannon was incredulous. When we finally arrived at our true destination and boarded the sailboat, he leaned back in the stern contentedly and said, "What a way to celebrate a birthday."

A Trail of Thank You

Betsy Baiker, a vice-president at Oppenheimer & Co. and member of the board of directors at Wainwright House, went to visit a friend in the Hamptons for a weekend. She left a trail of thank-you notes at the beach house behind her, each of them a play on words. She tucked them in places that retraced the moments she and her hostess had shared: in the tea canister, on a photo album page, with a collection of seashells they had gathered in an early morning walk.

I left a similar paper path after staying with Amy Weintraub, the playwright, in Newport, Rhode Island. Amy wrote to tell me how she had discovered my messages one by one.

"The last one beamed at me as I climbed into bed, and I laughed myself to sleep. Thanks for the generous gift of your spirit."

So trail notes are a pleasant way to say thanks.

Emily puts a load of wash in the washing machine one night and leaves a note on my pillow, "Please put the wash in the dryer before you go to bed." I am tired, ready to retire. I do not feel like going back downstairs to the laundry room. Begrudgingly, I go. When I lift the lid, there is a note taped to the inside of the dryer: "Thanks for remembering." Even at midnight it was worth a smile. Somebody has been here before me, someone who cares.

22
Be a Bon Voyage Person

Jesuit author John Powell tells the story of a man who was setting off for a dangerous sea journey. Everyone on the pier was discouraging him from going. Finally Powell himself ran to the end of the pier and wished him well.

I remembered this one day when some friends and I were in Friday Harbor, a port in the San Juan Islands of Washington, and a plucky fellow was in a kayak heading for Alaska. Alaska! That's fifteen hundred miles of open sea in an open boat. Maybe he was a bit foolhardy, yet I could not help but think of Powell's story, for each and every person on the pier was shaking his or her head and muttering while he packed up his gear.

"It's cold out there."

"You'll freeze."

"It's lonely."

"You might die."

"It's dark. You might be scared."

"Are you sure you want to do this?"

The fellow was determined, in spite of the negative send-off. He resolutely shoved his small craft loose from its moorings to begin his perilous journey.

How could I let him go with the echoes of despair resounding inside his head? What comfort would such mutterings be when he did get lonely and cold and hungry, and when the dark enveloped and scared him?

Remembering Powell's story, I mustered all my courage. If this fellow was willing to risk a voyage to Alaska in an open boat, I guess I could risk appearing foolish to these realists on the pier at Friday Harbor. I ran to the end of the pier and cupped my hand to my mouth so my voice would carry.

"Bon voyage, brother!" I called, "Godspeed! We're with you. The wind and sun are your friends. Godspeed! Bon voyage, brother!"

Life is like that. There are always plenty of doomsayers around to point out the perils, to tell us what we're doing wrong. We need to be, in Powell's term, "bon voyage people" to those around us, to cheer them on, to notice what's right and what's working, to send them on their way with smiles on their faces. Sending a note is one powerful way to do that.

Writing this book, I sometimes got discouraged. There were times when I was moved by a story and wanted to share it and its message with a passion. I was fired up. At other times I was walking in heavy boots through molasses fields and saw no end—or worth—in sight. At my darkest moments I took out a postcard I had received from a friend, a fellow writer whose work I admire. I had sent her some early pages of *Put Your Heart on Paper*. She sent me back a postcard with two sentences, *I don't know how you could have doubted it. It's a terrific idea.*

What do you think I did with that postcard? Smiled once and tossed it out? Not on your life. I photocopied it many times over and pasted it everywhere: in my journal, by my computer, on the desk pull.

My friend doesn't doubt—why should I? Keep on writing.

A Secret Energy Source

Once when I was doing a workshop in Atlanta, feeling overworked and kind of low, I woke up in a bad mood. I trudged into the hotel ballroom and started setting up for the workshop—adjusting the overhead, setting out handouts. I opened up my prop pouch, and there next to my Koosh ball and my pen that glows in the dark was a note from home—

Knock 'em dead, Mom. You're the best
—with a smiley face.

In that one stroke my whole mood shifted. I felt powerful, invincible, playful. I had a smile on my face and in my heart. That one little note made a difference in my whole presentation, in my ability to be all that I could be for my audience.

Now when I'm going on a trip, I pack my bag the night before and leave it out in the hallway, the way the children leave their shoes in front of their bedroom doors on Saint Nicholas Day, hoping for treasures to fill them in the night. Emily and Katherine get the hint, sit down with rubber stamps, and make a bunch of little notes.

They put one in a shoe, one in my cosmetic case, a couple in with my workshop materials. Funny part is, in the rush to catch the plane and in the frenzy of flying and settling into my hotel, I often forget that they're there. Until I open my case, and one flutters out.

Let your light shine.

Or I put my foot into my high heels and something blocks my toe. *You are bee-you-ti-ful. Tell me, who does your hair?*

And it gives me a jolt, a shot, a smile.

Notes from home are a recharge battery, a secret energy source. They warm my heart, radiating love, tickling my toes. They give me the courage to carry on.

Forward a Compliment

Years ago, I was in a carpool where the mother of one of the little girls said something that haunted me and made me feel so sad. She said of her little girl, who often looked forlorn, "I never tell Colleen that she is pretty. I wouldn't want it to go to her head."

Would it be such a terrible thing to be six years old and know that your mother thought you were pretty?

Unlike Colleen's mother, I believe the people you love in your life need to hear directly from you how wonderful, how talented, how smart, how handsome you think they are—and they also need to get the message indirectly, from other people, through you. That makes it stick more.

After a while they might even start to believe what is true. Think what could happen to the people in this world if we could live up to the potential of the truth of our talents. When you relay a positive remark that someone else said, it is the old "appeal to authority" used to advantage. It is not just me who thinks you are wonderful; the whole town is talking about it.

One time Peter had a piano teacher who called me at work to say, "Peter is doing very well at piano. But don't tell him I told you that." We found a new piano teacher within the week. A compliment, an acknowledgment of progress, is made to be passed on. When you overhear a tribute to someone you know, give it back to the original claimant. What is the use of a compliment you do not pass on? It is like the song from *The Sound of Music:* "A bell is no bell till you ring it."

Love in your heart wasn't put there to stay, and a compliment becomes real when the person it is directed to knows about it. Relaying it verbally is better than not reporting it at all, but when you put it in writing, it is sure to sink in. Grab a memo-cube-size paper and write it out verbatim, like an attributed quote from a famous person.

"James is a whiz at computer graphics. I'm impressed."
—*Irene, clerk at Olson's*

"Jim has a brilliant mind. He handled that deal like a master."
—*Joel Sullivan*

"Emily is so self-assured. She works well independently, and also bringspositive energy to the group."
—*Mr. Dave Baldwin, math teacher*

And then just leave it somewhere that the complimentee will find it and reflect, "He said *that* about *me*?"

For some reason forwarding notes are more powerful in the third person. It's a subtle distinction, but listen to the difference here.

"People were talking about you at the grocery store today. I heard them say what a fine athlete you are."

Compare that to,

"Peter is a fine athlete."
—overheard at the grocery store

"Trish told me she saw you playing with her two-year-old today, and she was impressed by your ease with little kids."
Or,

"Katherine has a way with little kids. I enjoyed watching her play with my two-year-old today."

—Trish, Becca's mother

The members of your family, the people in your life you care about, need to know not just what you say about them but what others are saying also. Consider yourself a letter-carrier; it is your job, come rain or hail or sleet or snow, to forward any compliment you hear to the right address.

I Love You Because . . .

Bob Pike, president of Creative Training, says, "People are like dry sponges waiting for a drop of appreciation. There is always someone there to point out what is wrong." Be the one to point out what is right.

My friend Helen Hesketh once gave me a pack of printed cards about the size of calling cards. They had red hearts in a border all around the outside, and inside that heart frame, in blue, it said, "I love you because . . ." and then the rest of the card was blank, giving me plenty of room to recognize a specific action or a delightful trait. This pad of cards put me on the prowl—I was on the lookout for good deeds to write up. I was like a meter-maid giving out tickets, but instead of being a fault-finder, I was a self-appointed "good-finder." The "I love you because . . ." cards were quick and small and helped me say something specific.

What to Say When There Is Nothing to Say

I have a letter from my dad framed and hung on the wall in my kitchen. I keep it there not only as a reminder of a dear man and our love for each other, but also to help me keep in mind how easy it is to write a short note that has an impact. My dad did not give me any advice here, he had no profound message, he used no fancy words. He just wanted to say, I think of you often and I love you.

When I pass your picture on the refrigerator, I say, What a gal! Sure would like to see her and enjoy her sparkling wit.

What I learn from that, every day, is that the emphasis in a bon voyage note is on the person you are writing the note to and on what he or she means to you. Bon voyage notes are "you" messages, not the accusatory, judgmental kind but the cheerleading kind. Whenever I am stumped about what to say in a quick note, I start with "You . . ." and something lively is sure to follow.

Now You

It only takes a few seconds to scratch out a message of care, yet such a simple act can have a long-lasting effect. A friend who saved a note her dad sent her told me, "It's like a conversation I can have over and over with him." That is how I feel about my dad's letter framed in my kitchen—it's a conversation we can have over and over, and it continues to give me solace and support fifteen years after his death. You wonder, "What can I say?" He did not say anything more than "you're the greatest."

And if you have a friend in trouble and you don't know what to say, chances are your confusion comes from not having a solution to their problem. Forget solutions (the best are within anyway); express support.

Be a bon voyage person to the people in your life. Cheer them on their way—let them sail the day's rough seas with your words of encouragement nestled next to their hearts. Tell them the truth: "You are not alone."

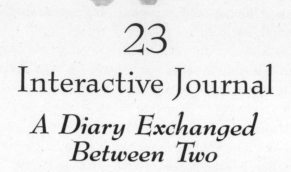

23
Interactive Journal
A Diary Exchanged Between Two

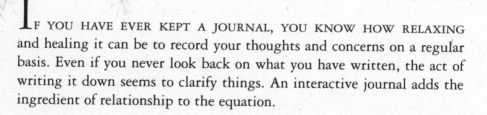

IF YOU HAVE EVER KEPT A JOURNAL, YOU KNOW HOW RELAXING and healing it can be to record your thoughts and concerns on a regular basis. Even if you never look back on what you have written, the act of writing it down seems to clarify things. An interactive journal adds the ingredient of relationship to the equation.

After giving a workshop in New Hampshire, I received a fat envelope postmarked Merrimack. Inside was a photocopy of a journal that spanned several years, alternating a young child's hand and drawings with an adult's answers. I took the package on the ferry with me, and surrounded by the Olympic mountains, the waters of Puget Sound, and several sea gulls, I read through the entire manuscript. The stapled sheets were a chapter from the life of Virginia Penrod, who was in that workshop, and her daughter, Tina. What came through on every page was the relationship between this mother and her daughter, the bond and the caring.

Virginia, a mother of five, sometimes felt overwhelmed by running the household and holding down a job outside the home as well. She was worried that Tina, the youngest, was not getting the same kind of attention that she had been able to give her older children before she went back to work. She started this two-way journal as a way to keep in touch.

I was thunderstruck by this interaction, so generously shared. Between the lines I read of a little girl growing into young adulthood, questioning yet eager, sometimes mischievous, and a mother whose heart was full of love for this little one and wanted her to know the right way. Tina's pages were complaining and explaining, a place to tell her stories and vent her frustrations; a great deal of trust was there. Ginny's answers were New England solid earth: sensible, maternal, never heavy-handed, but wherever possible wanting to use the occasion to teach a moral. Tina openly shared her annoyance with her sister Cindy, for example:

> *Cindy's always grouchy so when I get home from school I feel rotten. I don't know what she's grouchy about.*

While acknowledging and respecting Tina's feelings, Ginny sees a chance for a lesson. In reply, she asks for patience, since Cindy, who is getting married, is not thinking of others but of herself.

> *She only wants to be with John as his wife. Be patient with her, as we need people to be patient with us. It's no fun to kiss a "grouchy face."*

Another time Tina shares her struggle with controlling her anger:

> *Sometimes it's hard to be good. Sometimes it's hard to keep cool without losing your temper.*

Ginny answers gently,

> *It's good when we can notice if our behavior needs to be improved—and better still when we do it. Not only for all the people around us, but even more so, for how much better we feel inside.*

Tina is in trouble. She tries to win her mother over with good intentions.

> *I hope your not mad. I'm trying to be good.*

Ginny, wise mother of five, is not about to be fooled so easily.

> *About your trying to be good—I know you are—and I love you very much, even when you give in to being naughty (that is, thinking only of what you want or want to do for yourself). But sometimes you do pretend you're being good and that's fake. You won't be happy if you let yourself do that. It makes a person very sad inside even when no one else knows it. So, because I love you and want you happy—Keep trying and most of all, be "true."*

Back and forth between mother and daughter, with that practical Yankee wisdom sprinkled throughout. It was a touching thing to read this journal, to peek into the evolving friendship between mother and daughter.

Tina, down on herself, ends one letter,

> *signed your so-so-daughter*

Ginny, always on the lookout for ways to build Tina up, was not about to let that one pass. She came back quickly.

> *you are a so-so-daughter—so VERY so VERY special!!! Every drop of rain that hits you today is a kiss from me!*

As I read, I imagined what it would be like to be a little girl like Tina, reading those letters, so filled with warmth and caring and useful information.

When I finished reading, I sat for a long time without moving.

Then I looked down at the note Ginny had included for me. Tina, the once-eight-year-old who had written "Be Kind" in large letters across the front of her journal, was celebrating her twenty-fifth birthday.

Everyday Stuff

The issues and concerns Ginny and Tina wrote about almost twenty years ago could have been written in our house, or your house, yesterday. Their interactive journal inspired me to set up a journal with each of my children.

First and foremost, the interactive journal is for everyday stuff. It is a way of staying connected when your schedules do not mesh.

Where is my Tina? She's in and out so fast I hardly know she lives here! The only time I seem to be talking to her is when I have to tell her what she has to do. That's no fun! Stop by and say "hello" sometime. I miss you. Maybe there would even be time to ask—You know what??? I love you!!!!
—and just what is your world like lately?

What is your world like lately? One of the first entries that James ever made in our journal told me simply about his Fourth of July weekend with his friends.

I had a nice time with my friends this past weekend. It felt pretty good to just be relaxing around a brick patio—cookin' a few burgers and dogs and talkin' about old times w. my old pals. We played a game of croquet (I won, I might add!) and just a generally fun time was had by all!

When I read that, I thought, Well! that's exactly the kind of stuff I like to hear, the little scraps of information that fall through the cracks because we have so little time together. I did not know that James played croquet. Recently, Emily wrote me in her journal that she had joined the debate club, and the topic was comprehensive national health insurance. I would have felt awful to miss out on that tidbit. Now I can be on the lookout for articles and news headlines about the national health plan, and also I had a chance to write back to her about my own high school debating days and how we all had a crush on the forensics coach.

The journal is also a place for requests, like mine to James to be home for dinner more often and to let me know the next time he plans to stay out until three o'clock in the morning. And Tina has a request for her mom, pleading politely for the perfect birthday:

I hope you don't mind if I make a few suggestions about my birthday. You know if you don't get me anything I won't be disturbed. And if you give me anything I wish it would be a hamster. I know you give me your love on my birthday. And if I just happen to get presents I wish I could go on a treasure hunt to find them.

Since this is a two-way proposition, it is also a forum for the adult to share a bit about what is going on in his or her world. Ginny tries to explain what it's like to be a mom and sometimes having to be the one to say no; another time, she writes of the stress at work that week,

you know how hard I have been working this week . . . my body is tired and my brain keeps telling me to sleep-sleep-sleep.

A Place to Share Worries, Struggles, Problems

An interactive journal is like a friendly ear, ready to listen completely. It is the perfect place to share the hurts of the day and any worries, struggles, or problems. James tells me, over several letters, of his frustration with his truck constantly breaking down and finally how proud of himself he is for getting under the hood to fix it.

Trying hard to hide her hurt, Tina might never have told her mom in face-to-face conversation,

In school today I got on the bus and all of Janet's little friends laughed. So when I got in school I asked Janet why she laughed at me and she said I didn't laugh at you. But she did.

It is also a safe place to share things you are afraid you might get in trouble for. It is a good opportunity to tell the truth, and take responsibility and at the same time have a chance to plead your case. I will not forget the day Peter came downstairs and handed me the journal, solemnly, and I opened it and read,

Mom, I have just kicked a hole in the wall in the upstairs hallway.

Tina also knows their journal is a safe place to tell the truth.

I got a 75 on my math quiz. But mother I'm trying I really am. Please sign it. I know I discourage you but I hope you know I am trying (three underlines). Oh, don't forget the cookies tomorrow.

When Tina is worried, she goes to the journal to share her concerns.

Sometimes you look sad.

Ginny sees an opportunity to turn the concern into a game.

I'm really very very happy Tina, but if I look sad, it's really only that I'm tired like I told you. Once I let my body have some time off, it'll feel more like fun and games again. So don't worry your little head. Happiness I have!

Then Ginny makes a list of things that made her happy and challenges Tina to come up with her own.
 Still struggling with math but feeling a little more confident about it, Tina writes,

did you have trouble with math I don't anymore. I wonder if you have anything you don't want to put on your writing paper.

Ginny answers both questions and once again sees the chance for a lesson and a learning game.

No limits, Tina—you may write anything your heart desires in your notebook here. This is you and yours, and I enjoy it all.
 You know what, there was a time I did have a hard time with math, too! Division was miserable in 5th grade until one teacher showed me how I was just making it hard for myself—even then I never really liked it very much—and I always really hated addition—but boy, am I glad I was made to stick to it and learn even when I didn't want to because math is important every day all your life. Some day, for fun—just keep track of

how many times you use math when you're not in school—maybe we can try it together.

Sometimes there is scolding. Ginny chides Tina on not getting her homework in on time, asks her to be more cooperative in helping her sister pick the tomatoes after school, and once, coming home overtired and finding the place a mess, she scrawled in big letters,

Tina—I could cry when I find your things all over the place. Why do you do this to me—It hurts. Mother

I'm sorry mother (signed) sorry daughter write more next time

For an older son or daughter, the interactive journal is a place to work through teenage issues like curfew, dropping out of school, drugs, irresponsible driving. The more difficult it is to talk about it, the more welcome these pages will be.

My friend David and his son Taylor have kept an off-again, on-again joint journal ever since Taylor was thirteen. Now Taylor is nineteen, and he was planning a trip to Yosemite with his girlfriend. David told me, "I was in a bind. I had always encouraged Taylor to travel and to save toward a dream. I wanted to contribute to his fund, to encourage his excursion, and at the same time I felt real uncomfortable about the fact that he was traveling with his girlfriend. Finally I had to be true to myself, even though I was afraid he would be mad and accuse me of being old-fashioned. I wrote it out in our journal. I'll never forget his response; it began, 'Dad, there are times when you drive me crazy.' That made me laugh. It was almost a relief, it was so direct and real. If he had said that to my face, I might have reacted with anger, but seeing it on paper, I could accept it as a statement of fact. I'm sure I do."

Taylor went on in the letter to explain his side—how this was something he wanted to do and had been planning for a long time—and then summed it up with the line that David remembers most: "Dad, it's not about you. Please do not make this an issue separating us, because it has nothing to do with my relationship with you." David accepted that argument and decided to let it drop. He felt better about it, just knowing that he had expressed his true feelings.

Nothing more was ever said about the letters or the issue itself, but three weeks after writing his defense, Taylor canceled the trip. He never said why, but maybe the fact that his father was able to listen to his side of it and still be honest enough to share where he stood made it easier to make that decision.

When You Are Mad

All families have moments of explosion. It is part of what shapes our humanity, and it shows our children the way we deal with anger and aggravation. I never believe a person who tells me, "We never fight." I want to say, "Let me show you how." I want to say, "Maybe you fight in other ways, in ways that are perhaps less healthy, not by letting it out but by holding it in, not by yelling but by silence." When you live with other people, there have got to be times that you do not see eye to eye on everything.

Writing out your frustrations to share is often a healthy way to fight.

Katherine was mad at me for putting her on restriction. She said it wasn't fair, because I hadn't warned her that that would be her punishment for neglecting to hand in her monthly school assignment. She ranted and raved and cried and ran upstairs, confiding the whole story indignantly to her sister. She was sputtering, she was so mad.

Finally I told her, "Katherine, that's what your journal is for. If you're mad at me, write it out." She stopped midsputter, midtear, her eyes got round. "I can write down what I think? Write that I'm mad?!"

"That's what it's for," I told her.

Later, she came down, journal in hand, with a brave smile. "I feel so much better." And then she added tentatively, "Don't read it until tomorrow."

I honored her request and put the book aside until the morning. When I picked it up, I braced myself for an offensive attack. I made a mental note to explain to Katherine the "rules of fighting," which include, no name-calling. Instead, her entry was gentle, just letting off steam and expressing her side of the argument. I felt much better after reading it.

That was a good idea on Katherine's part—to write out the letter and then ask me to put it away until later. I remembered it a couple of weeks later, when Peter wrote me an angry letter in our journal about a money issue. We had been arguing about it and getting nowhere.

I was so mad when Peter handed me the book that I wanted to tear his letter up.

Katherine's earlier request made me realize that just because he wrote it did not mean I had to read it right away. My eye caught a phrase, "Let me remind you . . ." and I thought—or said out loud—"I don't need this"— and at that point, I didn't. I was still steaming. I put the journal in a drawer.

If Peter made a smart remark in a verbal exchange, I might have thought, What a nerve! and come back with an authoritative, "Don't you talk to me like that." Next thing you know, the scene would escalate, and one or the other of us might have stormed off mad. But since it was written, I could go back to it whenever I was feeling ready to respond rather than react.

The next day I put on *Ave Verum* and a pot of tea, and that helped. It is hard to stay mad with Mozart and a cup of strawberry tea to soothe the savage beast. Before reading Peter's latest entry, I reread some of the other letters, both sides, and that helped me remember the bond, and remember that we had been through tougher times than this, like the reckless driving charge at the Apple Blossom Festival, and the hole in the wall. So I had softened up a bit by the time I finally read his letter. It still irked me, especially the tone, but I was also more open to hearing his side and to sorting out what part of it rang true and what part not.

Longevity: We Go Way Back

An old entry from James makes me laugh.

My apologies for neglecting this book—it's been under some clothes on my desk.

Mostly we do not use our interactive journals every day or even on a regular schedule; sometimes several months will pass; sometimes a year;

sometimes there will be three or four entries in a single week. But when we do use them, and especially when we have a tough issue to address, we know that we are building on a long-standing willingness to communicate. Ginny can tell Tina when she is upset with her room being a mess and concerned about her grades in school, because their book also contains so much praise and love.

The journal gives a historical perspective on what is happening now: "We go way back."

Memory forsakes you, even though you may think, "I won't forget this." Looking back, you can see you've made progress, you appreciate the layers; the love and the richness of the relationship are all there. This is another reason why I encourage you to keep the exchanges together in one bound book: It's not just, here's a letter, here's a letter, but a backlog, a record, of what you have been through together.

When I went back and reread my journal with Peter, it made me feel more mellow. There is a lot of love there on both sides, obvious caring and working things through. For my part I do sound maternal at times, but what the heck, I am a mother. And I'm happy to realize I don't sound patronizing; in fact, far from it. I let him in on the workings of my mind as I struggle to find the words to share what's bothering me. Also, I like the way my pen runs away with me when I start writing about his good qualities and can't stop—for pages and pages.

Classroom Journals

I know a third-grade class in Connecticut that began journaling with the teacher on a regular basis. A lot of teachers do this today. The Connecticut teacher confessed to me that she had no design in mind, which paradoxically is probably the best way to approach it—as a clearinghouse, without too many rules. She was astonished by what the kids wrote. One little boy who had problems at home wrote about them in the journal; another student expressed her happiness at getting a kitten. The Iranian students in her class, during the Gulf War, wrote how they felt about it. Anyone in the class can give her a message or express a concern at any time; at least once a week she collects all the journals, reads them through, and writes a comment or answer back.

She said it helped her to be a better teacher, because she was sensitive to some of the mental baggage that the students were bringing to school each day, and she realized that they often had a lot more on their minds than last night's assignment or today's test.

Suellen, the teacher who tells her story in Chapter 50, has her fourth-grade students write every day and provides the time in class to do that. She tells them they can fold down the page of any entry they do not want her to read, and she will respect that. She takes the books home once a week, reads through the new entries, and writes back.

"There are certain things that they can share with me on paper that they are not able to say face to face."

Recently a little girl came to Suellen and asked her to please read her daily entry right away and not wait for the end of the week. Suellen read that the little girl's parents were getting divorced, and her mom was going away to school, and she would not see her for six months.

"She told me in our journal what she could not bring herself to say out loud. I found her in the schoolyard and just held her close."

A Place for Expressing Love

Mostly the interactive journal is a place for expressing love.

James, Here are some neat things you did this week, and I wanted you to know I noticed:

bought and made a BBQ dinner for the family
took Grandma on a movie date
brought flowers for Dorothy on her birthday

Emily, I overheard you on the phone today, and your voice was so full of enthusiasm, I thought, wouldn't it be nice to have a friend like that!

Tina, it was so nice to get home last night and get your note—gave me that loved-all-over feeling. I'm so lucky I have you! I think I'll give you kisses now instead of at the end! xxxxxxxxoooooooooo

I think your a great mother (most times) I know why you get mad at us.
Cause you don't want us to grow up doing the wrong thing all the time.

boy how I like writing to you. I'm glad you love me. I love you to.

Now You

It is such a little thing. An exchange of letters between two people; why, anyone could do that. It hardly seems worth writing about in a book. Until I see what Ginny and Tina have done, until I read between the lines in journals people have shared with me since, of the searching, and the caring, and the security, the maternal and paternal influence, and the filial trust. Of the friendship.

The last few months of pulling this book together were intense. I had to let go of many things I enjoy, dig my heels in, and write. I needed to get away to a midnight café, or on the ferry to write for long hours. I wasn't as available for the children as I like to be. I wasn't able to go to all the band concerts or the lacrosse games. I stopped reading the funnies with the family every night. Often I did not come home for dinner.

The interactive journals became my lifeline with the kids, especially with Katherine, just to share a thought I had about her during the day and to give her a place to jot down what was going on in her life—like Tina and her mom, like Taylor and his dad, like you and someone you love and want to be even closer to.

24
The Wizard of Oz
All You Need Is Within

REMEMBER DOROTHY AND HER STALWART GANG HEADING OUT to find the Wizard of Oz? He had all the answers, or so they thought. Then Toto pulls the curtain down, and they find out that the wizard they had counted on is a fake, a front, a phony. He has no power. Their dreams are dashed—or so they think. Then the wizard himself helps them to realize the real magic is inside each of them, and they had it with them all along.

Courage. Brains. A heart. And the way to get back to Kansas—what they needed they already had. It was not some wizard who would give it to them; they had only to stand still and give it to themselves.

Psychologists call it "knowing without knowing"—that part of us that senses a truth we have not yet learned to articulate. The problem is we are looking in the wrong place for the answer.

Perhaps you have heard that old Sufi story, retold by Robert Ornstein, Bernie Siegel, and others. A merchant has lost his keys and is searching for them under the street light. His friends come along and offer to help. They get down on their hands and knees and join him in his search. Finally, in exasperation, one of them exclaims, "Ali, where exactly were you standing when you dropped your keys?"

"Over there, in that dark alley."

Sputtering and incredulous, his friend asks angrily, "Then why in Allah's name do we search for them here under the streetlight?"

"Because the light is better here."

We laugh at the silliness of the Sufi merchant, and yet every day we ourselves do precisely the same thing. We look in our conscious workaday minds for the answers, because the light is there—even if the answer isn't.

So how do we get at that place in the dark? Jennifer James, author of *Success Is the Quality of Your Journey,* offers a down-to-earth image: "Listen to your stomach." Good advice. To put that gut feeling into words, grab a pen, set a timer, and start to write, fast, without analyzing—an approach I call rapidwriting. Rapidwriting provides a way of listening to that still small voice within.

We know what we know. We know what we don't know. The trick is to identify that part of us that we know without knowing. Writing is a way to delve into that part of us that knows but cannot articulate what it knows.

We get an aha! moment when the conscious and subconscious come together. We already knew it, but only the right brain knew it. The aha! comes when the information crosses over the bridge of the corpus callosum connecting right and left brain and lets the left brain in on the secret.

Writing without thinking, getting it out of your head and onto the paper, helps make those "aha!s" happen.

The Repository of Your Mind

Your mind is a compendium, a repository of ideas; your birth position in your family, every book you have ever read, the people you have met, the places you have traveled, the languages you have studied, what you had for lunch today, and the route you took to get to work this morning. All of that bundled together constitutes what makes you uniquely you. You have no doubt heard stories about people who have had near-death experiences; they speak of how their whole life flashed in front of their eyes. I used to think that mental review was a quick assessment and fond farewell. Bob McChesney, instructor in the Silva Method, suggests something different. He says that what is happening in those hypertense, life-threatening moments is that the brain is clicking fast through the replay, frantically searching: What have I learned in the past, in anything that ever happened to me from the time I was very little, that could save my life now?

Writing is another way to take a review of what you know—and what you do not know you know. "Writing goes to the core," says psychologist Richard Allen. Writing unlocks ideas inside.

A woman named Susan, a student at NYU, was in a workshop I gave in Manhattan. Susan spoke incredulously about a paper she wrote on systems analysis that she did not understand. The professor said it was her best work. That made no sense to her at all. "Where did that knowledge come from?" she wondered.

Another time, I counseled a brilliant young man who had no confidence in his own abilities. When he saw the A grade on his final term paper, he thought the professor was crazy. "Nothing I did that fast and without thinking could be any good."

I say both these students knew more than they gave themselves credit for, and writing helped them unleash it. Out of desperation, late-night pressure, or deadline panic, they did not have time to listen to the voice that said, "You can't do that." Outta my way, my baby is under that car, stand back while I single-handedly lift four thousand pounds to rescue my screaming infant. That strength, and that knowledge, comes from within.

It Does Not Come from Prentice-Hall

John Garner designed the More Time system, an engagement book that tracks not only "to do today" lists but larger life-goals and dreams. The course I took with John on time management was one of the benchmarks of my life; it changed the way I think and plan.

John taught me another important lesson outside of the class. I was working on my first book, *Writing on Both Sides of the Brain*. Several publishers had turned it down; I was losing heart. It was hard to stay motivated, to keep believing in this work. Then an acquisitions editor from Prentice-Hall called me. He *wanted* my book. He took me to lunch to discuss the terms. I was ecstatic; imagine, going to lunch with an editor, to discuss my book. He gave me a copy of "Prentice-Hall's Guide for Authors." Wow. That made it pretty official, in my eyes. I was in heaven.

He was eager and excited about the project and sent it on to the East Coast office with praise and promise.

I went home from that meeting and started to write again. I wrote and I wrote and I wrote. The words poured through me. *Prentice-Hall is interested.* I woke up in the middle of the night and wrote; I took my pad and my paper in the bathroom, in the car, on line at the supermarket; I could not stop writing; I was one with my pen.

Several weeks passed, high-energy weeks. I kept on tapping my teeming brain.

Then I got a letter from Prentice-Hall, from the Big Boys in New Jersey. "Thank you for your submission blah blah blah, but unfortunately at this time blah blah not right for our house, etc., wish you luck elsewhere etc. etc."

Pruuuushhh. All the air went out of my balloon. I stopped writing.

I called John to cry on his shoulder. I told him how all the energy fizzled out of me, how I had stopped writing. What John said next taught me a lesson for life.

He said, "Henriette, where did that energy to write come from? It did not come from Prentice-Hall—it came from inside you. Go back to your pad, and keep on writing."

John was right. I did just that. I have been writing in supermarket lines, at soccer and volleyball games, at red lights, and in the bathroom ever since.

This was eight years ago, and I have not forgotten it. I have used John's wise words over and over, whenever I am in a slump. "Where did that energy come from? Not from Prentice-Hall; it is inside you."

All you need is inside you. It is already yours. It is already there. It's just that maybe you cannot hear it, since the outside you is so busy about so many things and so occupied with "yes, but" kinds of considerations. Your conscious mind is like the father of a big family who is so concerned about providing for his family, he has forgotten how to play.

If your subconscious mind, the inner part of you, has the answers or at least can point you in the direction of where to find the answers that work for you, how do you get the conscious mind to come out and play? How do you pull down the curtain of bluster and busyness standing between you and your ability to create your own destiny?

Take a piece of paper. Take a pen. Set a timer, and write.

Now You

We can learn from others, but the best wisdom comes from within. Let your writing be a guide who takes you through the wilderness, rather than a court reporter commenting on the action, reporting thoughts already thought out. Let the writing do your thinking for you, with you.

Often as you start to write, you have no idea what you want to say, and that's okay. Write anyway. Allow for the surprise, when the writing takes you somewhere you had not expected to go.

The ruby shoes are on your feet.

25
The Transformative Powers
of Writing
Available to Everyone

THE HEADLINE IN THE PAPER DID NOT BEGIN TO DO JUSTICE TO
the seriousness of the accident:

"Girl, 13, Injured in Fall off Bicycle."

That made it sound like I had been sitting on my bike in the front yard
and it tumbled over. Instead, while vacationing at the family farmhouse in
Ludlow Asbury, I went down Suicide Hill without any brakes on my bike
and wound up a few feet from the railroad tracks with a concussion. It took
a team of doctors two and a half hours to dig the road out of my face; I
needed twenty-seven stitches within one quarter-inch of my left eye, and I
was hospitalized for two weeks. The boy in the bed next to me was
impressed because I had a Gil Hodges autograph, and I promised to get
one for him too. The nurses told me I would be scarred for life. I cried a
little, but not for too long. Instead of moping I wrote a story, which I sent
to a juvenile magazine I subscribed to. I wrote about my mishap (the line I
got kidded about for years after described "my empty scream echoing into
the forest"), my scars, and with the dramatic nobility only a thirteen-year-
old can muster, my vow that for the rest of my life, I would strive to be

beautiful on the inside, since I could not be beautiful outside. I called it, "A Band-Aid for My Soul."

Already at thirteen I was beginning to realize a principle that has guided my life: Writing transforms. Writing takes what is distasteful and makes it palatable, takes what is painful and helps you to heal. Writing that story *was* a Band-Aid for my soul, because it shifted my perspective. "Every crisis has a gift for you in its hands," says the ancient proverb. Writing a story about what seems to be a crisis in your life can help you unwrap the gift beneath.

Years ago I read Nancy Friday's book, *My Mother, My Self.* She speaks of some of the painful experiences she had in school, where teachers ridiculed her; she tells how devastating that was. It was curious to me to recognize some of the same cast of characters in my own high school experience, some of the same put-downs, a similar restrictive atmosphere and authoritative stance. Why had it had an opposite effect on me? How had I come through unscathed?

Then I remembered—I never made the connection before—*The Timely Turtle Type.* Throughout the four years of high school, I was in a club with three other girls. We called ourselves The Turtle Club, and we even invented our own language, called Yertle. For four years we put out a weekly newspaper, *The Timely Turtle Type,* with a circulation of four, and took turns co-editing it. It included satirical poems and stories, jokes and riddles. Where did we get our material? Why, we distilled the events of the school day and made it grist for the writer's mill. We saw everything embarrassing, defeating, and humiliating as perfect material to parody in the next issue. Once a teacher dismissed a question I asked with a wave of her hand and much disdain. "Sit down. Sit down!" she barked. "You are an oddball. You are as odd as Dickinson's hat band." Now that was choice. We milked that phrase for almost a year. First, we wrote a whole story about it; for the next year, it was prime "call-back" fodder. Whenever we wanted to get a laugh from the four club members, who had all been present in the classroom when I was humiliated, the phrase "oddball" or "Dickinson's hat band" was sure to pop up. We never did figure out what it meant.

Harsh words did not have time to stay and eat into the psyche; rather, we were relishing them as wonderful phrases to write about. While others around us were swallowing the repressive put-downs and shrinking smaller and smaller, we were embroidering them, rejoicing in the new material and standing taller and taller, eager with anticipation.

When you think of yourself as a storyteller—and we all are—and your life as a story, it helps keep you from taking yourself and the barbs and frets of life too seriously. If you have ever planned a "dream come true" trip, you know this feeling exactly. The closer you get to the date of departure, the more it colors your world. Everyday frustrations roll off your back. Traffic can be awful, people snarling and rude, and you keep smiling. You can afford to be pleasant and patient with everyone. Next week they will still be stuck in traffic. You will be in Paris.

Similarly, writing colors the events of your life and helps you see them through a prism. Writing takes what was painful and potentially harmful and forms it into a different shape. Like seeing your life as a movie, writing it down lets you see your life as a novel or a good book. And that transformation is available to all of us, not just for those who call themselves writers. It is a path that anyone can follow.

The Sacred Story

Michael Gurian, author of *The Prince and the King,* talks about the healing power of story and suggests writing your own myth to tell the story of your life. As he puts it:

> *The writing process is a transformative force—writing a poem about your feelings; writing down a dream; writing a story, even if it's never published. Writing the words down, forming them into remembered or imagined stories, alters your perceptions and can heal your wounds.*

Children often pick up on this truth intuitively.

Tim Koivu's daughter solved a playground problem with a story.

Tim is first mate on the M.V. *Yakima,* a Washington State ferry. I was riding across Puget Sound on the Edmonds-Kingston run, when Tim stopped by the table where I was writing. We got to talking, and he told me a wonderful story about his daughter, Chelsea.

For years, he, his wife Peggy, and their two little daughters have told stories at the dinner table.

"It started out orally, but to keep us from rambling too much, and to organize our thoughts beforehand, we began to write them down. We had five minutes to gather our thoughts and write out the story." All of them wrote, Mom and Dad and the children, now ages eight and ten. They wrote their stories before dinner, and each in turn got the floor during the meal to read the story they had written.

"It was a chance," Tim said, "to have three other people listen to you completely without interruption. You don't get that a lot in an ordinary day."

Writing stories to read to each other became a way of sharing what had happened during the day, and a way for the children to learn to handle the hurts that came up. One night Chelsea told a story about a little girl who had been pushed down in the playground. Tim and Peggy figured out right away that she was talking about herself. The end of the story was revenge. The little girl got even with the boy who had hurt her. The rules of story time in this house are "no comment," and "no judging another's story," so the parents said nothing.

The next night Chelsea told the same story, but this time with a different ending. She had gone behind the character of the boy in the story to try to figure out what made him mean; in her second story someone had hurt him at home, and he wanted to take out his anger on someone smaller.

Tim's little girl has already learned how to take the hurts of life and make them bearable, how to figure out from a distance what happened and resolve it, how to switch from a subjective, emotional response to an objective, dispassionate one, and then with that new perspective to return to the original situation with new eyes, empowered.

My own children now love this story, and they say to me, "Tell me again the one about the little girl who got beat up at school and made up a story about it."

The Bumpy Bumpy Bed and the Little Fish in the Pond

Dessye Dee Clark is a psychiatric nurse at Children's Hospital in Seattle. She was one of the participants in a workshop I gave there.

Dessye Dee told me how she writes transformative stories with her nieces.

"My oldest niece, Kelly, was very young when her mother remarried. Kelly and I wrote stories together as part of helping her with the distress. Kelly didn't understand that when Mommy got married and went away on a honeymoon, Mommy wasn't leaving her. We did some stories where I adjusted fairy tales like 'The Princess and the Pea,' focusing in on the bumpy, bumpy bed and making it into where she got to tell part of the ending. It's a bumpy life that you have when your mother gets remarried to somebody who isn't your daddy."

Dessye Dee had her younger nieces draw a picture and dictate a story.

"My three-year-old niece, Christina, is verbal enough to do stories with me. I have her draw a picture that she then tells me a story about, and I write it down as she speaks.

"My brother had built a pond with a little waterfall in the back yard of his house, and my niece was trying to get her feet wet in the water when she wasn't supposed to. She dictated to me this elaborate story about how she was trying to rescue this little fish from this big fish and got the water muddy, and that's what her picture was about. The muddy water was clearly her anger at being disciplined for getting her feet wet.

"I thought it was quite an imaginative way to come up with an excuse: 'Well, I was saving the little fish from the big fish in the pond.'"

A Story Within a Story

Writing transforms the events in our lives, turning our pain into promise, and sometimes when we pay attention, the writing has a message for us. This is an extraordinary example of just such a message. It reminds me how the act of writing transforms, not events, but us.

Michale Gabriel is a professional storyteller and my friend. We first met in 1986, when she was planning to take a group of American schoolchildren to Russia to tell stories to the Russian children. She taught our daughter Emily to tell the story "The Woodsman" when Emily was only eight. Michale stands like a tree when she tells a story, and the roots grow out of her feet and into the ground. She mesmerizes her audience as she weaves her tales, and she casts her spell with her whole body, drawing her audience with a twist of her hips or a wave of her hands into the magic of her words.

Michale wanted to write a fable for publication. At first doors opened up for her. An artist agreed to do the illustrations. A friend had a friend in publishing, who would look at her manuscript. So she wrote. And wrote. The story poured out of her. She wrote about a peasant woman named Sophia Petrovna, a master knitter. This woman is lonely and has no children. She decides to knit herself a family to love. One day Sophia Petrovna realizes that if she is ever going to have her dream come true—to have her family of wool stitches come alive—she must do a painful thing: unravel the yarn and recreate it into sweaters and mittens for the needy in her village.

The story took on a life of its own. Sophia Petrovna haunted her. Michale found herself thinking about the story all the time, even in her sleep.

"I was driven, getting up in the middle of the night, to add a word or change a phrase."

She was hurt and bewildered because the publisher never got back to her.

"I thought that they would at least notice it and get back to me. Were they or were they not interested?"

A voice inside her said, "It's not about publishing."

And then it hit her: "It wasn't a story; it was my own road map," she told me.

At first, I thought she meant that her story was a metaphor for the kind of reshaping that any artist does, and a call for the willingness to give away your gifts. It was so much more than that.

Michale felt an ache grow inside her.

"I've been a mother to children all over the world, and I've never been a mother to one—my arms are empty.

"My brother told me, 'You have had more adulation than people have in six lifetimes.' Yet something was missing. My work was not inspired, I was pulling back and closing down. I thought if I could write a book, get on the speaker's circuit, things would change, it would give me that break out of the 'treading water' mode I was in.

"Then I got the message that my writing was giving me: 'You will not grow unless you say yes to this child.' "

*   *   *

Unable to reach me by phone, Michale faxed me a copy of her story, with a handwritten note at the bottom. It gave me chills when I read it:

"I am taking myself apart, moving in a new direction. I have just filed papers to adopt a little girl from the Ukraine; my friend from Odessa is going to the orphanage this week."

I went back to her story and read it again. There was one paragraph there I had not noticed before.

Late one night when everyone was asleep, Sophia was awakened by something tugging at her heart. It was a dream, so long unanswered, Sophia was quite sure she had lost the thread of it . . . until this night of remembering. Inside her head, Sophia saw a small child running across a field, her face framed by yellow dancing curls burnished with orange and gold. A child with no parents of her own, searching for a family she could call her own. And so, with her heart pounding, and her needles clicking, Sophia began to knit the child of her dreams. And she named the child Lara.

In the process of writing, Michale, the teller of tales, had named what was tugging at her own heart.

26
The Invisible Interview

THE INVISIBLE INTERVIEW IS A WAY OF TALKING TO SOMEONE who will not talk to you.

In Chapter 3, Ken and his daughter Aria sat across a table from one another, and wrote out their hurt and their anger. They exchanged letters, and the breach in their relationship was made whole. But what do you do if the person you are at an impasse with refuses to come to the table? Then you have to write both sides of the dialogue and use what you learn to open up the lines of communication again.

Some part of you knows what is wrong, so let that part of you come out in writing. Write out an imaginary conversation, and pose the questions as an interviewer—this third-person distancing seems to help—and let the pen answer, rather than assuming what the response would be.

What comes up as you write is startling—and is often later verified, a dramatic way to get inside another person's head. The invisible interview clears the air and sets the stage for a new interaction.

For the invisible interview your stance is nonjudgmental, recording every response and each little detail as fascinating data, without becoming sidetracked by emotional impact or moral weight. A woman in a recent workshop in Cambridge told me that for four years she had been corre-sponding with a Czech student, and she is able to say things to him on paper she would not dare say face to face to anyone else. She thinks it is the cultural difference that gives her that freedom, that ease. If he disapproves or criticizes her, who is to say he is right; he lives in another country. If her mother, for example, or one of her friends, said the same thing, she would be defensive. With him, her response is, "Well, we do it differently here, and your way is okay for you, and my way is okay for me." There is a great freedom in that.

We often need that "be and let be" attitude toward ourselves and other people close to home.

Model yourself on your favorite English detective. Miss Marple, Adam Dalgliesh, and Lord Peter Wimsey are unfazed by dead bodies. "Well hello, what have we here!" they say; the attitude is, let's get on with the story, find out the facts behind the corpse. It is a challenge for them to get to the bottom of this thing.

When you see yourself as a detective, you want to find out what's at the bottom of the conflict. That's your dead body. And you are collecting clues. What are these characters doing? What do you think is motivat-ing that? What is it that you need to work with to get this thing resolved?

Interview an Object or a Project;
Getting a Boat Afloat

If you have not done this kind of imaginary dialoguing before, you might want to start by interviewing an object rather than a person. Whether the problem is a breakdown in a relationship or a breakdown in a project, the tendency is to place blame—blame ourselves, blame the project or the other person. The invisible interview defuses the blame and creates a welcome objectivity. A Boeing engineer in one of my Planning and Problem-Solving workshops interviewed the deck he was building. He laughed when he read this out loud in class:

INTERVIEWER: *What do you need?*
DECK: *Look, I'm going to be out here all year round. Give me water-resistant boards, treated wood. And there are a lot of trees around here, and the pine needles will clog me up if there's not enough space. Give me at least a half-inch space between boards, and that will save you money, because you will use less wood.*
INTERVIEWER: *That's reasonable. Anything else?*
DECK: *Yeah. Use good nails.*

I have been known to interview my tummy, when my stomach was in knots.

ME: *Good morning, tummy. Why do you have the flutters today?*
TUM: *It's almost like anxiety with a sadness mixed in.*
ME: *Tell me more.*
TUM: *It has white edges around the lining; it feels at once heavy and also light, as though it were floating or bouncing around in there disconnected. That is the strongest feeling—disconnected. It feels loose and rambling, like a once-tethered ball that has become loose from its stanchion.*
ME: *What does that remind you of?*
TUM: *It makes me think of the party last night and the way that Joel snubbed me. I thought I was his friend, and he treated me like pond scum.*

Before I wrote that, I had not connected my free-floating anxiety with the snub from my friend, but as soon as I listened to my tummy tell me it felt "disconnected," bingo! The words I wrote matched exactly the feeling I had. So I was able to name it, own it, and let go.

One time Jim interviewed our boat to find out what needed fixing. A marine mechanic had told him the outdrive was rusted inside and would cost a minimum of $2,500 to repair. In the interview Jim wrote out, the boat told him it was not the outdrive at all but bad spark plugs that were causing the problem.

Jim said later, "As I wrote, I just kept thinking about what it would be like to be inside that engine." He paused for a moment, then added, "People may think it's crazy to write to your boat; they can laugh all they want. I saved over $2,000."

To Understand Rather Than Be Understood

To seek to understand rather than to be understood: It is an ancient wisdom. To understand means to shift your approach, to stop trying so hard to get your point across, to make sure your voice is heard, and to open yourself up to the position the other person is coming from. What is it like to be inside?

The invisible interview is a way to walk a mile in his shoes, to experience the world from behind her eyes.

Asking Questions, Handling Hostility

When we did this exercise in one of my workshops, a Westchester woman asked me, "Could you provide questions?" That is hard to do, because each interview is different. The questions will depend on your relationship with the person you are interviewing, and the source of the breach between you. It is the attitude that you come from, not the specific questions, that move the piece along. The key thing is to ask questions that keep the answers coming.

Dorothy Parker says the most beautiful words in the English language are *cellar door.* I say, that's close; to me, the words people most love to hear are, *Tell me more.*

The questions you ask and the statements you make are nonthreatening ways to say, "Tell me more."

"What is it that you don't like about this plan?"

Even in the face of hostility, do not get hooked, stay calm.

"What could (your name) do to change that?"

"Any ideas?"

"You sound upset."

Make it safe for the other party to answer. No matter how heated the answers become, keep the questions cool. Do not get defensive. As a disinterested third party, it is not your place to defend, only to collect data.

You want to be careful not to steer the interview where you think it ought to go. You want to give the interviewee full rein and the comfort to tell you what is going on. One of the best ways I know to do that is by using the rule of three.

The Rule of Three

Years ago at a convention, a speaker somewhat abashedly explained a device for instant rapport. When you do not know what to say next in a conversation, he suggested, give back the last one to three words of the speaker in order to keep the conversation moving. He laughed and said he hoped his girlfriends were not listening to his presentation, because they all thought he was such a sensitive guy and a good listener. Fact is, when you use this device, you *are* being sensitive and a good listener. I have been known to carry on conversations for half an hour or more using this technique, and the person I am talking to never "caught on." Even if they did, it would not matter, because the repetition says, "I care. I'm listening. You have the floor. Tell me more."

In ordinary exchanges we are not used to having the floor uninterrupted. Give that stark and precious gift to your imaginary subject.

Here are some examples of the rule of three, and of the kind of breakthroughs in store for you.

A Trust Issue with a Teenager

Amy from Atlanta told me that she prided herself on her open relationship with her teenage son, Steven. Then an incident came up that shattered her trust. She judged that she was on the side of right, but she could tell he was not listening when she lectured him; in fact, he was becoming withdrawn and sullen. So she tried an invisible interview, and the rule of three.

INTERVIEWER: *What is going on, Steven? It's not like you to respond in this way when you know you were wrong.*
STEVEN: *That's just it. I'm not wrong. It was harmless enough. My mom wants to control, to hold me back. She takes down the posters from my walls, God! she won't even let me have my own room the way I want it, and then she gets Rachel to snitch on me.*

INTERVIEWER: *Snitch on you?*

STEVEN: *Yes, it isn't fair. Now Alex is in trouble and I'm in trouble and Rachel is in trouble, and it's all because of Rachel.*

INTERVIEWER: *Help me with this. I don't understand your reasoning.*

STEVEN: *What we did was not bad, and we all came home safe. Since we are safe and since we were good, why get so mad that we weren't where we said we'd be?*

INTERVIEWER: *I think your mom was worried.*

STEVEN: *I say she overreacted—and embarrassed me in front of my friends.*

INTERVIEWER: *In front of your friends?*

STEVEN: *Yeah. It was embarrassing. She made me feel like a little kid, and I'm grown up now. Boy! I can't wait until next year when I can move out.*

INTERVIEWER: *Move out?*

STEVEN: *You bet! I can't wait.*

INTERVIEWER: *You can't wait?*

STEVEN: *I want to be myself and make mistakes and not get caught and have my nose rubbed in it. Now it's like living with the Gestapo. We are under interrogation and surveillance all the time. She drills us and pries.*

Amy was on a roll. She kept on writing. What came out next was a note to Steven, written right at the bottom of the same page, which she later recopied and gave to him.

> *Dear Steven,*
> *You're always the one to write first to me to get us back in relationship again. This time I'm writing to you. I don't approve of what you did, but I recognize that maybe I could have handled it differently.*

Amy told me, "I never would have come to that if I just kept thinking about how mad I was and how he had broken my trust."

A Friendship That Had Cooled

When Lee did this exercise during a workshop, he interviewed a close friend who had suddenly become cool to him. What came up in class startled him. Lee knew that Stan and his wife were not getting along too well, so it was no surprise when the interview revealed marriage troubles as one of the reasons why Stan had been avoiding him. ("It isn't my fault it's not working out, and I'm afraid he would blame me.") But Lee was not prepared for what came next:

I: *It's the marriage, then, that's at the root of your distancing from him.*
S: *That's not all.*
I: *That's not all?*
S: *I'm hiding something from him. If we get too close, he'll find out.*
I: *He'll find out?*
S: *Yeah, he'll find out, and I don't want that.*
I: *You don't want that?*
S: *Hell, no. He thinks his kids are so perfect. How could I tell him Marie is on drugs? He'd think I'm not only a bum husband, I'm a bum dad.*

This exchange scared Lee when he wrote it. He said to himself, now you've gone too far, forget it; you are making up things you have no right to say.

"Then I started to think about it," Lee told me later. "If Stan's marriage was in trouble, and his kid was on drugs, it made sense that he might be putting me off. It explained a lot. It made it easier for me to approach him again, because now I saw him as hurting, and I realized that his anger was not directed at me.

"I gave him the opening to talk by first sharing some problems I had been having with my own boys. It turned out that the information from the interview was right on target, and Stan was relieved to be able to talk to me about it."

Now You

A psychologist friend of mine says that interviewing a person who is not present is "good Gestalt." The added dimension here is writing it out rather than acting out, to let the writing help you create the dialogue.

Also, when you write it down, you can look back on it later. Often the invisible interview reveals some stuff that you might not be ready to hear. It is all there, waiting for you, when you are ready for it.

Remember *Alice in Wonderland?* "Off with her head!" threatens the

Queen. Alice answers defiantly, "Who cares for you? You're nothing but a pack of cards!" A useful perspective. Don't get hooked. It is nothing but a piece of paper. Hold that view, as you write, at the same time that you hold on to the realization that this exercise might divulge some truths that you had not before articulated or recognized. Hold both these awarenesses at once: of its playfulness—and of its power. Now all the cards are on the table. Now you can understand.

27
Pen Pals

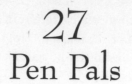

PEN PALS PROMOTE UNDERSTANDING AND CAMARADERIE BETWEEN students of different countries. So it was an appropriate title and a logical theme when two transatlantic schools took on an ambitious project: a high school drama class in Tukwila, Washington, arranged to co-write a play called *Pen Pals* with a class of students in London, England.

The staging was uncomplicated: Two girls who are pen pals read letters from each other, while their fellow students act out the scenes the letters described. The logistics of the joint project were just as straightforward. In their respective classrooms the Americans and the British brainstormed a list of experiences and problems they faced as teens, then students in each class wrote letters to a fictional pen pal. Each class evaluated their own letters on the basis of conflict, characters, and story line and wrote scenes to dramatize the stories. By phone and fax and letter, they started putting it together.

They chose tough issues—drugs and homelessness, gang violence, teen pregnancy—and because their teachers trusted them and let it be their play, the students wrote about them honestly and directly, not the way an adult would think these topics ought to be treated, but openly, as one friend sharing with another.

When the British sent their part of the script over, the Americans were amused by some of the cultural differences. They noticed first some differences in language. The British wrote about going to a *rave* (the underground drug-and-dance party popular in England), they wrote *nappies* for *diapers,* and they called their mothers *mum;* they used *smashing* to refer to something the American kids called *cool.* The Americans were intrigued by the references to British products, *The Manchester Guardian* newspaper, Areal, a *washing powder,* and *The Big Issue,* a magazine written by runaways.

What came through in the end though was what they had in common. *The Big Issue* might be unique to England, yet the runaway problem and the reasons kids run away were the same.

Domingo, a Tukwila teen, was struck by the similarities as he worked at fleshing out the scripts.

"When I first heard of this project, I thought the British would be close-minded, or conservative; I didn't expect them to be so open. I thought, 'Oh wow, they will talk about their parents, not problems.' I thought English kids stayed home and watched TV and *read* and recited Shakespeare. And then I read some of their part of the play and said, 'Oh wow, they go out and do some of the stuff we do. They go out and *party.'* "

Writing the play together was a learning experience; what would it be like to stage and perform it together?

They had a chance to find out when the British students got a grant to pay for transportation to come to America and put the play on with their American counterparts.

At one point in the show, the two girls reading the letters say in unison, "I know it sounds stupid, but even though you are thousands of miles away, you are my best friend. I can tell you anything. When I read your letters, I feel like you're reading them with me."

The grant made that moment real.

At first the American students were elated; then they worried about the responsibility. The way they saw it, it was not just their high school that was on the line but the reputation of the American people. If we don't study, they thought, and know our lines, it won't just look bad on us, it will look bad on America. If we don't work hard, they'll think that we are not only lazy, but a stereotype of all Americans.

The British arrived, sporting the United Colors of Benetton, and instant camaraderie replaced the apprehension. They were bonded together, like one big family. There was an agreement on both sides, to give their all.

They not only built a play, they built a relationship: a relationship based on mutual respect and deep sharing.

Afterward I asked Elaine, a tall blond girl from London, to tell me what she had learned. She answered,

"What I've learned is that teenagers have the same problems, from London, England, to Tukwila, Washington. When we were writing the script, we found out they had already done half the things we wanted to do. We had to *scrap* ours; they'd already got it. We have a lot of gang wars, for example, but they had already covered it.

"As we read what they wrote, we realized, the more we are different, the more we are the same."

Where did the play let off and real life begin? Because they had already set it up through the play, they were on a different level with each other. The night of the first performance, they stayed up until four, talking in groups at a sleeping party at school, talking in depth about issues that their fictional friendship had already established. Once you've delved into the alcoholism of a friend and your response when your best friend tells you she is gay, you don't go back to, "So how's the weather in London?"

Erin, an American, said, "They didn't have to come and prove themselves with some type of exterior; we knew them, we knew who they were from their play. We knew some of their deepest thoughts, and we accepted them. We liked them just because they were."

The airport scene when the British went back home was intense. They didn't want to part. Even the boys were crying. There was a flurry of paper back and forth, back and forth, as they exchanged addresses.

Two boys, both with baseball caps on backward, had their arms around each other in a shoulder-to-shoulder hug. Both of them were crying, and the British boy was saying, "I'll write. I promise I'll write." Elaine was sobbing and running around asking for signatures on a dollar bill, even though her teacher was worried about defacing American currency. Heidi and Stacy, newly formed friends for life, were each wearing half of a broken friendship heart necklace. The kinship they felt had been formed not just in the performance of the play but in the transatlantic writing of it together: a deep friendship, an abiding bond.

The plane was taxiing to the gate, and all around was the echo of voices. Through tears, the American accent and the British accent blended.

"I'll write. I promise. I'll write."

Now You

What are some ways you can bring together people from different countries working on a writing project together? Does your city have a sister city? (Even our little town of Edmonds has a sister city in Hekinan, Japan.) Does your children's school have a sister school? Does any organization you belong to have a parallel group overseas? Start something new, or use an already-in-place pen-pal program to have the youngsters collaborate, maybe a small collection of stories offering different essays on the same topic to distribute in both countries. Make our world a smaller place.

28
Sign Language

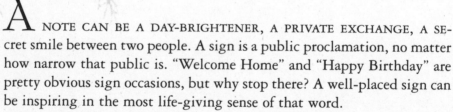

A NOTE CAN BE A DAY-BRIGHTENER, A PRIVATE EXCHANGE, A SE-cret smile between two people. A sign is a public proclamation, no matter how narrow that public is. "Welcome Home" and "Happy Birthday" are pretty obvious sign occasions, but why stop there? A well-placed sign can be inspiring in the most life-giving sense of that word.

A neighbor told me about the day he called home with upsetting news: He had just been given a pink slip. He was distraught, defeated, and embarrassed to face his family. Half an hour later, when he arrived home, his footstep was heavy and his head was down as he walked in the front door. His wife and children had been busy since he called. Inside the door, a sign greeted him, "We're with you, Dad," and then others in the kitchen, "We love you." "We're behind you all the way." "Something better is waiting."

Put yourself in his shoes, feel how he felt—and see those signs. His family could have said the same things verbally, but there was something about taking the initiative to sit there creating a sign, something about saying it so big and brashly, that solidified their feelings and made their caring more real, more believable. The signs were a tangible life-ring to grab on to.

In our house we make signs for everything. We keep a supply of butcher paper and newsprint end-rolls on hand. I might commission the kids to "make a sign for my pal who was just paroled from prison" or to "make some signs for James—he is having a bad day." Then there are congratulation signs: "Emily's average is 4.0—make a sign"; "Katherine just got accepted in honor choir—make a sign," and welcome signs: "Make a sign to take to the airport—your cousin Christine is coming to visit."

I let them figure out what to say; the only instruction is, whatever you say, write it in large and colorful letters.

A sign can say a lot in a few words because it says it big and happy. Advertisers know that eye-catching headlines have a maximum number of six words. Signs can have even fewer.

I got a lot of congratulatory cards from friends when I launched my first book, and I appreciated them all. What I remember most, though, is the two-word banner stretched across my cousin Mary Edna's living room: "Author! Author!"

Staging a Media Event

How do you think they stage media events? I got an inside view once, as I stepped off a plane at a busy airport. Someone connected with a controversial court case was arriving at the same time as I was. The local TV station had a bunch of signs on wooden poles, and they were handing them out to people waiting for the plane.

"Here, hold this."

"Do you mind holding this? You get to be on TV tonight."

So that's the way to do it, I thought. This was several years ago, and it is probably illegal now, but it taught me an interesting lesson. The next time we were meeting someone at the airport, we didn't just make our usual one sign—we made a bunch of them and asked other people at the airport to hold them.

I have a friend in Chicago whose sister was making a major move to come to Chicago to live.

"I knew she would expect me to greet her in a grandiose way," he said, "as a way to applaud her in this step, which had been a long time coming. I mean, she was giving up her job, her apartment, and the known to come to a strange big city where I was the only one she knew. I just couldn't have her get off the plane, and for me to casually say, 'Oh hi. Glad you're here. Let's go get your bags.' "

He made a bunch of signs, got to the airport early, and handed out the signs to people waiting for the same plane. Most people were willing to play along when he explained, "I want my sister to feel welcome."

By the time she stepped into the waiting lounge, it was like a celebrity was coming.

Small Signs, Large Signs

Signs do not need to be elaborate or fancy. Our friends the Greenes, Steve and Lorraine, celebrate everything with signs. Sometimes their signs are small, colored in crayon on the back of standard-size letterhead paper. They call these Chapman College Signs. A friend of theirs was a professor at Chapman College, and when the college moved to a new campus, he gave their children a ream of outdated letterhead as scrap.

"The kids like the texture of this paper, and the weight of it," says Steve. "They seem completely oblivious to the fact that it says Chapman College on it, with the old logo at the top. They don't even bother to turn it over. So we get WELCOME HOME Chapman College; GOOD LUCK ON YOUR TEST Chapman College; CONGRATULATIONS ON YOUR SOCCER AWARD Chapman College; even I LOVE YOU Chapman College."

The Greenes also like lavish signs. Their favorite place to mount gigantic greetings is on a tree in front of their house. That is their Sign Tree, because you have to pass it when you exit the driveway.

"I like the big signs best," says Andy, their oldest son. "The bigger the better." Andy is sixteen and has been known, on special occasions, to take newsprint, decorate it with some cheerful message, and then tape it, writing facing inward, to the bedroom door of a sleeping member of the family.

"In the morning, they have to break through the note to get out," he says with a big grin.

A Tribute

William Read was a classics professor at the University of Washington. He was kind enough to coach me, when I got it into my head that I wanted to teach my children Latin, and organized a little neighborhood school for them and their friends.

Professor Read and I met many times, often on campus, where he had been teaching for forty-five years; he had an office in the oldest building there. Sometimes we met at McDonald's, especially when I had one of the children with me. He shared books and props and ideas with me, and he helped me with my pronunciation, which was dreadful. He was so delighted at what I was doing that he encouraged me and helped me and gave me ways to make Latin lively, sharing names and addresses of societies for the promotion of Latin and the names of people I could write to for more information and material. He shared his own graded texts, which he had written to make learning Latin like learning to read.

It was a sad day for me when I got a call from the classics secretary, telling me that Professor Read was dying. He had slipped into a coma and was in a local hospital. They did not expect him to come out of the coma.

I went to his bedside immediately. I brought my Pliny and Seneca and sat by his side and read to him. They said he could not hear me, but I know he did because he winced at my pronunciation. And I thought, how fitting, because this has been his life. His life has been spent listening to students mispronounce Seneca.

His room looked plain, and that did not seem right to me. Everyone knew it was just a matter of time and not much time at that. It would not be appropriate to send flowers or balloons or even cards. But I kept thinking, some tribute must be paid to the life of this man. The nurses who changed his sheets and shifted his body position did not know this was a Latin scholar they were tending.

"I thought Seneca was a street in downtown Seattle," said one nurse when I told her who Professor Read was and what I was reading, and I swear I saw a little smile play on his face when she said that. That's when I decided, I cannot let this man die in a bare room. I went home and gathered my family together and said, "Help me make a sign for Professor

Read." We made a elaborate poster in Latin, and I went back the next day and hung it in his room.

I was not able to go to his memorial service, but someone who did go later told me that in the reception hall where those who loved him gathered after the funeral, his family had posted the sign.

I like to think that maybe Professor Read woke up and saw it before he died.

"You're a Star!"

Sometimes a single sign can get years of mileage.

Aimee Benson is a theater arts major. It is not too surprising that she chose that major; she has grown up in a theatrical family. She and her mom have both been acting in local shows, wherever they lived, since Aimee was in high school.

"My first show was *Biloxi Blues,*" says Aimee, smiling with animation at the memory. "I had eleven lines, and I had to kiss a boy. I was so nervous. I came home to shower before the performance, and when I came out of the shower, there was a giant, golden, home-made star on the door to my room, and in the middle, in big letters, my mom had written, 'Break a leg!' That was the beginning of a tradition in our house. For the next six years, I'd say, we never put the star away; it just shifted places."

Soon after *Biloxi Blues,* Aimee's mom played the Katharine Hepburn part in *On Golden Pond*.

"It was a really big deal for her. Everyone's seen the movie, so she felt she had to live up to Katharine Hepburn."

On opening night Aimee snuck backstage and put the star on the door to her mother's dressing room.

After a while the sign and the message, "Break a leg!" became the "Go for it, You can do it, We're behind you" symbol for all kinds of endeavors.

"Whenever I was nervous or scared about something, that star sign would show up. For a big test, a job interview, a big date. Once for a prom, my first. But the best fun we ever had with it was when we gave it to my dad."

Aimee's dad is a civil engineer. In order to be hired for a particular project, his firm presents a proposal to the company in need of their services. There was an important proposal he had been working on for six months. He had to fly to California to represent his company and present the plan. There was a lot riding on it.

"We figured that that proposal was his own little performance," says Aimee. "He had to convince them why his company should get the job.

"We put the star sign in his briefcase, and when he opened up his briefcase in L.A. in front of a whole roomful of important people, there was our sign, supporting him and loving him: 'Break a leg.' "

Although there were many other competitive bids, he got the assignment, and for a while they all moved to California.

Aimee tells other stories of how signs have made a difference in her life.

"My dad is a great guy, but quiet, kinda shy. He doesn't say much. We move a lot. One of the worst moves we ever had was when I was in the seventh grade. I hated to move, to leave my friends behind, to start a new school. And we were moving from the Deep South to the Pacific Northwest. It was like a foreign country to me. My dad was in Thailand, so my mom and I had to move by ourselves. That made me mad. Even though I knew it wasn't his fault, I was angry he wasn't there. I was crying and crying and crying."

One day, Aimee came home from her new school, still depressed, and found a sign tacked up in her room from her dad. He had mailed it to her mom and asked her to put it there. It said, "Aimee, You are so brave."

"That's all it said, but from that point on things started to look up for me. In those few words his sign said to me that he recognized how tough it was and that he was proud of me. That's all I needed."

New at the Job

It can be tough starting any new job, but if you are new at "pulling espresso" in a coffee town, it can be grueling. Both Aimee and her friend Don Jones speak from experience of the stress. Aimee says, "When I started working at Starbucks in Seattle, I was miserable. My head was spinning, trying to learn all the different drinks, with all those busy business people, lines out the door, wanting their espresso just so, and fast.

I had so many questions: Where does this go? Who do I give this to? What should I do now? I was afraid I was in everyone's way."

After one particularly harried day, Aimee says, "I went back to the employee spaces where we put our things, and as I was hanging up my apron, I saw a big sign taped to my backpack. A fellow employee, Reiner, had left it. It said, 'Aimee, you rock my world.'

"The tension just evaporated. It made me smile. To me that was his way of saying, 'You're doing okay; you're not getting in my way.' "

That was three months ago. Aimee still has that sign.

Don is a seasoned *barista* who knows now how to pour a perfect *crema*, but he still remembers how it was when he was starting out, and how a manager of the café where he first worked helped him over that lonely hump with encouraging signs.

"Mary had to close every night, and I was scheduled to open. When you're closing, all you want is to get out of there; you have been working hard all day, and all you can think about is getting home and kicking back. She would take the time, ten or fifteen minutes extra, to make these signs to greet me in the morning. And when I'd walk in at five forty-five to open, there was a sign from Mary waiting."

I can imagine how Don felt. It was a joy for me to come home one night recently and see a huge sign for Katherine, celebrating her good grades. If it made my heart sing, think what it did for Katherine. A kindness and a celebration touches us all, even when we are only secondary recipients or even further removed from it. Just hearing about it, just seeing it, reminds us of our own humanity and makes us feel honored—that's the word, honored—and loved.

Now You

The opposite extreme of hiding notes is to put them out in the open in a big way. For those times when you want to be sure the person gets your message of support and cheerleading, of welcome and congratulations, make a sign.

29
Make a Stranger's Day

THE FIRST TIME I CAUGHT THE MESSAGE WAS IN THE LADIES'
room at the Elliott Bay Bookstore Café, where the stalls are labeled
"politics," "religion," "sex," etc., so you can pick your graffiti accordingly.
There it was, in black Magic Marker scratched on a side slat:

"Practice random acts of kindness."

Later, I heard there was a book with that title, and I started noticing the
bumper stickers. Through anecdotes, the book suggests actions like, "Pay
the toll of the motorist behind you." It encourages you to do your own
anonymous nice deeds for strangers at unexpected moments, with no
thought of your own gain, not even waiting around for a thank you or an
"Aren't you sweet?" but simply spreading goodwill around, making our
world a nicer place to be.

On the Lookout

I carry thank-you notes in my bag, so I'm always on the lookout for places
to leave them behind.

No sooner had I written that sentence than I realized that, right where I was sitting, I was being unexpectedly entertained by a foot-stomping, melodic, fun, and smile-producin' group of jeans and jackets, playing in lively fashion a cello, a banjo, a guitar, and a violin. I had ducked into the Honey Bear Café in Wallingford for what I thought would be a quiet evening and a chance to write, over a mug of hot chocolate or cider and a cinnamon bun. Before I knew what was happening, the place was jammed and everyone was tapping feet and smiling broadly, listening to this virtuoso bluegrass band.

I put a thank-you note in the tip jar along with a donation—

I am a writer. You helped me write tonight—fast! I should follow you around to all your neighborhood concerts—I sure would produce a lot. Keeping up with you is a joy.

Thanks for the fun, and the heart lift.

Yours with a big smile, and a hot pen,
H. Klauser

I have my own cup at the Teahouse Kuan Yin. I knew I had arrived the day Miranda invited me to bring my own. I put it on the bus tray with a note tucked under the lid: "Thank you for washing my cup." Next time I went to the Kuan Yin, I ordered Pu-Erh, an earthy Chinese tea. I took my tray to a table and settled in. I took the cozy off the pot and picked up the strainer to position it properly. That's when when I lifted the lid on my teacup and was startled to find inside a fortune cookie and a note: "You're welcome." The smile that suffused me totally down to my toes made me feel welcome indeed.

Leaving notes for a waitress or waiter is a pleasant thing to do, but do not stop there. As you leave a restaurant, you might drop a note on a nearby diner's table: "I like your hat" or "I couldn't help but notice what a fine family you have."

One time Peter and hi friend James Hicks were having a Coke at Denny's. They were all of seventeen years old. They noticed two females at another table and decided to pay for their "drinks," their Coke and coffee. Peter and James wrote a note on napkin and sent the waitress as the intermediary.

To Table 32 from Table 18, the drinks are on us. Don't mention it, or actually, thank us later.

The two at the other table were startled. They smiled when they read the note and wrote one back: "Thanks!" On their way out, they stopped by Table 18. James Hicks asked outright, "Do you have boyfriends?"

"No. We're married."

And then they took out baby pictures and "I Love Mom" keychains.

"Peter," says I, when he tells me this story, "you made their day."

"Well," he says, grinning broadly, "when they walked out, they were smiling pretty big."

A Trail of Haiku

My friend George is a haiku master. He is a merry, mischievous man, like a gnome, the kind of guy who puts mustaches on his eight-year-old twin sons' wallet photos, so they match his own picture. He keeps his driver's license with his own mustachioed mug shot in his wallet next to the side-by-side pictures of Nick and Chris. Whenever anyone asks to see his ID, they get a jolt, followed by a smile, as they get the joke. Here's something else George does that makes people smile.

George was on the bus, and the passenger next to him was snoozing. George wrote a haiku:

> *nodding his head*
> *the man next to me has fallen*
> *asleep on the bus*

Before getting off at his stop, he tucked it in the window next to the man, so he would see it when he awoke.

Once he noticed a young woman on the bus who was knitting or sewing something. She looked lost in thought as she stitched. Suddenly a smile lit up her face, so George wrote a haiku about that and slipped it to her as he left the bus.

Another time he passed some street musicians and dashed off a haiku for them, which he put in the donation jar along with some coins.

171

A good haiku, according to George, "captures the moment, including the unseen connection between things that seem unrelated." For George, haiku is more than a form of poetry; it is, in his words, "a way of showing love."

Orchids & Onions

A friend of mine who used to fly with United Airlines told me that flight attendants have files they call Orchids & Onions. The onion file collects complaints; the orchid one is for compliments.

Since she knows firsthand that people are more apt to write, she created something she calls the one-minute orchid.

"When I want to tell the airline about the good service I've received from an attendant, I write the date, the flight segment, and the name of the person on the back of my own business card. Then I write a couple of sentences and sign my name. Because it's my business card, they know how to get in touch with me, and they know that it's valid.

"When I give it to the person who has done the good service, I suggest to them that they make a copy of it for their own files, then drop it in an envelope to send to the airline president. It winds up going into their personnel file, as though it were an actual letter."

It takes her a minute to do, and she gets it done right away, as opposed to thinking she will do it later and then forgetting about it or getting too busy. As a result, she gets letters from the airline company thanking her for her letter, as though it had been a formal business letter. And the flight attendant has an orchid to file.

Friendly Service

For several months I met weekly with a group at a coffee shop in Mill Creek. We had all taken Barbara Sher's eye-opening course, "Wishcraft," and we were following up on Sher's idea to have regular meetings as a way to support each other in being accountable for our own dreams, for following through on what we said we were going to do. We reported to one another, "This week I . . . ," and, "By next week, I will . . ."

We met every Friday morning, from eight to ten. Rosalee was our waitress. You have to give her a lot of credit. She always had a smile, and from week to week she remembered our order without being told. In Seattle "Latteland" that is no mean feat—"a single tall vanilla nonfat," "a mocha with no foam," "a triple grande two percent," "a half-caf/decaf with almond," and the like. Often that original order of steamed milk and flavored coffee was all we ordered. Six men and women, taking up space in Rosalee's section, for two hours every Friday. I think one time someone added scrambled eggs, but we were not what you would call big spenders. We were not there to eat.

Rosalee was nearby if we needed her, but she wasn't hanging over us, with a "May I get you anything else here?" that translates, "Are you ready to leave yet?" Now we tipped Rosalee generously, and we always had a pleasant word for her, but one day we decided to add something extra.

"Let's leave a note on the table for Rosalee," someone suggested, "and tell her how much we appreciate her smile, and her patience with us, and her friendliness, and always making us feel welcome."

On a single small piece of paper we each wrote something, a sentence or two. That's all. We left it on the table, along with the tip.

The following Friday, Rosalee seemed even friendlier, but she did not mention the note and neither did we.

We met there for three more months before another waitress told us something we never suspected.

"You know that note you left for Rosalee? She posted it in the back room by the order board, and it's still there!"

Joe Griffith of Dallas, Texas, tells a similar tale. Joe travels quite a bit as a professional speaker. He contends with the usual annoyances of the frequent flyer: lost luggage, delayed flights, and so on. One time in New Orleans he had a particularly rough time with a baggage problem and was feeling stressed. In that state of mind it was gratifying to receive friendly and efficient service from a shuttle driver named Stanley Watkins from Avis, who bused him to his rental car. Stanley grabbed his bags to swing them onto the luggage rack, handled his valise, and made him feel well taken care of. In trying to exit the rental lot, Joe encountered a problem with the person at the security gate; Stanley got off his bus and came to Joe's aid, even though that was not his job. Joe was so pleased at the good care that he wrote a letter about Stanley to the chairman of Avis, complimenting his service.

Four months later, Joe was back in the New Orleans airport, and "as I'm walking out, ready to board the Avis bus, Stanley Watkins hails me by name.

" 'Mr. Griffith! Mr. Griffith! I got a copy of that letter in my pocket that you wrote to the chairman of Avis four months ago.' "

Stanley had carried that letter around in his pocket every day for four months.

Says Joe, incredulously, "It was just like he'd been waiting on me to come back."

Now You

Be on the lookout for strangers whose kindness makes a difference in your life, and take a moment to make a difference in theirs. Notes you leave behind increase the niceness in the world, bring sunshine, because they let people know they are noticed and appreciated.

What can I say? You may think you are being altruistic; you may walk away not expecting or wanting anything in return. But when you do something nice for a stranger, it is like a boomerang. The good feeling you planned to leave anonymously behind starts following you home.

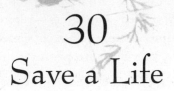

30
Save a Life

THERE IS EVIL IN THE WORLD, BUT THERE IS A LOT OF GOODNESS too, and writing can give that goodness a voice. Collectively it can tower over the evil and eventually triumph. You may think, what can one person do?

How would you like to know that your note to a stranger could stop that person from being tortured? How would you like to hear a political prisoner say, "Your letter saved my life." That's the kind of response that Amnesty International gets when it mobilizes its Urgent Action Network on behalf of a "prisoner of conscience" held for his or her beliefs.

This is no lightweight matter. It is a chance to make a profound difference, because you care about somebody you do not even know, except that he or she is a member of your family, the human family, and you want that person to know that he is not forgotten. The worst of it is believing no one cares.

"I've lost my faith in humanity," I overheard a woman on the street say recently. Who knows what irksome thing, what betrayal or slight, had set her off? Maybe somebody had wronged her or said something behind her back that was not true, and so she had lost her faith in human nature. What if you were being tortured, forced to live in darkness, denied food or water, beaten—and not for any crimes of your own but for standing up for your beliefs? You might well lose faith in humanity, in your fellow man. And then—imagine—a letter comes, addressed to you, and with it a glimmer of hope. There is some goodness in the world after all. Somebody knows what is happening to me. Somebody cares. A political prisoner in Paraguay aided by Amnesty International gives this chilling report:

"On Christmas Eve the door to my cell opened and the guard tossed in a crumpled piece of paper. It said,

Take heart. The world knows you're alive. We're with you.

"That letter saved my life."

Your letter makes a difference, and not just to the detainee. The governments detaining him notice too. They sit up and pay attention when their atrocities are found out. The bully in the schoolyard thinks he can torment others who are helpless, because no one else stands up to him; world governments are the same. Until you speak up, they think nobody has noticed. According to Amnesty International, even the most tyrannical governments want to keep their image intact in the world community; they, after all, want to engage in trade with other countries. They control through hidden means, like any bully who does not want to get caught, especially if those who might catch him outnumber him.

Amnesty International is a respected organization that monitors the situation of political prisoners around the world, who, although they themselves do not use or advocate violence, are detained and violently abused.

When they are alerted to a crisis situation, the Urgent Action Network can verify the facts through computers and then, with astonishing speed, be in touch with its members. Within hours, by fax, telegram, and letter, people express their support and indignation.

A single letter can bring hope; mass mail can bring freedom. John G. Healey, executive director of Amnesty International, quotes one freed prisoner:

"When the first two hundred letters [from Amnesty members] came, the guard gave me back my clothes. Then the next two hundred letters came and the prison director came to see me. *The letters kept coming.* The president called the prison and told them to let me go."

"The pen is mightier than the sword" sounds trite, but it is nonetheless true.

You can stop tyranny and torture with your pen and a piece of paper.

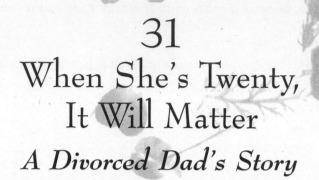

31
When She's Twenty,
It Will Matter

A Divorced Dad's Story

I'D KNOWN JOSEPH FOR A LONG TIME BEFORE I KNEW HE HAD A daughter. It wasn't something he talked about. I guess it hurt too much. When he finally did tell me about her, he told me they were not in contact, and that saddened him. Oh, he called her stepdad once a month to get a report, to find out how she was doing, but he says now he didn't think she even knew that.

He and Jennifer's mom were divorced when Jennifer was only nine months old, so he and his daughter didn't have much history together. He had seen her a few times over the years, but when she got to be ten, she asked for the visits to stop. He didn't know why.

"Maybe she was afraid I would take her away from the only family she has ever known. I had no intention of that, but maybe she was worried."

The visits stopped.

Joseph felt helpless, didn't know what to do. Two years passed. Then one day he got a letter from Jennifer that surprised him. She had a novel idea.

Could we be pen-pals?

Joseph liked that idea, so he checked with her stepdad to make sure it was okay, and then started to write her regularly. At first, it worked out just fine. He'd write to her, and she'd write back. Basic, get-acquainted kind of exchanges:

First, I would like to tell you about myself. My favorite color is blue. My favorite type of music is alternative, that is, Collective Soul, Pearl Jam, Alice in Chains, Smashing Pumpkins.

Do you have a favorite animal? I do. Mine is dolphins and whales.

I hate school. The only thing good about it is I am in Advanced Choir. My birthday is in April. You probably already knew that, huh?

My favorite channel on TV is the Discovery channel because I learn a lot from those programs about people, culture, and other parts of the world.

Then Jennifer stopped answering Joseph's letters, so he stopped writing any to her. After all, he reasoned, she was the one who had the pen-pal idea in the first place, so if she wasn't game, neither was he.

Then he remembered something he had heard a long time ago about parenting. It was an expression that stuck with him: "I'm the adult, and she's the child." He thought, I want her to always know, no matter what, that her father cared. Even if she chooses to reject me, let that be her choice, rather than having her believe that I didn't care.

The way he figured it was this: Jennifer could grow up to be a young woman, thinking, "My natural father never cared enough to keep in touch with me." Or, she could know, "My father wrote to me regularly, but I chose not to answer him." He imagined her at twenty, at thirty, dealing with those thoughts.

Joseph went to a card store and got a whole bunch of blank notes with lighthearted pictures on the front. What would a twelve-year old like? he asked himself. He picked one with Garfield on it, another with the moon and stars, a third with funny geometric shapes and fluorescent colors. Picking them out, he was thinking of her. He felt good about that.

Then he started to write again—short notes, not long letters. He told her what he was up to, and what was going on in his life.

> *I have been getting a tan this summer and going hiking on the weekends. I need to buy some new hiking boots.*
> *My basement flooded from all the rain. It is a bummer to clean up.*

He told her stories of himself growing up. Since she liked to sing, he wrote to her about being in a chorus as a boy. Simple stuff: This is what I'm up to, and I'm thinking of you as I do it.

He sent a note, like clockwork, every other Friday. Twice a month, on alternate Mondays, Jennifer could count on a letter from her dad.

Months passed with no response. Joseph kept writing. Then one day, I had a phone call from him.

"Henriette, I got a letter from my daughter." There was a catch in his voice when he said it.

Soon there was another and another. She decorated the envelopes with colored pens around the borders, put funny stickers inside, stamped them with rubber stamps. She sent him a drawing. He framed it and hung it over his desk.

She began to open up.

> *You know that saying that you wrote on one of your letters,*
> *"Keep your head high*
> *Don't let your dreams die."*
> *Well, I showed it to all of my friends and I have it written on my binder along with other poems and sayings.*

She didn't call him "Dad." She addressed him by his first name, and that was fine with him. It was never his intent to replace the affection she had for the stepfather who had raised her. He just wanted her to know that her biological father was a real person and that he cared what happened to her.

It took a long time, but the message got through. One day, Joseph got a letter from Jennifer that he especially treasures. The letter itself was unremarkable; just the usual chit-chat. What stunned him was the closing.

At the bottom, in a fancy hand in big letters she signed it, "Love always, Jennifer."

32
Turn Complaints
to Requests

"TURN EVERY COMPLAINT TO A REQUEST." THAT'S THE ADVICE OF my friend Carolyn Ann, who also happens to be Dr. Meeks, a pediatrician, and author of the book *Prescriptions for Parenting.* It is the kind of useful maxim that applies to so many situations, it would be appropriate to embroider it in counted cross-stitch and hang it on the wall or make a pillow out of it. Many's the time I have followed her injunction when I'm writing for relationship and turned what seemed like an impasse into an opening. "Turn every complaint to a request" can get a stalled situation moving; it can open the door to understanding, bring a breath of fresh air to a stale argument. It clears up confusion and takes away defensiveness; it points the way to compromise.

One Sunday after church, two of our children were complaining. It was a familiar refrain: Church is boring, we hate the homilies, why do we have to go? Jim and I feel strongly about going to church as a family, so we counter first with an explanation of tradition, like Tevye in *Fiddler on the Roof.* We share our love of the church, hoping it might catch on. Then we try our friend Father Ortmann's classic line, "It's not that you *have* to go to church; you *get* to go." Of course, the children had heard these arguments before, usually ending with the ultimate appeal to authority (even Tevye finally came to, "There *is* no other hand"): "As long as you're a member of this family, living under this roof blah blah blah. . . ."

This time we decided to try something different. We asked them to take a moment, go upstairs, and write us a letter explaining their position. They could say anything they wanted, as long as they remembered the rule to turn every complaint to a request. We thought we were leaving ourselves wide open on that one; we already anticipated the request—not to go to church. Then we'd be back in the same old circular argument again.

Instead, the requests they wrote surprised us and opened the way to a healthy alternatives.

Could we go somewhere else—to another parish—occasionally—on Sundays?

Could we go to an earlier service or an evening one to have more free time on Sundays?

It was not an all-or-nothing argument after all.

For years, I was a member of the Northwest Women's Health Club. They had a form at the front desk that I liked. It gave me a voice in the club, a sense that someone was listening, and it also steered my complaints away from whining into an action plan. Households could use a form like this sometimes.

The forms were printed on half-sheets in the club colors, with the logo in the corner:

Communication to Staff

To whom: _____

Regarding: _____

My suggestions for handling the situation are: _____

_____

_____

_____

_____

_____

_____

_____

It was that last fill-in-the-blank that got me. The space for the suggestions took up three-fourths of the sheet. It brought me up short more than once; it turned my kvetching into cooperation.

I try to remember this principle when I need to admit a problem, to complain, in order to be true to a relationship. Mentally following the "Communication to Staff" form, with its "suggestions for handling the situation," reminds me that there are two players. It keeps whatever I write from being a dump of frustration, and it encourages me to take responsibility for being part of the solution.

Jim and I take turns driving the weekly carpool to take our daughter and her friends to school in the morning. Since school starts at seven o'clock, that usually means leaving the house by six-fifteen, rounding up the various passengers, and hitting the freeway by six-thirty.

Sometimes Jim would come home after fighting early morning traffic with his stomach in knots. "Would it kill them to say, 'Good morning,' and 'Thanks for the ride'? They make me feel like a taxi driver."

I told him not to take it personally; it was the same when I drove.

Yet we dreaded our days to drive. We thought that if we complained, it would only make matters worse, make the students defensive and more morose.

I wrote a note and made copies of it for each student in the carpool. I started off with the request:

We have a favor to ask of you. Please be friendly in the morning when it's our turn to drive. Somehow it starts the day off wrong and sour when no words are exchanged, where a cheery "Hello" and a pleasant "Thanks for the ride" would be a day-brightener. You needn't engage in witty repartee or animated conversation, just be civil.

It was a little easier to swallow and respond positively to than the first note I had mentally composed, which was an attack on bad manners and rudeness and a threat to stop driving the ingrates altogether. Still, after reading the request over, I realized something was missing—what we were willing to do to make the situation better. I went back and added,

For our part, we'll not ask so many questions and will allow you the quiet you need to study or sleep.

Our willingness to meet them halfway cleared up the problem completely. They were happy to oblige; in fact, until they read the note, they had not even been aware that we were offended.

The Anger Letter

Dr. David Irvine, from Calgary, Alberta, teaches a communications course to high school students. He leads his teenage students through a formula for writing an "anger letter." He tells them first to write out their anger, then move from anger to the fear underneath the anger to the request, and finally to understanding and love. He shared with me a typical letter from a sixteen-year-old girl to her mother.

Dear Mom,
  I am very upset with you. I am mad at you for not letting me have more freedom, and for not trusting my judgment, and I am frustrated at not being able to drive like so many of my friends. Oftentimes I think you are

unreasonable and selfish. You want to control my life, always telling me what to do and where I can go or not go. I hate the way you lecture me, and it angers me when you base your decisions on the preface, "A sixteen-year-old does not . . ." I am not a "sixteen-year-old"; I am your daughter.

I am afraid to approach you as a friend anymore. A lack of understanding seems to exist between the two of us. I am afraid that we are drifting apart, afraid of a black hole in our once pure relationship of a friendship, a friendship that seems to no longer exist. I am afraid I will go away to college anxious to get away from home.

And then the request, the "So what?" or "So now what?" part:

Please stop treating me like a little kid, and trust me to do things with my friends.

Finally, the understanding and love:

I know that there are a lot of things that you are not happy with about me. I understand that you are frustrated that I spend little to no time at home. And when I am home, you probably feel that I talk too much on the phone, I am mean to my little sister, I don't do my jobs, and I shrink your clothes. I'm sorry. I understand that you have a lot of pressures in your life right now, too. Thank you for reading this letter. I know we will be able to work through these hard times. I love you.

Dr. Irvine tells teenagers to share the anger letter with a friend or, if they want, with their parents. Either way, it gives them a new insight into the relationship.

In a letter of this kind, it is often useful to include another "R": response. Put in some provision that gives the party you are writing to a chance to respond. Make it clear what you are asking, and then add some specific request for a response that will let you know the reaction to your proposal.

Could we meet to talk about this?

Would you write me a letter back to let me know how you feel about my suggestion?

Will this work for you? Please call and let me know.

Including a request and inviting a response recognizes the relationship and changes a complaint from a harangue into a dialogue.

Now You

If you are upset about something and you care about having a relationship with the person you are upset with, write your complaint through to a request. Sometimes the thing you are complaining about is a done deal—there is nothing you can do to change it—but you are mad and want to be true enough to the relationship to say so. Then your request begins with, "Next time, would you . . ."

Turning a complaint to a request is a compliment; it implies an ongoing connection with the person to whom you are writing.

33
Easing the Pain of Death
Finding the Words to Say Good-bye

PEOPLE LEAVE MANY THINGS BY THE VIETNAM MEMORIAL IN Washington, D.C. They leave cans of beer and high-heeled shoes, medals, flowers, and flags. But more than anything else, they leave letters. These are letters to the dead. Some say, "Here's the beer I promised you if I made it home," or, "Happy Anniversary, my darling." Many, many of them are labeled, "Do not open."

And every one of them is saved, unopened if requested, in the Memorial Museum. The Wall has been called "the final mail stop for the dead of the war."

These friends and relatives of those who were killed in Vietnam have touched upon an important truth. Putting your broken heart on paper can help it to heal.

Jan's Story

Because she is a giving and generous person and because she is my friend, Jan was willing to share this extraordinary and intimate view, a close-up of one person's grief work. "There's a reason why they call it work," she told me during a dinner conversation that went into the wee hours. "It's like putting a bunch of papers in an in-basket if you have an office. All your work is going in this in-basket. And you can let it stack up, but it's not going to go away till you tend to it." She is talking about a baby who died; the sorrow she walked through and the truths she learned could apply to the death of anyone deeply loved.

"Well, my baby, my little girl, Justine Elizabeth, was born with a birth condition that is often fatal, and in her case it was.

"She was a baby that we had wanted, she was planned and prayed for, and we loved her, couldn't wait to meet her, and it was the worst thing I've ever had happen in my life. And I think I started writing right away."

Jan wrote in her journal almost every day for twenty-one months, and filled seven notebooks. Writing about her baby made her real: "Instead of just a baby that died five hours after birth, she was my little girl, a person that I had carried for nine months, who I loved and was bonded to. Nobody knew her except me. You know, it's a lonely grief."

We went to a friend's house for dinner. It's so strange how no one asks how you are after your baby died. They avoid the subject like the plague. Put the lid on. Build up the pressure inside instead. Doesn't anybody know? How awful it is to suffer in silence and loneliness.

Jan told me it is music to a mother's ears to hear the name of her baby.

"The most appropriate thing to say to someone like me, if you haven't gone through this type of a loss, is always make sure that you say the baby's name. Say the baby's name. Say, 'How are you doing since Justine died?' or whatever the name is."

Jan needed to say the baby's name, to write her name, to make her "print" on this earth real.

"It's almost like sometimes you think you're imagining this. Your mind will trick you when you haven't got to really hold that baby, nurse that baby, and talk to that baby. I used to think, over and over, 'Was I really pregnant? Did I really have a baby? Did she really die?' Writing it down is kind of like etching her name in history."

Just seeing her name written is so precious to me, even though it makes me cry. So few ever say her name. They are afraid to make me cry. Don't they know I love to hear her name? To know that she really is a person who lived and died. That I am mourning a real person, special and individual, who came briefly into our lives and left way too soon.

Looking back on it now, almost two years later, Jan believes that writing helped her to survive and keep her sanity, especially through the darkest moments.

"You have such despair, and depression, and anger, and bitterness, and questions. Your mind is so bogged down with these emotions, it feels like it's going to explode. That's when I would write."

Not the Same as Talking

Jan had supportive friends who were willing to listen, but often writing was even more therapeutic for her, especially late at night, when she did not want to wake her husband or call her friends.

"Sometimes in the middle of the night, I would feel like I was in a nightmare, a nightmare I would never wake up from. Then the only way I could even stand to go on, would be to get up and write. I'd get up at two or three or four in the morning, and I'd be driven to go in there and just write."

It's 4:30 am and I can't sleep. I hurt too bad inside. I feel so betrayed. It's Halloween, and I got tricked instead of treated. I've been told it becomes more bearable with time. TIME—PLEASE FLY!

It's going to be Thanksgiving, and I don't want to do it. I'm not very thankful. It's coming up on the first anniversary in just six weeks. So here I am at 1:30 am, crying, unable to sleep again.

Jan might write a paragraph, or six pages, but she would write until she was finished. She would say just exactly how she was feeling, and then go back to bed, and fall asleep, feeling like she had taken a tranquilizer.

Her notebooks allowed her to be more present to her family, knowing she had this private solace.

"Afterward I would feel like I had been given a—I don't know—like a stream in a desert. I can't explain it. You're still sad, and you're still going through grief, but you've been able to express it on paper, where it'll always stay. And it does something. It's kind of a miracle."

Stages of Grief

At the time she was not consciously checking them off, but in rereading her notebooks now, Jan sees how she progressed through the stages of loss.

"It starts with denial, where you don't believe it happened or is happening. Denial is a state of numbness after a death, which is a very protective thing—and it's wonderful, when you look back. It's kind of like Nature's or God's way of protecting your mind from blowing up. It's like having a shot of Novocain in your brain or in your heart."

I still don't know if it has sunk in. My baby—*dead. It's so awful. I'm not sad or mad as much as I'm shocked that this horrible tragedy happened. I guess it's like the aftershocks of an earthquake.*

The next stage for most people is anger. Jan explains the transition.

"Over the last couple of years, I've talked to at least fifty mothers whose babies have died. Every single person, the ones who faced their grief, all had a day where the pain reliever or the Novocain wore off, and wham! it hit them full force in the face."

This has been the worst week since her death fourteen weeks ago. It's like the cocoon that was wrapped around me at the beginning has slowly been unwrapping and finally fell off this week, leaving my pain completely exposed like raw nerves. Pain so awful that I honestly don't know how my heart keeps beating. It is a searing pain inside. You'd think it would burn out your heart physically. I miss my baby so much that human words aren't able to even come close to expressing it.

I have been trampled like a bunch of grapes in a vat being crushed. My very life has been crushed out of me. This all sounds so depressing and so negative because it is.

"And then you go through your anger. Where you're angry at God. Angry at doctors. Angry at whoever or whatever you think may have been the cause."

Knowing she could be completely honest in her notebooks was a tremendous outlet. Then she knew she wouldn't explode in front of her other children or take her anger out on them.

"There's no place else I could get away with cursing when I wanted to curse. In the first journal it's not as bad, because I was still in shock. But then when I got really angry, sometimes four-letter words were the only way to express myself. And I would do it on paper, so I wouldn't do it out loud in front of my kids. Sometimes there are just certain words that work.

"There've been times when I wrote big letters, big big letters, saying, 'GOD, ARE YOU DEAF?' And then I'd have a real confused bunch of words. And then maybe a day or two, maybe three days later, I would write again, and I had come to a place of peace, at least for the time being."

The next stage is depression, which Jan went through a year later:

I am severely depressed. It's cutting deep today. All I did was cry and lie in bed all morning—having no reason nor desire to ever get up again. I am feeling overcome with despair today—such black hopelessness.

Shouldn't I be better by now? But how can I forget the baby I loved and was so excited to meet?

Writing provided some relief.

"Writing helps you sort through millions of thoughts that you have to sort out, to decide which are true and which are not, and what applies and what doesn't. It helps you get a grip on how valuable you really are. Because when you're going through grief and depression, it doesn't matter who tells you you're valuable, you don't believe it. Because you have a cloud over you and you can't see anything but darkness."

It was at times like this that Jan wrote out thoughts like,

I feel ugly and old and useless. Today I was looking at myself in a mirror at the mall and saw how old I look. My eyes seem to have these horrible baggy wrinkles underneath them. Maybe it's from all the crying I've done over the past months. Then again, maybe they've been there for a while, and I just now noticed.

I can't think of one thing good about myself. NOTHING. I DON'T KNOW WHY I WAS EVER BORN. This is Hell. I feel like a BIG ZERO, the biggest zero that ever lived.

Somehow just writing it down, having it stare back at her from the page, helped to reaffirm her value and go on.

Jan's husband has read her journals, but she is not sure if she would want her children to read her candid notebooks quite yet. But someday it might be appropriate.

"As adults, if they go through a tragedy, there'll be days when they will have those same emotions, because we're all human and we all have those. Whether we admit it or not, we do."

Talking to Justine

Jan often uses her notebooks as a chance to talk directly to her little girl.

"It's not like you're in some kind of delusion, where you believe they're alive here with you. It's just a way to be able to say what you want to say to a child you never got to say it to."

Dear Justine,

I miss you so much. You know, I never got to rock you and nurse you, and I never got to hear you say "momma" and "dadda" and all your first words. How come you left me? Why didn't you stay?

If you can hear me, just know how much I love you.

Dear sweet Justine,

Today is your first birthday. If only you had stayed with us, we would be having a cake, and little toys, and beautiful little girl dresses, and pictures and relatives. We would have watched with joy as you went from babyhood to toddlerhood.

"You know how you remember that first birthday. And in writing that down, it's like I got to have that. An experience that I really didn't get to have with her, and yet on paper I could celebrate that and be glad for her short life.

"Writing made it like I still got to be her mother."

Sad Associations

When you are going through the grieving process, you forget how "un-healed" you are until a trigger reminds you.

I was at the Penney's in Snohomish today, and I started to cry when I walked by the saltwater sandal display. Justine would have been fifteen months old now, and I would have been buying her little saltwater sandals.

For some reason I cannot get those little tiny sandals out of my mind. She didn't live long enough to get her sandals and go to the beach. It's so odd to be so sad over something so small.

Never Too Late

Jan believes that anyone recovering from the death of a loved one could benefit from writing.

"I have encouraged two friends of mine whose babies died to turn to writing for healing. I told them, 'It's just you and the paper, and the paper is not going to judge you or talk back.' "

One of her friends took her advice and found that it did help. The other one keeps putting it off because she says she is not a good writer. In answer to that Jan says, "I tell her, 'You don't have to write well; don't edit, just write. Your pen will not be able to keep up with you once you start.' "

This is true even if the death happened a long time ago, and you never worked through your sorrow. Says Jan,

"A friend of mine is seventy-nine, and her son died almost sixty years ago, at the age of ten months. Her daughter says she's never heard her talk to anyone about it. Never heard her mom mention it. Nobody's ever acknowledged that child's life. And yet the daughter knows, by the look on her mother's face at times, that she thinks about him and that she's never forgotten him. Sixty years ago they weren't into working through grief and talking things out, and they didn't know what we know now. Back then they didn't talk about that. 'Nervous breakdown, oh, shhh.' I am convinced that that woman, even now, could benefit from writing. Writing helps us deal with events of the past that have been so painful that we block them out. Hearing about my story could give her a cue, 'Maybe this could help me.'

"And nobody would have to know. It can still be secret, but at the same time it won't be secret anymore, because she will have put in on paper."

Jan expects that, because of her willingness to lean into her own pain, she will not be dealing with grief at the age of sixty or eighty.

"I wanted to find out how do I do this, so it doesn't have to last my whole life.

"If you don't feel the pain, you can't heal. You have to feel in order to heal. I don't know why that is, it just is."

Hope and Acceptance

The final stage of the grieving process is acceptance. Jan realizes that the worst is behind her, and she has learned some important lessons.

"It's twenty-one months now; I've started to accept it and integrate it into my life. I can still enjoy my life. I can go on. I'm smiling again, and I can laugh now and mean it. My life isn't normal yet. It'll never be the same again. Thanks to the support of family and friends—and thanks to my notebooks—I'm getting better, but I'll still always be a mother whose child died, and I'll always have a part of my heart missing."

By the fifth notebook, Jan started to jot down positive signs and thoughts.

"I started to write things in the back pages that gave me hope. Words of encouragement that people would have, some quote I came across.

"I used to cry, 'Why me?' and even now, it comes across my mind, 'Lord, what did I do to deserve this? Well, are you mad at me? Did I do something?' Through writing, I came to the place where I realized that this stuff does happen. It happens because we live in a world where stuff happens, and I'm not being singled out as a victim because I was bad."

It is my time of encouragement. The days of hopelessness are over, and they'll never have power over me again. My restoration is in process. Now I'm starting to actually feel it coming forth from the depths of my wounded spirit. Joy is returning, the balm of healing is touching my broken and crushed heart and making it whole.

Jan says philosophically, "As far as the answer to why it all happens, I don't know. There's got to be something valuable that comes. I'm in the process of finding out what's the importance of this tragedy, what can come out of it."

Jan's awareness has changed:

"Now when I'm in a store and I see someone who looks sad or unhappy or who's in a bad mood, I don't ever ever anymore go, 'Oh, that old bag.' I stop and think, 'I wonder what that lady's going through today?' Or that man, or that solemn-faced girl, I wonder what's going on.

"You don't know their story.

"I have a sense of wonder at people's lives and how they survive. And how they make it through their life and are halfway normal. Or maybe they're not normal, and now you know why. I give them more slack, I give them a break."

Somehow, Justine, I feel that you have and will continue to teach me more about life by your dying than anyone ever has or will by their living.

34
A Book for the Bride
and the Groom
A Network of Support

Iᴛ ʙᴇɢᴀɴ ᴀᴛ 11:32 ᴏɴ ᴀ Mᴀʏ ᴍᴏʀɴɪɴɢ ɪɴ Nᴇᴡ Hᴀᴍᴩsʜɪʀᴇ. They turned off Kenny G. and began Pachelbel's *Canon,* and Daniel, the ring-bearer, came across the grass wearing sneakers with a tux shirt. Mark, the groom, was pacing nervously back and forth.

When Beth, the bride and my cousin, rounded the corner of the garden on her father's arm, her red hair shining in the morning sun, her gown sparkling, all alençon lace and satin bows and pearls, everyone gasped. "Oh, she looks beautiful."

Roger Paine, the minister, began, "Beth and Mark have asked these people that are most important to them to be with them today—their strength comes from you: their hopes, their ideals, their values. Without their love you would not be here today; without you they would not be."

The birds were singing and darting in and out. They wanted to see what was going on.

"Marriage has always been," Roger Paine reminded us, "uncharted territory. Whether you live across the street or across the country, you are their network of support."

The Wedding Book

At Beth and Mark's wedding I passed a blank book around to capture on paper the thoughts, the feelings, and the pithy advice of the guests at the wedding party—the people who were, after all, their particular network of support.

At first people were flustered.

"What should I say? What should I say?"

I gave them three guidelines: Tell them what you noticed, tell them how you feel, give them your best advice. Write anything. They are glad you are here and will be glad of whatever you write. There is something almost sacred, no matter what people write, to know it was written on this particular day. Any entry says, "This is me on the day that you were married. This is what I was feeling and thinking and noticing about you."

Beth's dad filled a page exhorting the young couple to include both "giving and forgiving" in their marriage, and then, like a hand opening up in a gesture of satisfied resignation, ended almost with a sigh,

It's been a long, wonderful, happy, and tiring day. I hope this makes sense. If not, "I love you both" should say what I mean.

—Dad

The father of the groom wiped away a tear when I asked him to sign. "What a lovely idea," he said. The mother of the bride read through every page, reading out loud some of the entries that particularly moved her. She was not just reading the words—she was thinking of the people behind the words, and that made the simplest entry special.

My friend Shelley heard about the wedding book and decided to pass a blank book around when her brother, Larry, married Kim at a Jewish-Christian ceremony in Connecticut.

Kim and Larry had put out a guest book with large unlined pages, hoping that people would get the hint and fill up a whole page. Shelley checked the guest book during the reception and noticed that people had only signed their names, because that was what they were used to doing.

On the other hand, in the wedding book, Shelley told me, "People said the funny things, the warm things that were missing from the guest book. My brother and his bride loved it!"

A Teachable Moment

A wedding is a "teachable moment." The importance of the occasion, the overwhelming courage, the lifelong commitment, open the celebrants' ears and hearts to take in and act on the wisdom of the ages. A bride and groom want every piece of inside information they can get their hands on. So the couple is open for advice, even eager for it, and because of their heightened awareness, the magnification of all things associated with this day, chances are high that if it is good advice, they might even heed it.

Any wedding book you orchestrate will be unique. There are always personal touches, significant to this couple. Larry had played the part of Don Quixote in the musical *Man of La Mancha*, so several people in his book made comments about his impossible dream coming true. One of Beth's cousins wrote simply, "Happy camping," because the newlyweds were planning a cross-country Amtrak and camping trip for their honeymoon. "Happy camping": that could be a motto for living. Another cousin took the image even further; "Pitch your tent on the high ground." Then there are the bits of homespun family wisdom, now become metaphors for life: "Always spread the peanut butter to the edge of the bread"; or "Fake to the right, cut to the left, and go out for the long one."

Some people draw pictures. Larry is six foot four and Kim is five two; when it came time for the groom to kiss the bride, someone brought out a little stool decorated with flowers for her to stand on; a little cousin was so tickled by it that he drew a picture of it.

These personal touches are another reason a book like this is so special; these are things that only people who know the bride and groom well and care about them can say.

Now You

A wedding book can be as low-maintenance or high-maintenance as you want. Use it as a chance to circulate among the other guests at a wedding, to introduce yourself to people you do not know. Or let the book and a pack of colored pens go around a table by themselves, asking one table to pass it on to another. Every hour or so, locate where it last landed, and if it has stopped going around, put it back in circulation again.

Keep it simple. If people need a formula, share the notice-feel-advice trio. Encourage people to take a full page; save the opening few pages for the parents and grandparents. Invite each individual to write separately rather than "couple" entries.

Often those who say "I can't write" are the ones who write the most touching things.

What stands out in a wedding book are the funny "inside" stories, the welcome to the family, the affection, the reflection of the couple's joy. Most of all, what emerges is the image of two people whose love is infectious, and that is a good thing for a couple to know about themselves ten, twenty years from now. The bride and groom years later will read these entries and remember who they are.

35

Passing on the Torch
Religious Milestones

ADOLESCENCE—THE BRIDGE BETWEEN CHILDHOOD AND MATU-
rity—is a perilous passage," says Arthur Davidson, commentator for the
photographic collection, *The Circle of Life*. "To become fulfilled members
of their society, adolescents must understand when childhood ends, adulthood begins and what their culture expects of them."

There are many different kinds of ceremonies to mark this bridge, to
publicly acknowledge "growing up." Certain aspects of the ceremony may
change—for example, the traditionally male bar mitzvah has a female
parallel, the bat mitzvah, in many Jewish communities today—but the
core reason for the rite remains the same. It is an acknowledgment that the
young adolescent is passing to a new level of ownership and responsibility,
of accountability, in his or her faith and community. Such rites of transition in the lives of our children are an opportunity to establish a link
between generations, and one more chance to tell someone near and dear to
you just how dear they are.

When Emily made her first communion, a cousin wrote,

Dear Emily,

What a bright and shining person you are. Did you know that you can light up a room when you walk in? I'm telling you it's so. Your good nature and happy heart are qualities about you that I love (along with your humor, your intelligence, your etc. etc.!)

Holy Communion may be for you another way to keep your light aglow. Long may you shine,

Your cousin

Grandma Klauser wrote about her own first communion, which was sixty-five years earlier, as though it were yesterday,

As you know at that time we had to fast after twelve midnight before we went to Communion. What do you think I did? I had a sunflower seed that morning. When I told the Sister, she was upset but let me go to Communion after scolding me. It's all very clear to me, though it happened a long, long, long, time ago.

According to ancient decrees of the Catholic church, the first communicant has officially reached the "age of discretion" or the "age of reason." Katherine's first communion letters, including one from her brother James, talk about this "growing up."

Katherine, my little sister,

Every time I turn around you've grown up even more. You're becoming quite a grown-up little woman! I'm so proud of you.

Peter recalled his own feelings of being scared that day and reassured her not to worry.

I went up feeling like a monster and came back feeling like a flower. Have a good one.

Letters like these are an important addition to the family album. They give the young person a sense of belonging, of being part of a tradition that goes way back, experienced in many cases by brothers and sisters, parents and grandparents before them.

Family History and Color

Times of ritual passage are engraved in memory; often an older person might find a grandchild's, a niece's, or a nephew's ceremony bringing back vivid memories of his or her own special day. The shared memoirs not only remind families of tradition and the continuing link, they sometimes add color to family history, painting a scene of long ago.

Bertha Sangiori, a woman in her late seventies, gave her grandson a special gift when he made his first communion. She wrote him an account of her own communion day in Switzerland more than half a century earlier.

> *Nearing your first communion day, a lot of beautiful memories awaken my thoughts. All at once those ideas of yesteryear are racing through my mind. Little by little, I remember more of it.*

She first sets the scene in the Swiss village where her family lived. With much warmth and affection, she tells about the long-awaited Sunday,

> *called "Der weisse Sonntag," the white Sunday, where we were crowned as good family members, receiving for the first time the holy communion.*

She describes the preparation and in an aside tells her grandson a funny story about her brothers—his granduncles.

> *By the time my younger brother received his first communion, things and times had changed a bit. My younger brother was eight years younger than I. When it came to his day, my mother's heart gave her a lot of trouble and she wasn't able to buy her youngest the first new suit. She gave me the money and all the orders, and I went by train with my little brother to the next big town to buy his suit.*

When they came home with a navy blue suit with long pants, white shirt and tie, and a new pair of socks, everybody was excited about it, except her older brother.

I finally found out what the trouble was for his crazy behavior. He was boiling mad that his younger brother got to wear a pair of long pants on his big day, not a pair of knee-high ones like he did. He was awfully jealous of his brother, and the two brothers were feuding about this for a long time.

For her own communion day, her father had a "wonderful surprise." She is as thrilled to recount it now as she was the day it happened.

My father, your great-grandfather, had a wonderful surprise for all of us. But the gentleman he always was, I shouldn't have been surprised. As I told you once before, my mother was a sickly person who suffered from heart and kidney troubles, and any extra activity left her short-breathed. My father knew she couldn't walk with us to church, that was out of the question. And we sure hated to leave mother home, not to see us in our new outfits.

Sunday morning, after we were all dressed and ready to go, after being warned a dozen times not to touch this and not to do that in order not to get dirty again before the big moment, my brother stormed in the house saying,

"Mommy, they're here! They're here!"

"Who is here?" Mother asked.

"The horses! The horses! And the carriage!"

Meanwhile my father got hold of the situation. And in his calming way he accompanied his two ladies to a well-dressed-up two-horse carriage. That sure was the ride of the century! The carriage brought us right in front of the church, so mother didn't have to go any further than necessary.

Perhaps it is because we are paying attention that the smallest details are intensified and easy to recall with astonishing clarity even more than half a century later. Bertha remembers well, and tells her grandson, her feelings of impatience, of happiness, of reverence.

Saying a few prayers and waiting for the big moment, I watched all around myself, all these somber faces of the parents and the impatient faces of the first communicants left a big impression on me. Through the lovely stained window glass was a ray of sunshine stealing its way into church and our hearts.

She was astonished at the details that came back to her, right down to the number of communicants on either side of the aisle.

We all got settled in church at our designated pews with our hearts full of new expectations. The first few pews were taken up by the lovely white-dressed girls on the left side and the handsome-looking boys at the right. Behind their children sat all these proud parents.

The priest and his helpers held mass, and at the time of giving out the bread, we well-dressed little people moved up in rows to the communion rail, six girls at the left and six boys at the right; kneeling in front of that rail so the priest could give out the host to each and every little waiting heart. That sure was a very memorable moment. And then we walked, hands held together in prayer, in a solemn step back to our places. After Mass, the priest talked to the whole community and everybody seemed to shine with a happy face.

Then she lovingly tells her grandson about the reception after with his great-grandparents.

Very slowly we walked with mother to the Hotel Sternen where father had ordered a lovely festive dinner for the occasion. I remember how happy my parents were, and their love and respect for each other radiated out of their faces, making us happy and thankful as well. After a well-prepared dinner and lots of desserts, we had to rest our full bellies for a while.

Continuity and Connection

Rites of passage are about connection—connection to family, to community, and to history.

I talked with my friend Dan Rose about his son Alex's bar mitzvah five years ago.

"Alex and I went to Europe the summer before his bar mitzvah. The point of the venture was to talk to some of our relatives who survived the Holocaust, which began, with *Kristallnacht,* fifty years before our visit."

The two had many adventures.

"Incredible things happened on that trip: talking to relatives in Belgium and France who bribed and charmed their way to safety, relatives who had luck on their side."

A few weeks after, Dan went back to France alone to further the research.

"I found myself in the Marais, the old Jewish section of Paris, where I'd gone to buy Alex the tallis that he wore at his bar mitzvah, and I wound up talking to a man who was Alex's age when the Holocaust took place. This man was thirteen, he had just had his bar mitzvah when his entire family was deported. He himself was not deported because he was in a sanitarium with tuberculosis, and the Nazis were good enough not to come in with a stretcher and haul him away. So he was separated from his family, all alone, and one day he got a message from his father that had been smuggled out from a faraway concentration camp in the handlebar of a bicycle.

"The father was Polish and didn't speak French very well, so he had to write the words out phonetically, the way they sounded, rather than the way they were supposed to be spelled. And full of misspellings, not knowing if he would ever see his son again, this is what the father had written:

> *My son. Do not be sad. Have courage. We shall survive. Rip up this message. Au revoir.*

The son was eventually deported himself; one day the Nazis did come into the sanitarium and took him away.

"He never saw his family again. But somehow the son managed to survive, and here he was, standing with me on this street in Paris, telling me this story with tears in his eyes. And I thought, what fitting words for a father to tell his son in any age, war or no war."

The day of Alex's bar mitzvah, Dan wrote him a toast and read it out loud at the reception. He told him how proud he was of him, and he told him the story of the man he had met in the Marais. And he ended his toast with the ageless injunction,

> *My son, "Have courage. We shall survive."*
> *That you did what you did today, Alex, so beautifully in the chapel,*

proves that we are surviving. And that so many of us gathered today to help you celebrate—Jew and non-Jew, old friends and new friends, family and ex-family—proves that we are all surviving, each in our own way and all of us together: surviving very nicely.

Alexander Edward Rose, you are an original boy, a talented boy, not always an easy boy, but always an interesting boy. Today, you became a man.

Dan read his tribute to Alex, then gave him a hug.

"He was a little bit embarrassed by the last line. He said, 'Omigod.' Yet he kept what I wrote on his desk for months after, and he's not a pack-rat type of guy."

Alex and his dad have a great relationship today, five years later.

And someday perhaps Alex will lovingly embarrass his own son as he passes on the torch.

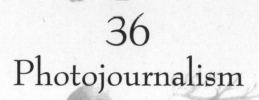

36
Photojournalism

KATHY HUSEBY, WHO TEACHES CLASSES ON ARCHIVAL-QUALITY photo mounting, tells a story about a woman who came to her with a long face and a shoebox filled with old photos. After the woman's mother died, she had found this box in the attic, stuffed with fading photos and tintypes. The serious young boy sitting on the pony, the smiling girl on an old man's knee, the bearded man in uniform, the solemn couple in their wedding finery—all of them were related to her, and not one picture had a notation or clue.

The Box of Germans

Her mother had grown up in Germany and immigrated to America as a young woman, so her daughter called the treasure-trove the Box of Germans. Sometimes she would take them out and look at them long-ingly, wishing photos could talk. Their stories, even their relationship to this new generation, were forever lost.

Kathy uses the Box of Germans to illustrate the future fate of our photos—even those carefully mounted in albums—when we fail to caption and date them.

She always concludes: "Don't lament, document."

Several times I have read stories about people fleeing from toppling governments or burning houses, and what they go back for, or what they miss the most if they are not able to go back, are their photo albums. The first house, the new baby, the graduate in cap and gown. Looking at those images brings back a flood of memories—that is, provided you were the one who took the picture or posed for the picture in the first place. The once-removed or twice-removed can only guess what your thoughts were and what was going on. The film cannot capture the sayings, expressions, or background of an event.

We have a framed quintet of my grandmother, my great-aunts, and my great-uncle, taken in 1902. The original of this picture hung in the hallway in my house when I was growing up, a single long rectangular frame with old-fashioned oval cut-outs for each portrait. Now I have a copy of it. Many times my mother would tell us why the cherubic face on the little girl with the ringlets of blond curls, who was my grandmother, looked so sad. Her six-year-old's eyes have that haunted look because her father had recently died.

My children and their children will know that about their great-grandma's picture, and they will even know that the great-great-grandpa who died young was Edison's patent attorney, because I taped the story to the back of the picture.

Words and Pictures Together

Once you start thinking of your photos as illustrations to a written text, you open up all kinds of possibilities. A man in one of my workshops showed me some samples of a precious gift that he has been giving for years. He has been putting together a series of birthday albums for his now-teen-age daughter ever since she was a toddler. Whenever he has pictures developed, he routinely orders "doubles." Right before her birthday, he selects the ones that highlight her year—her championship volleyball game, the prom—and collects them into a *Your Year in Review* book for her. He mounts the pictures in a small album, and around them he writes a birthday letter to her, recounting her year and how he has enjoyed watching her grow.

Somewhere we have an audiotape of Katherine's birth. On it you can hear me say, "Oh baby, you are beautiful," and hear Jim ask, "Is it a girl? Is it a girl?" This might be nice for Katherine to have when she is grown, but I am sorry to say I do not know where it is. We did not notice for a long time that it was missing, because from one year's end to the next, we rarely listened to it. The album of pictures of that memorable day, however, are well-thumbed. Katherine loves to look at that album so much that I had to tape the spine. It fell apart from being opened one too many times. I am glad we had the foresight to copy the quotes from the tape recording right into the album.

When Katherine was learning to read, we made her a storybook of her own. It was a way to let her learn the written words for simple things associated with her own life. Also using double prints, we mounted photos in a lined fabric book, only one to a page. There were pictures of Katherine with an aunt and an uncle, her grandmother, her brothers and sister, and the family pets. We asked her what each picture meant to her, writing down her response in block letters in her own words as she spoke. We spent many happy hours with her reading this custom-made book. What had started out as a reader has now become a memory album.

Annotated Albums as ''Directed Life Review''

Dr. Paul M. Lerner, a clinical psychologist in Asheville, North Carolina, says that elderly folks in nursing homes who review photo albums regularly, in what he calls "directed life review," have less stress, need fewer medications, are easier to be around, and are generally happier with their surroundings.

Della Bellamsky of San Jose writes in *Woman's Day* about her ninety-six-year-old great-aunt, who was moved to a convalescent hospital after living independently for many years in her own small house. Della asked her aunt if there was anything she could do to make it less painful for her, to make her feel more comfortable. She thought her aunt might ask for a warm blanket or maybe a comfortable chair. What could Della give her?

"Memories," the elderly woman said. "Can you give me memories? Sometimes I lose them."

At first Della did not know how to answer that need. Then she realized she could do it in pictures and words.

"I began by photographing her home inside and out, including her beloved garden and the surrounding neighborhood. I took photos of her favorite parks and the benches she used to sit on to enjoy nature. I found some old pictures of important events in her life, and wrote to friends and relatives to get more."

Della assembled the pictures in a book and called it a memory book. Whenever she went to visit, they would talk about the scenes and people, as Della added the stories to the pages.

"During the year she lived in the hospital, she spent her happiest moments recalling all of the wonderful times and places in her life."

If Pictures Could Talk

Kathy Huseby describes with warm affection a recent visit to her husband's home in eastern Montana. His mom and dad were homesteaders. The farm has all kinds of fascinating old-fashioned farm equipment and abandoned trucks and tractors. Kathy decided to take black-and-white pictures and asked her brother-in-law to accompany her as she snapped, to explain what some of the equipment was used for in the old days. Not only did he name and explain each piece of machinery, he started telling her marvelous stories about a father-in-law she had never met. At first she thought, "I'll remember this"; as the stories kept pouring forth, she realized, "I'd better write this down."

She grabbed a small notebook and entered the frame of the film next to the narration about the machinery's use and the family stories connected with it. He told her things like how many bushels of grain this old battered truck would hold, then expounded on outlandish tales about getting the grain to market. Kathy said that writing these notations to her photos "added reality to my relatives."

A Dating Scrapbook: Portrait of a Courtship

The children were fascinated when Jim and I brought out a faded scrapbook of our dating days: theater tickets, napkins, matchbook covers, Shakespeare in the Park, La Crêpe. It was crudely assembled, I must say, only the month and the year, no comments. Soon after, Peter began assembling a dating scrapbook to give his sweetheart Carolyn for her summer birthday. They met in November, so the book is a chronicle of their first seven months together.

The difference is, he is assembling it as it happens, while we reconstructed ours after the fact. The bigger, more important difference is that he has annotated everything, at length. The tickets from the football game in our old scrapbook stare back at me mutely. I have no idea even who won the game.

Peter's scrapbook is a compliment to Carolyn—to make even the smallest memorabilia like a ticket stub important because it was something they shared together. Mounting these trophies and writing his reflections elevates and recasts the mundane. It says, You are important to me, and the time we spend together is worth recording and remembering.

All of us have a feeling for this project. If I find a color brochure advertising *Pelléas and Mélisande,* I pick it up for Peter's scrapbook because I know he is taking Carolyn to the opera as a Christmas present. Emily gathers the throw-away mailings about a local show she knows they saw; I pick up a map of Puget Sound on the ferry to immortalize the trip they took to Port Townsend. Katherine cuts the movie ads out of the weekend edition of the newspaper. When I was listening to the bluegrass band at the Honey Bear Café, I started thinking that Peter and Carolyn would enjoy this place and the free entertainment on Thursday nights. The idea to tell him about it evolved backward. First I saw the Honey Bear logo on a flier, and that made me think of how Peter could paste one of those in his scrapbook if he came here with Carolyn. So they'd better come. Emily says it is like living backward: First think of the effect, and then figure how to get there. Throw the marker out in the water, and then swim toward it.

Even though we are all part of his scrapbook, Peter is the one who cares enough about Carolyn to want to notice what it is like to fall in love. Peter creates special dates so that he can put them in the album, and he pays attention to what happens so he can record it later. It makes him alert to detail—not just a café, but the Sound View Café; not just any ferry, but the M.V. *Hyak,* not just dinner together, but you had the tortellini with pesto and I had the steak and mashed potatoes. These are the details that recreate the scene and reactivate the memory later.

Because of his dating scrapbook, all his senses are attuned. Adventures abound. Life presents him with things to do, because he has provided a place to record them.

George's Journals

I met George Klacsanksy and learned about his unique kind of photo-journalism one night in the Teahouse Kuan Yin, the "tea drinking establishment." I had started to leave, because the after-movie crowd was coming in, the Raven Moon duo, Willow and Kaija, were tripping out on bamboo flutes and Celtic harp keyboard, and there was a skinhead with earnest eyes (we talked for a while; he had heard the Raven Moon ten times) sitting in the lotus position on the floor by my table next to the fishbowl. And there at the round glass-topped table by the exit was George, George with his books on Zen, his computer-generated haiku manuscripts piled high, and an open journal of photographs, heavily annotated.

And wouldn't you know, once we stopped to talk, the piled pages and photographs were not about clever scrapbooks or livening up of photo pages, they were about a way of life. Keeping a book like this is a way of paying attention to life, and George was speaking of enlightenment and mindset and heightened awareness. I decided not to leave after all.

In answer to my questions, George explained that in Japan there is an ancient tradition, called *haibun,* of writing journals combined with poetry and illustrations. Sometimes, he explains, the pictures elicit the stories; sometimes it is the other way around. Soon the stories annotating your photos create "moments of enlightened awareness." After a while you begin to have those moments more often.

"The more you write it, the more you develop that mindset, and then you start seeing things to pay attention to around you that you might otherwise have missed."

A car drove by on the street, and George remarked how its horn sounded like a toy horn, and he noticed as well a lovely moth that was flitting about our heads. I had been oblivious to both until he pointed them out.

"Anything can become a vehicle for enlightenment," George continued, "mowing the lawn, sitting in the teahouse, you become one with what you're doing: The teapot becomes part of your hand. When you write about a tree, you become that tree. When you drive a car, you are one with the car, it is an extension of you, or how would you know the boundaries, how to park? When we write, we give the things we write about, life, just as a painter gives life to his brush."

George explained that the Zen approach stresses being in the moment, seeing the world as purely as possible, taking things for what they are. A tree is a tree. His photojournals, his *haibun,* help him to achieve that presence, using stark, "camera-eye," commentary, without comment, followed by a haiku that gives a fresh look.

In 1988, when his twin boys were three, George compiled a poetic journal he calls the cowboy journal, to commemorate a family trip to a ranch at Sun Lakes in eastern Washington. It includes pictures of the boys riding ponies, a rodeo, and campside meals, along with George's account of the vacation.

"Once in a while, I read it to the boys. They laugh and remember. They are really there. Kids' long-term memory doesn't seem to kick in until later. The boys, now ten, don't remember what they did at three."

In his commentary George simply relates the occurrence, forcing the reader to relive the experience.

"In the cowboy journal, I do not say what we were feeling, only 'camera eye.' When something happened, I might laugh at myself, but I don't say in my diary that it was funny. For example, I have an entry that every morning I made peanut butter and jelly sandwiches for breakfast because I forgot to pack the cereal. The reader can add, 'How funny!'"

Or when a cowboy is injured, he does not add that he and the boys are upset, although it was a terrible thing to witness. Instead he tells the fact. The cowboy got thrown off his horse and didn't get up. It says something between the lines about the shock of seeing someone get hurt that badly.

Your vision, the way you see things in the world, comes out in your writing. George sums it up: "Sight is a faculty, seeing is an art."

Pictures are for sight; *captions* help him to see.

Now You

Set aside a couple of hours on a weekend and sit down with your photos, a marking pen, and other members of the family. If you use magnetic albums, write on sticky-backed address labels and mount them right on top of the plastic. Who are these people? What is the date, or approximate date, and what do you remember about that occasion?

Sit down with an older relative and your own Box of Germans. Take notes on the stories that unfold as you look over the photos together, and mount the stories on the pages right in with the pictures.

Make it a practice that as soon as your pictures come back from the photo finishing lab, you mark on the back, at very minimum, the date and the place and the people, or write the information on labels and affix them to the backs of the pictures until you have time to put them in the album.

"We won't forget that," you might say about some fact or feeling that goes along with a photo. Write it down in case you do forget it. Write it for when you are not here to tell it.

When you add a comment to your pictures, you are not only helping yourself remember years later, you are creating a conversation—which may ultimately reach across generations—with the person who looks at your album in the years to come.

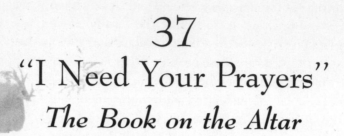

37
"I Need Your Prayers"
The Book on the Altar

IN OUR PARISH THERE IS A SIMPLE LOOSELEAF BINDER ON A SIDE altar. People asking for prayers can write their intentions in its pages, where others can read them and join in their petition.

Reading this book of other people's prayers touches me. People express their hurts and their hopes so candidly here. The facts are often stark:

I need a job.

My daughter has cancer.

Help my son in his swim meets.

Let my husband come home safely.

Please, Lord, help my daughter and her husband to work out their differences to heal the hurt between them. Help their little ones; they are so confused.

In Sunday school we learned there are four kinds of prayer, following the acronym ACTS. Adoration. Contrition. Thanksgiving. And Supplication.

"The book," as everyone calls it ("Write it in the book"; "Put my name in the book"; "I'll put your name in the book") is almost all supplication and some scattering of thanksgiving.

> *Lord, please be with me this week—I need your guidance and direction.*

> *Help my brother to have the strength to go to his meeting and be substance free.*

> *Please give me a remission from cancer. Bless in a special way all who pray for me.*

> *Help me to forgive her, Lord, and give me an increase in faith.*

> *Thank you for all the years I had my little mother.*

It is a precious thing to join your breath with another's in prayer as you read their heartfelt cry for help. It is an intimate moment to be let inside another's mind and soul and pray with him as one voice.

Some entries are addressed to the reader.

> *Please pray for my son who will be married this week.*

> *Please pray for a safe delivery for my granddaughter next week and that she may be a healthy child and also for her mother Karen.*

> *Please pray for a little baby Justine Elizabeth who was born tonight and died hours later. Pray for her family, her brother and sisters, her heartbroken mom and dad, and give them the grace to face the days ahead.*

And some directly to the Creator.

> *God, help us to be good parents. Give us patience. Let us learn how to let go!*

Or to a specific saint.

> *Saint Anthony, I would like to ask your assistance in helping me to find my digital watch. I have searched everywhere and cannot find it anywhere. Amen.*

217

Some switch midstream as the emotion overtakes the writer.

> *Prayers are asked for my brother that he'll get back on track and be sober again after his brief relapse. Please, I ask for strength for him. Also if it is not your will to cure my aunt, please keep her comfortable and take her quickly to you. I love you God the Father.*

Often you can read between the lines, underneath the words, to the pain.

> *Give all rape victims peace and understanding so they may continue with their lives.*

> *Thank you Lord for James's accident not being too severe. May he get full use of his fingers again so he can work safely and play his beloved piano.*

> *May my wife be better, and may they get her eyes and health under control so she can be with us longer.*

> *Please let my insurance agree to pay for the new medicine and let it give me the help I need with my cancer. Please let the Mason Clinic be able to do something with my eyes to help me to see better.*

Many reflect concern with global events like floods and famine, cyclones, war and political upheaval, and chronic crises: Bosnia, the Middle East, Northern Ireland. They remind the reader that we are all part of each other's losses and hurts.

And who can understand or fully appreciate the power of prayer?

Now You

Start a book of common prayer in your church or in a place you go regularly where people gather for support. When you write a prayer in the book, you are no longer alone. In your admission of need, you become part of a community of caring.

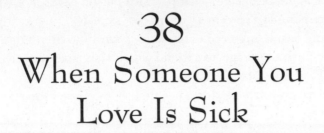

38

When Someone You Love Is Sick

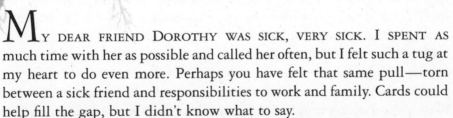

MY DEAR FRIEND DOROTHY WAS SICK, VERY SICK. I SPENT AS much time with her as possible and called her often, but I felt such a tug at my heart to do even more. Perhaps you have felt that same pull—torn between a sick friend and responsibilities to work and family. Cards could help fill the gap, but I didn't know what to say.

Would optimistic and hopeful seem insensitive? Would solemn and serious be depressing?

I worried so much about what to say and how to say it that I was not sending anything at all. I went to see my good friend Bob Barnes, who is a doctor. Bob recently completed a pastoral care program and was now working with hospice patients. Maybe he would know.

I told Bob that I could not be with my sick friend as much as I wanted to be. I explained how I wanted to send her letters of support but did not know what to say.

"I don't know much about writing letters or notes," he began as we sat in his sunny solarium breakfast nook, and he poured strong coffee into two big mugs.

"My work is visiting patients. I know about that. I know that the hardest thing for me to learn when I first started this work was the importance of going into a room and just being there. I had to learn to empty myself and be open to what that sick person needs, not what I need. Being there is ninety percent of it, maybe more."

A clearing inside my head. This sounds familiar. Step number one: A note, a card with a message, to a friend who is sick, does not have to say the right thing, it has to be there.

Bob says when you walk into a hospital room, leave yourself outside the door.

"Stop worrying about the meter running or the errands you need to do as soon as you get out of there. Stop worrying, 'Am I wearing the right tie?' 'Is this too loud?' 'Is it okay to tell a joke?' 'Oh, I shouldn't have said that.' Stop thinking about you, and think instead about the person who is sick. What does he, she need?"

Different people have different needs.

"In medicine, we say, 'Know your patient.' You will know what is appropriate to say. As you let go and concentrate on her, on him, you know in your heart if this is the kind of friend to whom it would be appropriate to say, 'I'm praying for you.' Maybe they would rather hear, 'What a bummer that you are sick.' "

The trick is to move outside of yourself and focus on the other person.

"Don't tell them about your tumor, your problems," says Bob. "That's like visitors coming from out of town and saying, 'Oh, we have places like this in New Jersey.' Don't you hate that? Her story is not the same as your story. Do you understand her story?"

And let them know that you are there.

"The patient needs to know, 'I'm here for you. I will not abandon you.' "

Listening to Bob, I was beginning to realize that a note to someone sick can be like a visit.

No matter *what* you say, that note is your way of being present, of saying, I'm here. I care. I worry about you. I know it must be tough for you right now.

The stuff that's on the card has little import. The healing power is that you're there.

I think about you every day.

Isn't it awful that you're sick?

I remember that night we had dinner.

You Don't Have to "Fix It"

The next thing Bob taught me is to let go of trying to "fix it."

"When your caring comes from the heart and soul, you are quiet. You have no agenda to fix this thing, not even the agenda of making her feel better. You don't have to give any advice. Great things happen when you are not trying to 'fix it.' Don't feel compelled to find the power to save this person. The only power you have is yourself, so give yourself."

People want to make a difference. That is why we want to give advice—to do something constructive, to take away the pain, to cure the sickness.

Bob has an answer to that. He says knowingly, with a kind-hearted smile, "The best way to make a difference is not to try and make a difference. It is the most healing thing in the world to know you don't have to fix it.

"It's freeing, isn't it?"

Permission to Have It Be Hard

The third thing to know is that it's okay to be angry. It's okay to be sad. This is what Bob calls "permission to have it be hard":

I got angry that my good friend was going through this.

I'm pissed. You lost your hair; it makes me mad that the medicine they give you today does that.

Acknowledging the reality can be a relief, especially if the sick person has been holding back emotions, trying to "keep a stiff upper lip" for other people's sake. It can be a comfort to know that somebody understands, and that it is okay to be real.

Even if your sick friend lives close enough to visit often, a handwritten note can mean a lot.

Bob tells me a story about a fellow he plays tennis with. There are sixteen of them who get together regularly to play. One day this man explained to the group that he had been experiencing double vision and was afraid that he was going blind. Everyone expressed sympathy, but Bob did something more. He went home and wrote him a note.

"I used some of my wife June's notepaper—you know, that cutesy jungle animal stuff; I told him I was aware how frightening it would be to have double vision and loss in one eye. I told him I was thinking of him, that's all. Now this man is my bosom buddy, my pal for life. Of all the people in the group, I was the only one who sent him a note. Before we were acquaintances; now we are dear friends. You would think I had done something extraordinary."

Dorothy's Cards

I called Dorothy to ask her if I could take her to chemotherapy; she said, "It is more important to work on your book." Then she told me about the wonderful cards and letters she received from all over. Typical of Dorothy, she asked, "Would it help you write your book to see these cards?" I said it would, and then I had an idea. Why not combine the two? She could show me the cards when I took her to chemo, and that way I would still be working on my book. She agreed.

"My daughter gave me this card," she said when I picked her up. "My friend who lives out of state sent this." She had tears in her eyes as she showed them to me.

These were cards and notes that she saved, and read and reread, because they touched her so deeply.

I'm thinking of you.

I'm here for you.

You are a dear friend.

You are in my thoughts. You are in my prayers.

You are one of the most special gifts that life has given me.

This road is a real rough one—you'll come through shining.

If you are afraid, call on me to listen and encourage.

I love you.

Simple words, from the heart.

Writing in relationship need not be immortal prose.

When you are writing in relationship, the person receiving it reads you into the words; it's like a conversation when you are not there. It means something to her, to him, because it is a symbol, a symbol of your presence, of your friendship, of your caring.

Why did I think writing to someone you love who is sick would be any different?

Bob Barnes helped me see what was right in front of my nose.

When I got home, I looked again at Dorothy's cards. I cried. Then I sat down and wrote this note to my friend:

Dear Dorothy,

Thank you for sharing your precious mail with me. It is no wonder you have such caring friends and family. They only reflect you, and the kind of mother, wife, and friend you are—caring, nurturing, available.

Count on me to be that kind of friend for you. I am here for you.

I treasure our friendship.

You are a fighter, and we are all fighting for you now.

Simple words. From the heart. I meant every one of them.

Why did I think it would be any different?

When Someone You Love Is Dying

Today, thanks to the pioneering work of Elisabeth Kübler-Ross and others who followed her, we know a great deal more about the needs of people who are terminally ill. In *A Hospice Handbook* Christine Longaker tells us that the needs of a dying person often include the need to "feel that dying is a natural process and that it is okay to let go." And Maggie Callanan and Patricia Kelly, the authors of *Final Gifts*, tell many stories to illustrate the principle that a dying person often knows that he is on his way out of this life and may be holding on until he senses or has a communication from those around him that he can leave.

When you are honest with a dying person, then they can be honest with you.

A teenager taught me this lesson.

Three years ago, my close friend Phil died of bone cancer. He spent his final days at the hospital, as friends and family gathered sadly around and relatives flew in to be with him. His eighteen-year-old niece, Angela, could not come, but she wrote him a letter and asked her dad, Tony, to read it to him.

Before Tony arrived we were all in a stupor. The thought of Phil's death was too awful to comprehend, to accept, to deal with—maybe if we denied it, it would go away. Perhaps we could will it away, pretend it wasn't happening, and have him back with us, healthy once more. With the slightest revival we'd say, "Doesn't he look better today?" We knew in our hearts he would not recover, but it was too hard to face that, to say it out loud. While there was still breath in his body, there was some chance.

The vigil at Phil's bedside was round the clock. As we changed shifts with each other, we offered empty platitudes of false hope in whispers—"He seems a bit better this morning" "He's breathing more regularly now"—and all the while our hearts were breaking.

Tony told us later that he practiced reading Angela's letter on the plane, reading it over and over to himself, so his voice would not crack when he read it to his brother. His voice cracked anyway.

Angela wrote about the good times, and she said the things she wanted her uncle to know before he died. It was painful to write, but a worse pain would be having him die, leaving her for the rest of her life wondering if he ever knew how much he meant to her.

She didn't pretend that he was going to get better. She told him not to be afraid, because his mother would be waiting for him in Heaven. She told him in her letter that she herself was less afraid of dying now, knowing he would be there to greet her. It's the kind of thing we sometimes say to soothe ourselves at funerals and memorial services; Angela had the courage and the clarity to write it out and say it to Phil directly, before he died. There was a completion in that, a sense of rightness, the way you feel when you have been open with another human being. Angela told the truth. And because of her courage, the adults could tell the truth. The adults could say good-bye to Phil because of Angela. And if Elisabeth Kübler-Ross is right, that made it better for Phil. He didn't have to pretend anymore—he left this life in truth.

Dear Uncle Phil,

I feel so incredibly lucky to have you as an uncle. During the hardest part of my life, you were the only member of my family to give me courage and support, which I will never, never forget. I cannot picture my family without you. I selfishly want you to stay here in this rotten world to see me perhaps make something of myself, or so you could be eventually a great-uncle to my children. But truly I want you to find the peace and happiness I know is waiting for you. I like to think of heaven as Yosemite, filled with brilliant wildflowers in the spring with a soft warm breeze, and the loved ones that have already arrived anxiously awaiting your arrival. I never got to meet your mother, my grandma, since she died before I was born, but I know she was a great lady just by the sons she raised. She will be there, and the love and comfort she will give you will take away any pain you have about leaving this world. Uncle Phil, you have already given me more than a lifetime worth of love and encouragement, and I will not fear or dread the day I must go because I know I will be with you again.

Love forever,
Angela

Now You

When someone you love is very sick, when someone you love is dying, don't worry about what to write—write.

39
It's Not Easy to
Say You're Sorry

OUR DAUGHTER KATHERINE WAS SEVEN WHEN SHE RECEIVED the Sacrament of Penance. The second-grade teachers taught the children a simple ditty they sang in unison:

> It's not easy to say, "I'm sorry."
> It's not easy to do.
> It's not easy to say, "I'm sorry."
> But it's good for you.

The next verse substituted the phrase "I did it" for "I'm sorry," and then the third verse culminated the progression in the same tune,

> It's not easy to say, "Forgive me."
> It's not easy to do.
> It's not easy to say, "Forgive me."
> But it's good for you.

That pretty much sums up the whole mystery of reconciliation at any age. Saying "I'm sorry" is tough enough; "I did it" is even harder. But only

"Forgive me" speaks to relationship and asks for a response from the injured party. And all three steps are "good for you"—a relief, a cleansing, a new beginning.

Often it is easier to say, "I'm sorry, I did it, forgive me" on paper, especially when the words stick in your throat or you fear the consequences.

Adam, our neighbor, is only six years old, and he knows this. Adam comes over to our house in the morning to wait for the schoolbus with Katherine. One morning Katherine was still sleeping and the rest of us were busy upstairs. Adam was downstairs in the living room alone.

When Katherine and I came down, there was a huge circle gaping in our sectional sofa, with puffs of stuffing hanging out of the hole. It was a clean cut, and an incriminating scissors lay on the pillow. Katherine and I let out a yelp in unison when we saw it.

Hearing a ruckus, my husband Jim came down the stairs. He threw his hands up in the air when he saw the hole.

"Oh, no! What happened!"

Adam began to cry, denying it all.

"I didn't do it. I didn't do it," he sobbed helplessly. "Just because I'm the only one down here, everyone thinks I did it."

He wiped his eyes, gathering himself together. In a little voice he said, "Maybe the cat did it."

After the children left for school, I called Adam's mother at work. She didn't think the cat did it.

That night there was a knock on the door. A puffy-faced and red-eyed Adam stood on the stoop with his dad. His dad propelled him forward into the house.

"Go on. Give it to them."

Silently the little guy proffered a giant yellow card of folded construction paper. Covering the front of the card, in childish script, it read with mounting urgency,

Oh No! Oh No! Oh No! Oh No! Oh No! Oh No!

over and over. Inside, a picture. There was the sofa and, quite clearly, a gaping, wounded hole. The offending scissors was carefully drawn and laid out on the pillow. The track lighting of our living room crossed the ceiling top of the card. Two figures stood by, one presumably me, and the other, Jim, with his hair standing straight up on his head and his hands thrown up in the air in horror. Down the side of the card, starting in big letters and echoing off into a margin of misery,

Oh No! Oh No! Oh No! Oh No! Oh No!

And there in the middle of the card, under the penciled track lights, the bravest words:

I did it and I'm sorry. Adam.

He handed us the card and sat down solemnly. His little legs dangled in the air above the calamitous cut. I could see he felt nervous yet relieved. I remembered the words of Katherine's song and said gently,

"It's not easy to say you're sorry. It's not easy to say you did it. But it feels good, doesn't it?"

He nodded. He didn't have to say anything. He had said it all on the card. He had put his apology and his anguish on paper and let the words speak for him.

It's never too late to learn the lesson Adam learned at an early age. Norman Vincent Peale tells of writing and asking forgiveness of an organist he had fired unjustly twenty years earlier. An insurance agent wrote a letter to Abigail Van Buren (Dear Abby), saying that because of her advice to make restitution, he had received a check and letter of apology from a former policyholder who had cheated the company with a fraudulent claim in 1974. The agent says, "This is obviously more than a story about insurance fraud. It is a triumph of conscience and courage and should be celebrated."

I am reminded of an astonishing letter I received once from a woman named Miriam. She and I were neighbors years ago when I first moved to Seattle; she had since moved on to California. I hadn't heard from Miriam in ten years, so I gasped when I opened her letter and a check for seventy-five dollars fell out. The letter began,

This is the most difficult letter I have ever had to write.

Miriam went on to tell me that she was the one who had stolen my briefcase, which I had inadvertently left by the car after strapping my baby son in the back seat. All these years it haunted her, and now she wrote to repay me and ask my forgiveness. Can you imagine what a burden she lifted from her heart the day she wrote that letter?

Now You

What are the events in your life that need to be forgiven, either recent like Adam's or long-term like Miriam's? What did you do? Who did you hurt? What do you need to do or say to resolve it? If it sticks in your throat, write it out.

40
Ethical and Ritual Wills

Rabbi Vicki Hollander lives in the Lake City area of Seattle. In addition to guiding Eitz Or Congregation, she is a bereavement coordinator in a local hospice. I went to visit her at her home when I heard about her work with ethical wills and ritual wills. She explains the difference, "An ethical will leaves behind for progeny what you believed in, what was important to you. A ritual will takes you through the dying process and how you want things and why. It also includes what you don't want and why."

ETHICAL WILLS

We spoke first about ethical wills.

"Ethical wills are part of ancient Jewish tradition, now being used by many different people, including Buddhists, born-agains, atheists," explains Hollander. Ethical wills incorporate and spell out the values one wants to pass along to one's children; they are transcultural."

Rabbi Hollander believes that ethical wills are popular today because families are spread out geographically.

"Earlier communities shared similar values. Today we lack that; our elders had more support from the community and from extended families living close together. These days, because we lack that embracing and grounding, there's more need to write it out as a legacy to leave behind, a tangible message to our children."

Overcoming Resistance

Florida rabbi Jack Riemer, author of *Ethical Wills: Guides to Personal Growth,* tells how his friend, Rabbi Joel Zaiman of Providence, Rhode Island, led a group of healthy young men and women through an exercise of writing an ethical will.

"The group's first reaction," he says, "was resistance: 'How can we pretend we are dying?' 'My children already know what I stand for. Why should I put it on paper?' "

One man shared what a letter like this from his own father had meant to him, how he read it over and over. Then the others in the class were willing to try it. Many wept openly as they wrote.

To show how broad the interpretation of an ethical will can be, Rabbi Riemer begins his collection with a letter written by an expectant father in the hospital waiting room, because it "speaks simply and touches themes that parents feel are important to their lives." The father, waiting anxiously for news about his wife and child, writes first of his eagerness for the baby to be born, "I wish you would arrive already. . . .

> *I am full of expectation for you. Though not about your sex. I don't have the least interest in whether you are a girl or a boy. . . . There are other matters that seem far more significant now. It is, for example, very important to me that you be fun, not so that you should keep me amused, though I shouldn't mind that, but more significantly, that you should be joyful.*

Next Riemer presents some advice from a father who was "a prominent New England scientist and businessman." He was healthy when he wrote it, and never guessed the solace it would bring his family when he died unexpectedly shortly after.

Never turn away from anyone who comes to you for help. . . . That which you give away, whether of money or of yourselves, is your only permanent possession.

Let your word be your bond! Those mistakes that I regret most keenly are the times when I let human weakness forget this. I know it is hard to learn from the experience of others, especially of parents, but if there is one thing I beg of you to take to heart, it is this.

A mother, in her will, reminds her children of the importance of lifelong learning.

Remember to always study, not just for book reports or piano or guitar lessons as you do now, or soon in college to prepare for your role in life, but even more as you grow older. Never grow too old to learn.

She encourages her children to stay close.

As you grow up, you may move far away from each other, and with families of your own. You probably will teach your children the important things you learned as children. . . . Remember not to take for granted your relationship with Daddy, your brothers and sisters; take time, make time, to call, to visit, to share your new families with each other.

The ending of this ethical will is particularly poignant.

If as you read this now or in the years to come, you ask yourself, "Why is Mom writing us all this? We already know it—this is what she's taught us, this is how we have always lived and are still trying to live now," then I will be thankful for having been so fortunate.

With all my love,
Mother

Know That You Are Loved

Rabbi Hollander was kind enough to share with me her own ethical will, addressed to her daughter, Miriam, and to explain the motivation behind her inclusion of certain points. She laughed as she handed a typed copy to me, declaring, "This is a rough draft, 'hot off the presses.' I see myself revising this every five, or fewer, years."

Although some of the content may change with subsequent revisions, Rabbi Hollander is very clear about why she wrote it.

"I wrote it because there are things in there I could see being helpful to Miriam, as she goes on her way. That's what it was written for. It was written for imagining her without me in the world.

"The first thing I wanted her to know is that she has worth, she is a greatly loved and wanted child. I have met adults who don't believe that about themselves."

You were a planned child.

"So I started with that as the first value. I wanted Miriam to know she has a place here, she was wanted."

Then she goes on:

Secondly, a hope I have for you. . . .
I would wish for you that it be a goal to develop a good heart. That you strive to be a mensch *and live with* derech eretz, *with decency toward all life. This is something that I have tried to live by, sometimes succeeding, other times failing, but always striving toward. I would pass this on to you to continue, for there is wisdom and well-being embedded in this teaching.*

Throughout, she shares with her daughter in a tender way her own struggle with the truths she espouses for her to follow. For example, she enjoins Miriam to take care of her body while admitting it is advice she needs to remember for herself as well.

This was a difficult lesson for me to learn. I still work on it. Please take care of yourself, of your body and of your mind, and of your soul. Learn to nurture yourself in healthy ways. . . . you are with yourself always through thick and thin.

There are practical considerations to this nurturing.

Take care of your body. Exercise. Eat well. Learn to play in a healthy way. Take care of your teeth, your eyes. Get check-ups annually. Do activities that bring joy. Walk carefully as a woman, in certain neighborhoods, in the night. Guard and replenish your energies, so that you may flow like a stream and not be drained out. For only those who are whole can touch others and the world for good.

Rabbi Hollander wants her daughter to know the importance of knowing how to support herself economically, once more sharing her own experience.

Do not rely on anyone else for financial support. I've seen the winds of life bestow gifts and in the next gust blow them away. Learn the balance of saving for unforeseen days of roughness as well as enjoying life currently. Thank G. I had the savings I did to weather storms. Do moor yourself for the winters of life.

It is probably not always easy being the daughter of a rabbi, and the mother acknowledges this, with her wish that Miriam will find her own relationship to God and to Jewish tradition. A last thought, and one that is "hard to put into words," is that Miriam would care about developing her soul.

Although you may view this as "my mom's thing" and avoid it, please don't throw it away. Keep it for a while. For those who exercise and grow, their souls shine in this world in a wondrous way. It can be of aid to you, in joy and in sorrow and in times in between.

Miriam is eleven now; Rabbi Hollander thinks she might even show this ethical will to her a few years from now, when she grows up and moves away. "I would love for her to see it when she leaves home. When she has to operate on her own, which is why I wrote it."

A Place to Get Re-moored

Writing an ethical will for Miriam and projecting what that might mean in later years has brought to mind how dearly Rabbi Hollander wishes her own parents would write one for her.

"I talk to my parents each week, and through the years they've given me insights or encouragement. And when there were things that were hard, they've been present. So when I think of them not being there anymore, not getting this weekly phone call, I need a place where I can get re-moored."

She likes the thought of their ethical will being a reservoir of encouragement, to give her courage to go out and do the things that she wants to do, "knowing that they love me, that they care about me, that they believe in me."

She sent them a copy of the ethical will that she did for Miriam, with a request: "This is what I've done for my daughter; would you do one for me?"

You Don't Have to Be Sick, or Old, or Jewish

Writing an ethical will is a growth experience; you need not wait for old age or sickness to do it, and it is not just for Jewish people. A friend of mine who is, in his phrase, "an unbaptized Unitarian" and a healthy man in his early forties, said to me, "An ethical will seems like a lot of work, but people take an inventory of their house for insurance purposes, and that is a lot of work, too. I will just set a day aside to do it. I could get killed walking across the street, and I would regret it if I had not left that behind for my kids."

Ethical wills sum up a life of learning and what you want to pass on, so of course they are not exclusively written from parent to child. Hollander explains,

"Single people without children bequeath their ethical wills to the places where they put their energy—a neighbor, an organization, a friend, a church, a niece or nephew. It's a place to put down, to tell them, what you believe has value."

Some Simple Options

An ethical will can be as plain or as elaborate as you choose. A book for writing your memoirs suggests a simple lead.

I would like to leave the following advice, attitudes, opinions, philosophies and predictions:

Answering that with as few or as many sentences as you want constitutes the most basic kind of ethical will.

I recently heard of a woman who was dying, who sent each of her friends a letter and told them not to open it until after her death. In each letter she put a recipe, so that the friends could remember her each time they made that recipe.

That reminds me of the lead character in Laura Esquivel's *Like Water for Chocolate,* who left her cookbook behind when she died. Her descendant, who tells her story, concludes:

"Tita, my great-aunt, . . . will go on living as long as there is someone who cooks her recipes."

Saying Good-bye

Arthur Ashe, the well-respected tennis player who died of AIDS in February 1993, wrote a long letter to his young daughter, Camera, which constituted a kind of ethical will. According to *Life* magazine, the message he left for her included "his love for her, his hopes for her, his fears for her."

I may not be walking with you all the way or even much of the way. Camera, wherever I am when you feel sick at heart and weary of life, or when you stumble and fall and don't know if you can get up again, think of me. I will be watching and smiling and cheering you on.

Very soon after penning those words as a legacy to her, Arthur Ashe died. Says *Life,* "He had no time to bid his daughter farewell."

The letter he left behind became that good-bye and will help sustain her in the years ahead.

RITUAL WILLS

A ritual will addresses the practical concerns of the ceremonial traditions that are important to you surrounding your death and burial. It can be comforting to your survivors to have your wishes so clearly spelled out, and just as with the ethical will, it can also be a source of satisfaction and completion to the person writing it.

Rabbi Hollander shared her own as an example. It is touching to read, between the lines, her gentle faith, her trust and peace, and her guiding belief in an afterlife.

First she explained some traditions to me.

"Jews are buried facing eastward, so they know which way to walk to Jerusalem. They are buried in white garments without pockets, which they wear throughout life at different holy days as well. I have an image of all these people walking toward Jerusalem in white garments. Some of the soil of Jerusalem is buried underneath the person's head. These are traditions that are important to me."

The beginning part of Hollander's ritual will speaks of the dying process and asks that no mechanical means be used to keep her alive. Then she goes on:

> *It is my request when I am dying, that someone be with me, and if possible, hold my hand.*
>
> *As I am dying, if I am not able to say the Shema, I would appreciate it if someone could say it for me. It is my hope that I will be able to say it myself as my breath leaves me.*

She mentions that it would help her "rest more completely" if words seeking forgiveness for any she has hurt be said at her funeral, then proceeds to detail which rituals she would like her relatives to include, and why.

After I die, a number of Jewish traditions are very important to me. They speak to honoring the body, and human dignity.

She would like to have her body washed and not embalmed. As for her prayer shawl, if she has lived long enough to acquire two, she asks that one be buried with her and the other given to her daughter. Otherwise,

If I should die before I acquire a second tallit, I would like Miriam to have my tallit, and be buried without tallit. I've never liked those skimpy little tallitot. According to Jewish tradition I wish my casket to be a plain unadorned wooden box. If the cost of one without nails but wooden pegs is not too costly, fine, if it costs a lot more than a plain casket, I would rather my funds be among the living.

Rabbi Hollander's love of tradition is clear, but so is her thoughtfulness toward her family.

It would please me to have a little sack of dirt from Israel under my head. Should this prove difficult to locate, not to worry. If Mashiach comes, I'll experience the soil yet again.

She includes some notes on the eulogy. She wants as few words said as possible.

I've always been shy of being spoken about and have attended too many funerals where eulogies wax eloquent and speak untruths. I have done what I can in my lifetime. I've done deeds both good and bad. I am human, striving to be, trying to figure out how to live in the fullest way possible. I would rather words be simple, if any said at all. Words are to comfort those bereaved. I've never liked phoniness. I would rather stories are told at a later time and that each have a moment to connect with me in heart, but I bow to that which those who are mourning need.

Her friends have been her mainstay throughout her life; she hopes they would be there for her in death as well.

It is important to me that from death to burial my body is kept company by changing shomeret of friends. . . .

I wish to begin the natural process of returning to the earth with as little as possible delay. I would like to be buried in a Jewish cemetery, my feet facing eastward, as is our custom.

It would greatly comfort me to be accompanied until my grave is filled and I am at rest in my new home. That feels like a circle come round, grants me a sense of completeness, to have been born amidst people and to be escorted back to earth amidst friends.

What's Not Important

A ritual will also spells out the customs and procedures that are not important to its author. Rabbi Hollander already indicated that she does not want any fancy speeches. In addition, she humbly lets her dislikes be known.

I do not want any kind of things in the casket, i.e.: pillows, silk. I came into the world unadorned and so I wish to leave it.

As tradition holds, I do not wish in any way for the casket to be opened or on display. Those who love me I wish to remember me as I was alive. I want to retain my dignity in death as in life.

I do not want any flowers. I want all expenses to be as minimal as possible. I would rather funds be devoted to tzedakah or to aid surviving family in trust.

The gentle tone she has displayed throughout her ritual will is captured in its conclusion.

I thank you for honoring and fulfilling my wishes as much as is humanly possible. You have my deepest gratitude for aiding my passage to the next world. . . . May you go from strength to strength, and may you know joy and wellness.

One Family's Response to a Ritual Will

What is it like to be on the receiving end of a ritual will? Mikki Eggebraaten's family knows firsthand the comfort and consolation that such a document, even simply inscribed, can bring. Mikki was forty-five when she died. At forty she had been diagnosed with breast cancer and had a mastectomy. She did fine for about four and a half years. Then she got very sick; the cancer had spread to her lungs. She died from the tumors in her lungs.

Before she died, Mikki planned the ceremony for her funeral, from A to Z. She planned the flowers, she planned the scripture readings, the theme. She left instructions on what to speak on, her favorite songs, her favorite singers. She wanted the service late in the afternoon, so that after it, everyone could go to the Fellowship Hall for dinner, to "eat and laugh and have a good time."

A year after her death, I spoke with some members of her family, including her husband, Glen, her sister, Kathy, and an eighteen-year-old niece, Kari Ann. Glen said, "Mikki faced dying openly and dealt with it for five years."

She died three months short of their twenty-fifth wedding anniversary. Her requests to him give an insight into the kind of loving relationship they had.

"Mikki made me promise her that I would never ever bring flowers to the grave. She told me, 'You gave me flowers many times in my life; buy them and touch someone else's life. Flowers are for the living. Don't come to the grave—get on with living. I am not there. I'll be with the Lord.'

"And then she told me, 'If you marry again, be sure she loves our boys.'"

After Mikki died, Glen went to the church with her list of instructions.

"The pastor said it was highly unusual, and it made his job so much easier. He said it was the easiest funeral he'd ever planned. Our meeting to plan the funeral lasted about ten minutes, and then he said, 'Okay, let's go for coffee.'"

I asked Glen what it felt like that Mikki did that.

"It was a tremendous gift. The most tremendous gift that's ever been given to me. At the time of death, you are so emotional, it's hard to remember a person's favorite song.

"So many of us avoid addressing our dying, and because of that we don't leave anything. Mikki's list of instructions brought all of us, her friends and relatives, peace."

Mikki wrote notes concerning her wishes as a letter to her sister, Kathy, who explains, "It was left for us in her jewelry box, on ordinary stationery in her own hand. It is very matter-of-fact and yet gives much consideration to those she loved. We have laughed and cried many times while reading through it."

"For example," says Kathy, "we have cracked up a hundred times over the line written across the top of the letter: 'If Glen remarries, take the good china!' "

Perhaps the greatest gift Mikki gave her family was the realization the will implied that she had come to terms with her own death. As her sister says, "She had lots of faith, and she didn't want to die, and yet she realized in the end it was coming, and she accepted it."

The service was a celebration of her life.

Kari Ann comments, "We actually left the service uplifted. We were able to smile through our tears. At the dinner after in the church hall, I can honestly say, the mood was festive. There was a feeling that we too could inspire one another to greatness in common ordinary life like Aunt Mik had us."

What the Will Included

The details of the service were written as two numbered lists. The first was headed, "What I Would Want," underlined. Listed were the names of those whom she wanted as pallbearers and her preference for the time of the service. She asked that the service and the songs, selected from the Hosanna tapes, be upbeat, the kind of funeral "that I would want to attend myself."

Don't make the day sad and morbid.

She named the people she would like to give a short eulogy on her life story and asked the pastor to include in his message the assurance of eternal life. In addition, it would please her to have

Memories from a couple of friends (if they would want to).

The second list indicated the things she did not want: an open casket, a fancy headstone, or viewing times for the public. And

I do not want a lot of flowers. I would like my memorial money given to the missions.

The numbered items have some crossings-out of misspelled words, and double scratching, and after the second, emphatic, "What I *Don't* Want" list, Mikki went back, as though it were an afterthought, and squeezed in an extra item at the end of the "What I Would Want" list. It was a note to her husband and three sons: "Go to Hawaii!"

Only the Best

Mikki Eggebraaten's sister Kathy sums it up: "You cannot, unless you have experienced the gift of a ritual will from a loved one, possibly know how precious and meaningful a gift it is.

"It was a wonderful service. She was very creative and very artistic. The funeral was just her. When you went to the funeral, you knew Mikki planned it, you knew she had produced this funeral. Even down to the food—it was what she would have wanted, down to the fact that she had real butter and real cream served with the coffee at the reception after, real whipping cream. Not half-and-half, not two percent, not Cremora. Cream. When people got to the coffee and saw that real cream, they said, 'Mikki planned this too, didn't she?' because we never had coffee at her house without real cream.

"She lived her life like that, lived a fullness of life, not pending. Emotionally, spiritually, she lived according to the best, everything the best she could give; even if she had nothing, she gave the best listening, she gave a listening ear.

"So everyone who poured the cream at the reception thought, 'How Mikki. Only the best.' "

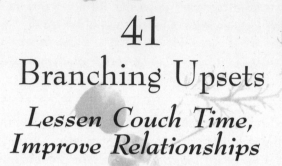

41
Branching Upsets
Lessen Couch Time,
Improve Relationships

You KNOW HOW IT IS WHEN YOU ARE OUT OF SORTS WITH EV-
eryone, yet cannot put your finger on whatever is bugging you? You have
this queasy rumble below the surface. Being near you is like walking near
land mines. People need to be careful where they step; you are volatile.
That is what it was like at one point for Lalita and her husband, Kent.

In addition to her regular job, Lalita and Kent worked together in a
small family-run business. She had concerns she was not voicing, and he
was not pleased with the way things were going either. The business
pressures began encroaching on their personal life; it got so they were not
having too much fun, either at home or at work. Kent and Lalita seemed
like they were at each other all the time; the slightest remark on either side
could cause friction.

Lalita thought she knew what she was mad about, but she is a wise
woman, a thinker. She knows the danger of the automatic answer, of
thinking you have it all figured out.

"Insights," she told me later, "are sometimes blocks that stop me from
growing, when I see the insight as a 'resting place.' Labeling verbally why
something is so solidifies what I think. 'I have a headache because of

tension in my neck.' If I say it three times, to three different people, it becomes so, because I say so. The 'insight' becomes solidified, and it is hard to move on from there."

In my class, Lalita had learned "branching," a non-linear method of organizing ideas. She decided to apply this free-form outlining to her relationship with Kent, as a way to sort out what was behind her bad mood.

Branching, in contrast to linear outline or list-making moves on and back and invites additions and emendations. Branching keeps the insights flowing and guards against the danger of being locked into an insight. Branching is perfect for delving into things and getting beyond the surface. You keep adding more branches instead of thinking that "the truth stops here."

Lalita knew that it was not the obvious things that were causing the freeze—the file cabinet drawers left open, the dishes in the sink, the invoices unfiled—there was something driving her frustration beneath the surface. Her branch dovetailed the technique I taught her with a commonplace of good communication:

YOU ARE NOT MAD ABOUT WHAT YOU THINK YOU ARE MAD ABOUT.

When you name what is underneath your anger, it no longer controls you or dictates your response to things.

So Lalita sat down and did a "branch" of her upsets, starting from the middle of the page. Letting go of conscious thinking about logic or form, she "let her rip," radiating outward lines and ideas as fast as her pen could move.

What poured out was:

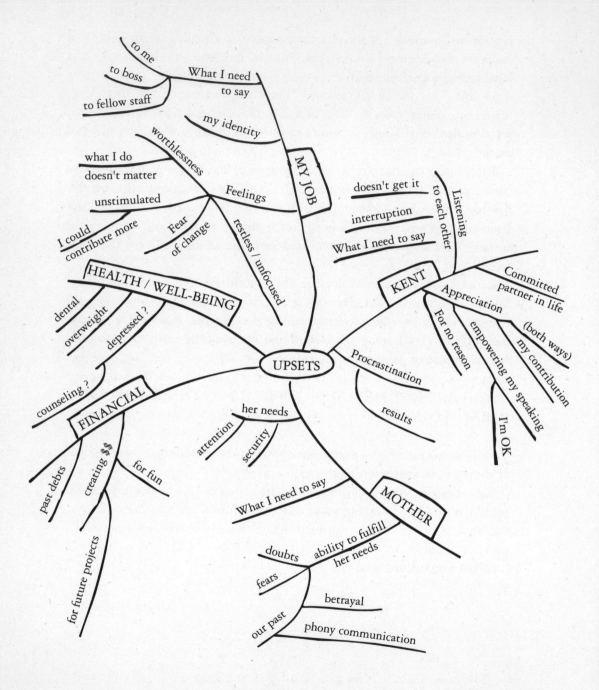

Even as she wrote it, Lalita felt the clouds parting and a smile playing in the corners of her mouth. Identifying the upsets behind her touchy mood was a relief, it was like light bulbs popping—"aha!" "oh, of course," "yeah, that's it!"

The branching brought up some things she did not know were bugging her—health, for example, surprised her—she hadn't known it was an issue for her.

Then she dated the paper. And put it in a drawer and forgot about it. What she did not realize until much later was that by branching out her upsets, she was giving them over to her subconscious to work on. One thing she did notice, however, was that things seemed to improve between her and Kent—the air had cleared. They started being more open with each other. The road seemed less rocky, the pallor had lifted.

Lalita made this branch of her upsets in November. One day in early January, when she was cleaning, Lalita found the dated branch. Her eyes opened wide in surprise: Most of the items on the branch had resolved themselves—the thorns were out of her side. *Without Lalita's trying to find a solution to any of them,* almost all of them had cleared up. She was eating more wisely, letting her needs be known, and she was no longer feeling depressed. She had even gone to the dentist, although she had totally forgotten that was on her branch. She decided to show the branch to Kent. The beauty of this was that she didn't have to start by harping on all the areas of discontent but began their conversation by acknowledging the changes in the past few months that had made the difference; they were able to talk openly about whatever was left that was not working.

"Handing it to him on a piece of paper was like a gift," she told me, "a gift from my subconscious, which I loved him enough to share, a jumping-off point for discussion, without accusing or shouting."

Lessen Couch Time

I call what Lalita did "therapeutic branching"; I use it myself frequently now as a swift and easy way to settle my nerves. Therapeutic branches grow before your very eyes, under your pen, like "magic flowers"—those intriguing little Chinese pellets that, when dropped into water, crystallize into shards of different colors, send off shoots, and grow and grow and grow.

Therapeutic branching can also be used—surprise—to help in therapy. Ron told me how he used branching before and after seeing his therapist.

"Before, when I went to see my therapist, I came out remembering things later I wished I had said. Or when I was in there, I felt tense noticing the clock ticking away the hour, hoping I was covering everything I needed to say. The thing that was bothering me most often did not come until minutes before the end of the session."

Ron began branching while waiting in the reception area for his appointment. He would quickly branch out all the things that were bugging him, things he wanted to be sure to remember to bring up. Next to each branch, he scribbled incidents related to his concerns. Now he went in for his session armed with a little piece of paper that took him maybe five minutes to compose and used it as a springboard for talking points. Soon he added a capper: When he came out of the session, he took a moment in the waiting room before driving away, to branch out all the insights gained, the advice offered, the homework assignment, the new attitude or direction.

"Before, when I left a session, there were so many images crowding for my attention. Would I remember to apply the points I had realized? Then branching became a kind of basket to catch it all, to gather it up while it was still fresh in my mind and to sort it out later, to make the connections I did not realize were there until after I had written them down."

Several times during the week, before the next session, he pulled this second branch out to refresh his memory and steel his resolve.

A useful question for a therapy session is, "What do I hope to gain by being here today?" Let branching help you answer that question with clarity. Afterward, branching can quickly summarize the session, let you collect your thoughts, clear your head—and act.

Ron was delighted with the results of his therapeutic branching.

"I am convinced that branching cut my therapy time in half; made what could have been long-term therapy, short-term. It saved me a bundle and let me get on with my life sooner."

Now You

You can branch your way out of frustration. Write the word *upset* in the middle of your page, circle it, then randomly branch out from that center all the things that are stressing you. Include everything that comes to mind, the things you know you can change, and the things you think you have less control over. Work yourself into a tizzy, a flurry of writing. It is a free-for-all.

Branching is a way of hanging out the laundry on the line: "Yes, there's that," "There's that," and acknowledging what is. Then move beyond the obvious, to get at what is beneath the surface—what are you really mad about?

Branching brings your upsets out of the mind's closet, out to where you can see them in front of you. Once you have them down on paper, you can put the branch away and forget about it.

Be sure you date it. Your subconscious is already working on it.

42
Butcher Paper Launches an Actress

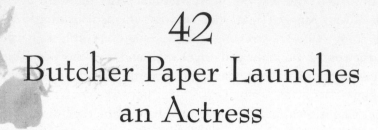

It never even occurred to her to be shy about it or worry what they would think, when, on her forty-fifth birthday, my friend Judy Sanders asked four of her closest friends to give her a special gift: the gift of a total day devoted exclusively to her.

Maybe it was because she would have done it for them in a minute, maybe because her need was so great that she could not stop to be self-conscious. She was the mother of five children, the youngest then ten, and she was getting paid thirty dollars a month to write a column for *Northwest Baby*. She wanted more. Looking back now, ten years later, she is not even sure what motivated her.

"I knew I did not want to grow up and be an old lady with those little purse marks around my mouth—I hate that look!"

She stops to purse her lips and in a mock whiny voice says, " 'I always wanted to go to the Grand Canyon, but I could never get Harold to take me.'

"I hate it when women blame men for the things they didn't do in their lives."

Somehow forty-five scared her more than any other milestone birthday.

She suddenly realized that in five years she would be fifty, and she did not want those pursed lips at eighty.

"I want to be eighty and say *wow,* I can look back at this year, and this year, and this year, and I did this, and did this, and enjoyed that, and enjoyed that."

But for now, it was family first and volunteer stuff second.

"Whatever time and energy was left over, was for me. Nobody asked me to do that—that's what I did myself. I willingly let myself be absorbed by everyone else's needs. That was the way life was supposed to be. That was being a good mother. I'm not saying that that was wrong to do. It just is a fact. And at forty-five, I figured I had at least thirty years of good health left, and I wanted each year to count."

The Setup

They met at a friend's apartment on a Saturday: "I had it at someone else's house, so there would be no distraction from my family coming in and out, or a phone ringing, or anything like that. It was a very focused day."

Of the four friends, two went "way back," and two were new.

"I would encourage anyone doing this to have that span, someone who knew you when you were young and someone who just recently met you, because you are many people in between. You want to invite people who know who you were and people who know who you are."

The most recent friend there was Karen Pryor, whom Judy had known only two years, although Karen's book, *Nursing Your Baby,* had influenced her greatly.

"And my friend Diana, who had had such success leading groups."

Judy says the friends that you choose for such a day need to be nonjudgmental.

"Choose the kind of friends who love you for who you are and have no interest in checking up on you. I have aversions to people who think they know what other people should do."

Judy had a wonderful breakfast ready for them and made her famous *cioppino* for lunch.

"I provided the food, and then the day was to be devoted to me, and they couldn't talk about anything else. I was allowed to call them back to the subject at hand if they got talking about something else."

Another rule was that this day of planning and dreaming had nothing to do with improving relationships or with other people in her life.

"I didn't want to get into 'Well, I want my marriage to be better' or 'I want my kids to—whatever' or 'My daughter whatever' or 'My son whatever.' 'Nothing to do with relationships' was a very important part of it for me. Because one of the things that happened at about this time in my life was a realization that I have control only over my own behavior. All I really own is what I do."

Paper on the Walls

Diana had been at business conferences where they drew up an agenda with a group and went through the points together. She appointed herself instant facilitator.

She put sheets of butcher paper on the walls, masking-taped them up, and then with a large marking pen started making lists of all the things Judy always wanted to do.

Diana wrote across the top of the first sheet, "What I want by age 50." And under that, she wrote, "Theme: Keep discovering things I didn't know I could do—and can do."

Judy asked Diana to put up there things like,

a condo and beach property
no dogs
an office
secretary
travel
running medal
national recognition
dancing
play the fiddle
theater
unlimited books and presents, etc.

"At fifty I wanted enough money so I could buy as many books as I wanted and as many presents as I wanted, without having to consider the amount. To me that was luxury, complete luxury."

Then they divided the primary list into two lists, one sheet apiece.

"One was for things that would make money, which I was interested in because I was making thirty dollars a month, and the other, just for things for me myself that I had always wanted to do personally."

Probing Questions

Judy's friends did not supply answers; they asked her questions. Says Karen Pryor,

"We were relentless. We kept asking her, What are your dreams? And then narrowing it down. She might say something like, 'Well, I want to be more physically active,' and we would say, 'Well, what is it you really want to do?'

" 'Well, I kind of always wanted to take dancing.'

" 'Well, what kind of dancing would you like to do?'

" 'Ballet, ballet, that's what I want.'

"And then Diana would write *ballet* under *dancing* on the personal list."

It's easy to make generalizations. The questions helped Judy to be specific.

"They would probe. Friends can do that for you; they did that for me. I said I want things to be 'hassle-free' and 'peaceful,' and so Diana wrote those two words down, and then they said, 'What do you mean by that?' and I said, 'It's balance and blend, that's what it really is. I want a balance of the stuff I want to do, and a blend of it, so there's people, and there's alone time, and there's making money, and there's time for fun."

So Diana wrote, *Balance and Blend,* on the last sheet.

"I wanted to try theater work. And they said, 'What do you mean by theater work?' and I said, 'Well, I really want to see what it's like to be in a play.' And they said, 'Okay, you do that,' and next to *theater,* Diana wrote down, *Actress.*

"You see, they would help me get more particular."

The First Step

The next important thing that her friends did for Judy that day was to help her come up with action steps, specific suggestions on what to do and how to start.

"It was a lot of work, and it took all day. Once we divided the main list into two lists, we came up with a first step for each item."

Diana hung up more sheets, and with everybody contributing ideas, under *Actress,* for example, she wrote:

take an acting class
make a list of little community theaters
find out casting calls
go there
read cold
get role—have friends fly in
"rave" section of fans

Then after much animated discussion, Diana circled "make a list of little community theaters" as the first step. (Judy never did take an acting class.)

"It's so wonderful to have a first step just written down. Because then you start making choices, and options become available to you that you may not have even seen before."

Writing It Down Helped Her to Focus

Judy admits that she could have possibly pursued her dreams without this. But writing them down helped her to focus.

"Seeing them on the walls like that was concrete. Writing them down gave me a sense of commitment. If I make a list, I work hard to cross everything off. Once it's on a list, I won't change my mind. If it's on paper, I'm committed to it."

And having friends there to help her generate ideas and write the list gave her focus and direction.

"Clarifying your thoughts focusing your thoughts and coming up with one action step is all you have to do to find yourself headed in a different direction."

Life upon the Wicked Stage

Even though it was number ten on her first page, of all the things listed the one that jumped out at Judy was "actress."

"I just wanted to see what it was like to be in a play, because I'd never been in a play in my whole life."

Soon after the butcher paper party, she auditioned for and got a part in a community theater play.

"It was terrifying, and I had terrible stage fright. I didn't know what I was doing, but I just sort of did it, and the thing is that it was, and it is, so much fun. I could hardly stand it, it was so much fun. The first play I was in was a French farce, and the third act was one of these insane acts where everybody is running in and out of many doors, with flashlights in the dark and jumping over furniture, and it was such a kick."

Acting had another surprise in store for Judy.

"The thing that startled me was that I was wanted for who I was as I walked in the door. Just me, just me, the person me; I wasn't even carrying my purse. That's who they wanted. What I brought to that part was who I am as a person. And the other amazing thing was to have to leave the house at seven o'clock at night because I had a rehearsal. Whether the kids had their homework done or the sink was full of dirty dishes, the rehearsal took priority. That's sort of heresy for a mother, you know."

After this first foray into the acting world, Judy got more and more parts, including a singing part as Aunt Eller in *Oklahoma!* Then a director from the Oregon Cabaret Theater saw her work and asked her to come to Ashland to do *Quilters*. This was professional theater.

In quick succession after Ashland, Judy was in *The Crucible, Fiddler on the Roof,* and *Our Town.* Then she played the part of Madame Rosemonde in *Les Liaisons Dangereuses.*

Judy found an advantage in taking on acting later in life.

"In acting what you bring to the process is who you are inside. What I had within me was my own life experience, and that helped me, especially as I got into heavier kinds of roles."

Keep the Sheets in a Special Place

Judy still has those sheets from a decade ago. She keeps them in a precious place.

"I have them folded up and I keep them on a shelf with grandmother's wedding pictures and a little glass thing that my son Rick gave me for my birthday when he was thirteen. He rode the bus all the way to Seattle Center and back to get it for me. It's my treasure shelf, and this is where I keep these sheets, folded up, because that day was one of those historic events. They are like a map, and it is so interesting to go back and look at them and see how different I was then. There are many ways I've changed, and looking back at these sheets reminds me of that."

She spreads the sheets out on the table and one by one checks off almost everything on the lists.

"Today I am able to buy all the books and presents I want to buy. I'm making enough money even without acting, because shortly after we made these lists, the publishers of *Northwest Baby* asked me to become editor of the paper. So now I have my own office, too.

"I wanted national recognition, and that's happened because I've gotten awards from the National Association of Press Women.

"I haven't yet learned to play the fiddle. I want to learn to play 'Turkey in the Straw.' I don't care if I go beyond that. But I've always wanted to just scratch at a fiddle."

"As for, 'get a role, and have friends fly in and see it,' Diana flew to Ashland to come and see me in *Quilters*, as a matter of fact.

Something else Judy learned that day of the butcher paper. She learned to be who she was, without pretense, and to value that. It changed forever the way she saw herself.

"All my life I denied who I was. Because who I was was not okay, for some reason. It was like my hair—straight hair was not okay.

"I believed that bending my hair was what I was supposed to do, bend it and color it. I finally figured out that when I bent it and colored it, it became unhealthy, and it was not my hair. I finally thought, to hell with that. My hair is straight. It's straight, it's brown, it's gray. That's what my hair's like, and I'm going to wear my hair.

"It takes a lot of courage for a woman my age to say, This is who I am, and not play some of the games."

"Because of that day, I found out it was it okay to be me."

Learning to Crawl

Judy acknowledges now that it might seem that she was being selfish, demanding time of her friends.

"But it was a time in my life when I was going through a period of unrest. A fact that I would encourage every parent to remember about their children and about themselves is that right before a period of great growth, great stride, there is a period of unrest. A time of feeling ill at ease with things that aren't going right. A baby who's trying to figure out how to crawl or a baby who's preverbal can be going through a terrible time. The baby doesn't even know that the baby wants to talk. And the baby who is trying to learn to crawl doesn't even know that he's trying to learn to crawl. He just knows that this isn't working anymore the way it is. There's something else, but he doesn't even know that. And he's just trying, by trial and error with his body, and then he gets over this hump. So every time there are wonderful strides made developmentally—and I think that's true all through our lives—there's a period of unease. And I was in that spot.

"I realized the other members of my family have their own life, including my husband. Everybody lives their own life. And I needed to find out what I wanted to do with the rest of mine.

"So that day with my friends and the butcher paper and the marking pens was kind of like learning to crawl, learning to walk. It was like growing up."

Now You

Organize a day like this for yourself, or gather friends together and give it as a gift to someone you love. All it takes is marking pens, butcher paper, good friends, and maybe *cioppino*.

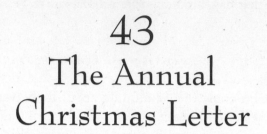

43
The Annual
Christmas Letter

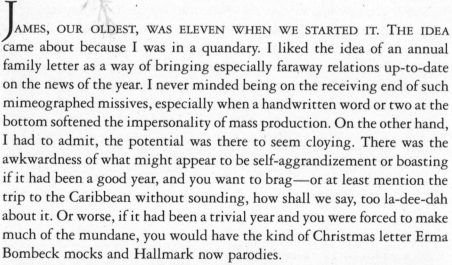

JAMES, OUR OLDEST, WAS ELEVEN WHEN WE STARTED IT. THE IDEA
came about because I was in a quandary. I liked the idea of an annual
family letter as a way of bringing especially faraway relations up-to-date
on the news of the year. I never minded being on the receiving end of such
mimeographed missives, especially when a handwritten word or two at the
bottom softened the impersonality of mass production. On the other hand,
I had to admit, the potential was there to seem cloying. There was the
awkwardness of what might appear to be self-aggrandizement or boasting
if it had been a good year, and you want to brag—or at least mention the
trip to the Caribbean without sounding, how shall we say, too la-dee-dah
about it. Or worse, if it had been a trivial year and you were forced to make
much of the mundane, you would have the kind of Christmas letter Erma
Bombeck mocks and Hallmark now parodies.

Let James do it. It seemed the perfect solution. I thought the audience
would be more forgiving of an eleven-year-old and that James could get
away with recording things simply, without worrying about what people
would think. I counted on him to unwittingly say something childlike
that would amuse, as only a youngster can—that unexpected twist or
phrase or hint at family secrets.

What I never considered was the effect on James and on the whole family.

One of the effects on James was that it helped him be a good writer. He rose to the occasion. He was pleased that we had such confidence in him. We took it for granted that he would do the job, and he lived up to it.

And to my delight, the relatives responded. Several of them wrote back to James as though he had written to them personally. That was fun for me, because it gave me a chance to talk about these people who meant something to me, who had been part of my childhood, and whom my own children did not know, having been born on the opposite coast.

"Who's Uncle Dan? He sent me a letter."

"Well, it's actually my Uncle Dan, which would make him your great-uncle. He's Grandma's brother. When I was a girl, he bought me my first camera and took me to Prospect Park to teach me how to shoot it."

James began to feel as though he knew his extended family better, and they knew him.

After four years, James passed the torch to Peter, and now Peter has passed it on to Emily. Recently, I visited on the East Coast with Heidi, a friend from college days who has never met my children. I was pleased and surprised to hear her speak knowledgeably, personally, about each of them. She seemed to know not only their exploits but their personalities. Over the years, from their styles of writing, she knew that this one had a sense of humor, that one was serious, this one creative. She spoke of them as though she knew them. I guess she does.

The other thing I was not counting on was the effect the annual letter has had on the family.

It happens every year. Whoever is writing the Christmas letter that year gathers the family together or corners each of us one by one and says, "What have you done this year that you are proud of? What events do you want me to mention? Give me a list."

The first response is the same. We each think, "Oh great, I haven't done anything this year that is different or exciting, just the same ol', same ol', 'wood products times ten,' " as a friend who worked at Weyerhaeuser for ten years once described his expertise. Sometimes it seems we live our lives that way too, "wood products times ten"—nothing remarkable, nothing different, nothing changed.

Then we are forced to stop and think about it. It becomes a kind of detective game, to remember, to find the clues. We look back over the penciled entries on the wall calendar or check out the pictures in the family album to jog the memory. "Was that trip this year? It seems so long ago." "Oh, right, this was the year—it was in May—I met Kiri Te Kanawa."

We ask each other.

"What did I do this year that you think matters?"

"Well, you took your friends for tea; you planned a surprise party for Hally; you went to the Paley exhibit."

"Wow. You thought that was important?" "Oh yeah, I forgot about that." "That counts?"

"You took art lessons."

"Was that this year?"

Gathering these items worth remembering builds self-esteem, that elusive attribute we are never sure how to get or give. It says, you had these milestones. I am proud of you. I noticed this. You have grown.

Guess what? We adults need this too. It is not just children who are growing up. Sometimes it is so much easier to see their progress, especially in the years when "Katey learned to read" or "Derrick rolled over" are feats worthy of mention. As adults, we think we cannot say, I read a book this year, but now we have to, oh, say, *write* a book to merit inclusion. Yet often it is the little specific details that bring the Christmas newsletter alive. Kudos to you for some of the risks you took, however small, the things you did that were different—and your hanging in there at the things that are the same.

The annual Christmas letter is a way to acknowledge and validate (that great eighties word that sounds like a passport stamp) the differences from year to year, however small, and a chance to also feel secure in some of the similarity, the comfort of knowing we are still with that company, involved with that organization, teaching and taking those classes, going to the opera, belonging to the guild.

So the annual letter is not just for the people we send it out to; it is for us, to help us take stock, to acknowledge in ourselves growth and change, adventure and risk—and consistency.

It is a little like writing a résumé: First you dread it, or think you have little to include; then, when you see it all in front of you, you give yourself some credit for your accomplishments and feel pleased at remembering the places you have seen and the people you have met.

The kids even tell me that knowing the Christmas letter is coming helps them to grab at opportunities and to follow through on goals. "How would this sound in the Christmas letter?" they ask themselves, only half-kidding. Peter says, tongue in cheek, "I live my life around the Christmas newsletter. Before I do anything substantial, I ask myself, 'Will I want to see this in my paragraph this year?'—whether it be winning an award or going to jail. Let's see, which will it be"—here he mimics a scale of justice with his two hands—"jail? Or award?" His hands go up and down, as though struggling with the contest. The "award" scale goes down further and wins the weigh. Peter grins broadly. "This year, award!"

More seriously, he sums it up: "It's about creating good times."

Implicit in that statement is a profound awareness. Early on, he and his brother and sisters have learned a guiding truth: Life is a narrative that they have a hand in shaping.

44
Trip Log
A Way of Paying Attention

FOR TEN YEARS WE WENT BY BOAT EVERY SUMMER TO THE SAN Juan Islands, cruising in and out of the maritime towns of Friday Harbor and Lopez Village, dropping anchor at the elegant resorts of Roche and Rosario's, hiking the rustic trails on Orcas and James Island. And I recorded it all, year after year. One summer day one of the children picked up my log and unceremoniously dropped it over the side of the boat. Although I retrieved it immediately amid much hysteria, it had instantaneously returned to its native state: pulp. We tried to dry out the pages, carefully layering paper toweling between each leaf, and were able to rescue some, but at least six years of entries were obliterated.

I felt sad, but not for long. It did not matter. I rarely reread it anyway. The drowning made me realize that the log itself was not important. It was the act of writing it that made me pay attention, that made my experience richer even as I was living it.

Keeping a log engages all of your senses. Writing it down sharpens your eyes to notice the sights, the names of the towns, the streets and the signs and the slogans that capture the essence of the place (Cannery Row, Positively 4th Street, "Don't mess with Texas"). It is writing that tickles your nose, bristles your nostrils so that you can notice the smell of saffron in Grenada, and the whole town smelling like chocolate in Hershey, Pennsylvania. It perks up your ears to hear the dialogue, the funny expressions, the idioms of speech; the music of sounds intermixed in the Amazon jungle: birds, insects, frogs, the splash of the caiman crocodiles— and far off in the distance, like a thunderstorm on the way, the low rumbling of the red howler monkeys. When you know you're going to record it, you pay attention.

Survival and Solace

There are as many ways to keep a travel log as there are ways to travel.

Aaron Camp, who is nineteen, travels on a shoestring, often without an itinerary, sometimes with a one-way ticket. His log, an extension of the journal he keeps at home, is like a friend he turns to for comfort.

Here I am in San Francisco, I don't know where I'm staying.

Writing down this simple fact, he says, grounds him, helps him to get his bearings.

"When I write in my log, I feel at home. Keeping a log helps me survive."

He likes the freedom of writing on the go.

"It's freer; there are no deadlines, no time frame. Plus, interesting things happen when you are are traveling. Writing them out makes them more real."

Writing Makes It Happen

When you keep a travel log, you not only record, you become part of the action. You are a receptor, sending out signals that say, "Okay, world, I'm ready."

Sara Rashad is twenty-three. She wears colorful berets and exotic head wraps and has a certain drama about her. Born in Hawaii, raised in Alaska, she moved to Seattle to go to college. Her mother is Irish, her father Egyptian, the first from his family to immigrate. All of her relatives are in Ireland or Egypt. That is part of why she travels.

The other reason is the adventure.

Sara talks with animated passion, punctuating her narrative with sounds like rockets exploding: "Whoo!" "Whow!"

"All the Egyptians are like this because the place is so big; people *express* themselves and savor every moment of life, and they know how to sit down at a table and talk for eight hours, laughing at the flower, the simplest thing—an amazing capacity for laughter and joy out of nothing."

Sara tracked her travels in writing; she says it made things happen.

"For me, knowing that I am going to write in a journal every day puts me in tune with every moment. It puts me in a position to take advantage of opportunities. If you are talking to people and you know you are going to write it up in a journal, you end up in conversations that you wouldn't normally have. The things that you wind up talking about are fascinating."

Buying a ticket for the metro, boy says "Where are you going?" "Sadat."
"O.K. You be friend for me." "No." As we walk to the subway near each
other, he turns around and apologizes. "O.K. I sorry I ask for you to be my
friend." "That's O.K."

"May God give you plentiful children." A woman in the street rattles off
several of these proverbs, kind words as she begs for money. She has two kids
and a constant smile of genuine need and kindness on her face.
"May God give you a long life."
"May God give you good health."
"May God give you happiness." As we walk away she continues to smile
at me with eyes of desperation until we are completely out of sight. It was
early, she was dressed in black.

Noticing Detail

In the journals of her travels that Sara shared with me, there are such snippets of dialogue and character sketches everywhere. She has an ear for language and nuance and an eye for detail, and her pages reflect this. Or is it the other way around? Is it because she is writing it down, that she notices detail and celebrates the rich tapestry of whatever country she is in?

A cross-eyed man gave us a tour of the room where the men knit the cloth. The men push a ball of thread back and forth while pushing pedals with their feet, and a beautiful piece of cloth is created. I took many photos. A boy kept on trying to be in every photo. A man yelled at me because I took a photo of him. He is a true Muslim. His head wasn't covered, so he got very upset.

In keeping a log in Egypt, in Israel, in Palestine, Sara says she learned about things that were important to those people as a culture.

"Family, religious values, and basic attitude—I would hear the same things being repeated. And because I was writing it down, I began to see patterns in the culture, patterns in the things that people say, things that people find important, as opposed to American culture."

What emerges from the patterns is a sense of the particular character of a nation, the quality that defines a country.

"I have traveled through a lot of places, and I have learned that every place, every country, has a basic attitude, a basic feel, a basic philosophy. You can taste it, feel it." She rubs her fingers together, and then continues, "In Paris, people are flamboyant and artsy, and it's very romantic; romance is in the air. In Egypt, there is an apathy, no control over the government, whatever happens is the will of God, 'Insha'allah.' Creating this attitude has made them able to deal with their reality. In Palestine, the people have nothing, I mean, *nothing,* and they are filled with hope, because without that hope they would die."

In Israel, she says, the people are full of stories.

" 'My son was shot,' 'My aunt died,' 'This happened, that happened,' but they are so full of hope, and I find that inspirational. In keeping a journal and in noticing this, it is one of the things I learned. They are telling you that their house was raided a week ago, and their eyes are glimmering, 'But we have hope.' 'But things will change,' they say. 'You can't get around it.' And things have changed—to see it happening now!"

''Tidbits''

When Sara is traveling, she keeps two journals: One is a tiny book she carries in her pocket throughout the day. Here she records and jots down what she calls "tidbits"—notes that will evoke a longer response later.

"Whenever I saw something I never saw before, I'd write it down in my small book."

Woman walking across the street with pot on head, carrying a baby

"Then at night, I'd go back, and I would spend an hour writing.
"I would write down everything I saw."

Egypt—women standing on the street, and men blatantly looking at their butts, so obvious.

". . . which maybe I would not have noticed if I weren't writing it down. When I am home in America, I am not paying attention to that kind of small look."

Egyptian museum, man proposes to me.

"I see that one sentence, and I have an entire story. I remember everything that happened exactly, everything, just from this one note, 'man proposes to me.' He follows me throughout the museum, I look back to say, 'Leave me alone.' It's a cultural thing, he interprets it in a different way, he thinks I love him, ooh-lah-lah. Here they would catch on that the look said, 'Leave me alone.' In Egypt it is brave of a woman to look a man in the eye."

nose-picking people everywhere; everybody picks their nose

"Here it is a big deal or you try to be discreet—you don't want anyone to see; there it is second nature."

Four Saudi Arabian women eating, hands up under their veils woman sitting cross-legged picks the bugs out of her daughter's hair

"Those were the kinds of things I wrote down, because these are *priceless—* these little details add the flavor."

Put People in the Picture

I learned an important lesson when I was writing "day trips" up for a local paper, *The Everett Herald.* The first piece I wrote was about a little town on the Olympic Peninsula, a ferry ride across Puget Sound: "Port Gamble: a Sure Bet for a Sunday Afternoon." Port Gamble was originally a mill company town, built for the homesick loggers from the eastern seaboard. It looks more Northeast than Northwest. I wrote about the seedlings of the New England elm trees planted there, the old cemetery, the unexpected Victorian woodframe and Cape Cod houses, the shell museum, and I wrote about St. Paul's Episcopal Church, the oldest continuously operating church in the state of Washington, a replica of a country church of the same name in East Machias, Maine.

I took a picture of St. Paul's to go with the story. When the editor saw it, he told me the picture needed more life. If this was a still-operating church, the editor said, "Put people in it. Go back and take a picture with the people coming out of the church after services."

I returned to Port Gamble on a Sunday. I positioned myself with a tripod across the road from the white spire of the church, waiting for the congregation to pour out. The singing stopped, and no one came out. I wondered if it was ghosts I had heard with voices raised in song. After about ten minutes I ventured over and inside. The church was empty. Then I heard the convivial noise of people downstairs. The mystery was explained. There was an inside stairway, and the entire congregation had gone down to convene after the service for coffee and homemade sweet breads.

I introduced myself to the pastor and explained my confusion. He laughed uproariously, then summed up the philosophy of St. Paul's for over a hundred years: "First worship, then fellowship." As soon as he said that, I thought, What a good quote for my story. That's when it hit me— what was missing from my story was the same thing that was missing from my photo: people. A Baedeker's guide can tell you the hours of a museum, but only you can add the people part. I spent the rest of the day interviewing townspeople and the proprietor of the museum. Now my story, as well as the picture with it, had more personality.

Lauren's African Safari

Lauren Ciminera, a classmate of Katherine's, was nine when she went on an African safari with her dad. Like Sara Rashad, she knew this people principle innately. The little metal-cornered journal with the blue ribbon marker that she shared with me faithfully includes accounts of all the animals seen;

> *Today we saw lots of elephants, crocodiles, two small dik-diks (dik-diks are antelopes), baboons, a water buk, eagles, some impala, and bushboks. Some of the elephants had babies.*

But more significantly, Lauren tells of the people she met and their stories. Whenever she meets anyone new, she notices their name.

> *At ten-thirty a.m. this morning, my dad and I went to St. Christofer's School to visit. I saw the classrooms and met the principal, Mrs. Leh Ngini. Two girls, age nine and ten, named Susan and Josephine, took me around the whole school and out to their playground where everyone was having recess. I had a snack of orange juice and two crackers.*

> *At six-thirty we went to our friend the schoolteacher's house and met her family. She has three girls and a boy. Their names are Susan, Elizabeth, Nonni, and Waiyaki. Nonni is age three and very playful. Elizabeth taught me how to make baskets. It was hard! I still don't understand!*

In her innocent observing and her caring for people, she displays an understanding beyond her years; in Coleridge's phrase, "common sense in an uncommon degree":

When we stopped to look in a shop window, my dad noticed a woman dressed in traditional Somali dress and stopped to say "hello" to her. Before I knew it, my dad was in a deep conversation with her. I started to pay close attention when my dad explained that there was a war going on right now in Somalia. The lady was named Sarah. Well, her husband and her mom and her dad were killed, and she ran away with her two twin girls, age seven. We felt so sorry for her because of her sad tears. We gave her three hundred shillings, which is twelve dollars, and our home address, and asked her to join us for some drinks.

She came at five and could stay only until six. She explained to us her girls couldn't come because they didn't have any clothes except rags, because they had to leave everything and run away from shooting guns and exploding bombs. I decided to give some of my clothes to the twins. I gave them two T-shirts, two pairs of socks, a pair of shoes, two shorts, and one long-legged pant. I feel so good! We will try to sponsor them and figure out how we can get them a plane ticket to Washington. It will be difficult, but we are determined to help this desperate family. Tomorrow, we're going to meet the girls, at noon. Their names are Jacklyn and Mary. They are both seven years old. Their mother, Sarah, was so grateful, she gave me all she had, a little leather purse. It is very small but very nice. I hope we can help them more. If I was Sarah, and had two daughters, and was all alone, I would want help, too. She can't get a job because not even all the Kenyan people can get a job, and they would especially not *give a Somalian a job because they don't like Somalians for reasons that might not be true.*

Think what our world might be if more of us had such sincere, unaffected wisdom.

''Belles Lettres''

Postcards and letters to home are also a way to pay attention. A good way to write a travel log is to send a series of letters back home to someone you trust.

When I graduated from college, before heading off to graduate school, I took the Henry James tour of nine European cities with my friend Alice Jean. When I came back, my mother presented me with a huge scrapbook—she had kept and mounted every letter and postcard I sent home as a record of my trip. I am eternally grateful to her for the only written record I have of that odyssey; the journal I kept was left behind in a hotel in Rome and never returned to me.

Sydne Johansen set up this kind of arrangement ahead of time, before she left to spend five months traveling in Asia.

"Almost every night, I'd sit down and write letters to people I worked with, my family, my friends. Some of my letters were ten pages long, and by the time I finished writing the letter, I wasn't going to sit down and write it all again in a book. So I asked the people to save them for me before I left, and most of them did. My parents, my sister and brother-in-law, people I worked with at Virginia Mason Hospital in the intensive care unit. I'd write to two or three different people every night."

To end the day, Sydne would sit out, watch the sunset, and write.

"I can't imagine not having done it. It was a way for me to process the day. I couldn't go to sleep without writing things down, because there had been so much."

Letters like these say something about your relationship with the person you are writing to. The things you choose to emphasize, what you learned and share, you see through their eyes. Collectively, they show many facets of your experience.

"I wrote to my brother-in-law about the Taj Mahal, because he's an architect. But I wrote to my mom about the Amber Palace in Jaipur, because I just sat down and cried. I was so overwhelmed; it was so beautiful; it was so old. I wrote to my mom about the emotions. But I wrote to my brother-in-law about the Taj, because of the architectural optical illusions that have been built into the design."

Sydne says that at the time she did not see that she was writing different things to different people.

"I thought that I was writing about these experiences because I wanted to express them. Looking at the letters now, I see the pattern."

She wrote funny letters to her dad.

"There was always something funny in them, something funny happening that made me think of him. He'd been raised in Kansas, and I never experienced being landlocked until I was in Nepal. I wrote a funny letter to him about how I had to get my feet into an ocean."

And she wrote special letters to her fellow workers on a political campaign, "because I realized how old India was, and how new the United States was. I compared the United States to a temper-tantrum-throwing toddler, a brand-new, spoiled-brat country compared to India, which had been there for five thousand or more years. I wouldn't have written that to Virginia Mason; we didn't talk about politics at the hospital."

The logistics of "letter logging" were fairly simple.

"I always had stationery with me. I had writing tablets in my bag. And stamps. In Delhi once I had to wait in line for three hours to buy stamps, but it was an adventure. The most amazing thing happened. In came a Sikh, surrounded by bodyguards. Long swords, beards, turbans. Dressed in bright, bright yellow and royal blue; big brown flashing eyes and white teeth. Their shoes matched their robes; royal blue with the royal blue, yellow with the yellow. I had 'another planet' sense of wonder.

"Waiting on line that long, I could have been miserable. I had a good time. I remember talking, reading—I always had books with me—and of course I wrote letters."

What's Missing

For all its usefulness, writing letters is not the same as keeping a log.

The letters to my mom from Europe were filled with the eagerness and wonderment I felt at seeing firsthand things I had read about and studied. When I look back on those letters now, I smile at my own naïveté and greenness, and I laugh out loud as I read between the lines all the stuff I left out.

I wanted to make sure my mother knew how sophisticated I was. She is an artist, so I especially told her about the artwork and the museums—the thrill of seeing Monet and Rodin in Paris, El Greco in Madrid, Botticelli in Florence.

What I did not tell her about was the Italian sailors who offered in French to take us to the Lido—oh yes, we had heard of that. But we did not figure out until we were on board a boat that the Lido we had heard of was a night club in Paris, and we were in Venice, now heading toward a deserted beach at night with two sailors who did not speak our language.

Sydne admits her letters, too, did not tell all.

"I spent a month on a nude beach on the west coast in India, and I notice in my letters that I didn't write to anybody and tell them that.

"Oh, and I didn't write about almost getting killed on a train one night in Sri Lanka.

"I had fallen asleep on an all night train. The train stopped and was boarded by thirty to forty men in camouflage, with machine guns. I thought, 'Oh, my god. This is it, I'm going to die tonight.' Then my next thought was, 'Well, it's been a great life.' But it turned out to be a bomb threat.

"If I wrote my family about that, I was afraid my mother would write, 'Come home right now.' "

And Sydne didn't want to come home. She wanted to stay and have more adventures to write home about.

Now You

Next time you travel, pay attention in a special way—write as you go.

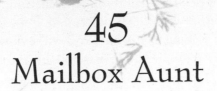

45
Mailbox Aunt

I WONDER IF AUNTS AND UNCLES KNOW HOW MUCH THEY OFTEN mean to their nieces and nephews. My uncles told me it wasn't enough for Jim to ask my father's permission for my hand in marriage; they claimed he also had to pass the Uncle Test. They would not allow anyone to marry me without their approval that he was a great guy. And my great-aunt Gerry, a free spirit and an artist, inspired me with her wild tales. She was a lawyer at a time when there were few women lawyers, ran for and was elected district attorney.

Aunt Gerry wrote to me only a few times, and each time only a few sentences. I mounted her notes in a scrapbook, and I still have them, over twenty-five years later. It brings a happy feeling to my face to talk about her—I can't help breaking out in a big grin.

My friend Dort, who lives in Arkansas, is creating memories like that right now. Dort has carried on a fifty-year correspondence with her nieces and nephews, grandnieces and great-grandnephews in five states—Idaho, Maryland, Michigan, California, and Texas. When she talks about them, she almost purrs.

"I had them all counted once—I must have forty. Knock on wood. They are all good kids. Here I am in Arkansas, and they live all over the country. We keep in touch. When I write, I try to say something that they might be interested in. Today I wrote, 'The dogwood is blooming outside my window,' and I wrote about the redbud tree—the flowers come right out of the bark. Redbud trees are the first to bloom in the spring here; they don't have them in Michigan. I tell them about the trees and all the spring flowers—they know I like to garden. In fact, the older ones know I am the past president of the Bella Vista Garden Club; whenever there was a piece about me in the gardening section of the paper, I'd send a clipping so they'd know what I was doing—cut it out and photocopy it and send a bunch.

"And I ask them questions, 'How's school?' 'How're you doing?' 'What are you up to?' "

They are pretty good about responding, and because they write back, Dort is involved with the life of three generations—she knows that Nicole, who lives in California, is doing a science project "about the disgusting slimy hagfish, with six hearts and an open circulatory system, who has a rough-tooth tongue and preys on helpless fish, oh yuck." She knows that Julie won first prize in a declamation contest in Texas, for reciting a sonnet, in French, about an albatross and sailors. She knows Rylan loves Power Rangers (Zack wears black), and that Beth has seen *The Lion King* on video sixteen times, that Sieren is reading the *Dragon Riders of Pern,* and that Therese has an "I (heart) New York (Denver, Austin, Portland, Paris)" collection, and that Katy is into trolls.

She enters into their fantasies, learns their vocabulary, relates to them and the world that they are in on their level, keeps current of their fashions, notices what kids their age are wearing and doing.

If they send a thank-you note for a gift or card, she sends them a "thank you for your thank you" to let them know their courtesy pleased her. She remembers them with a card or note at Halloween and other holiday occasions, and of course she always remembers Valentine's Day and birthdays.

"I have a birthday book; a month before, just to be sure, I buy the cards. I pick out one that suits them. If I didn't have a chance to get a card, I send a little note with Happy Birthday. I wouldn't let their birthdays go by."

Some of the children don't write back. Children are often like that. It isn't until their graduations and wedding days that Dort realizes the impact that her little notes have had. She is a part of their lives. They write to her and say,

> *Of course you're not going to forget my graduation day. It's (such and such a day), and you certainly are coming.*

They just assume that she cares enough to make it possible to get there. And they're right.

"Last year, I went to a grandniece's wedding, and the year before to her brother's wedding in Michigan. The bride and groom let me know ahead, and I drove eight hours to be there."

They arrange the date with her in mind.

> *I'm just not getting married if you don't come—you just have to come to the wedding.*

They turn to her when they need help. One of the nieces wrote,

> *I'm in trouble—can I come live with you?*

And so she did, for one month, until she straightened things out at home.

"I love 'em all, and they love me back. They are possessive about our relationship; we have a special bond. When I visited in Michigan, Melanie was seven. All the kids in the neighborhood would come over when I came; one little girl, Melanie's friend, Bethie, who was also seven, said, 'Hi, Aunt Dort!'

"Melanie was incensed.

" 'She's *my* aunt Dort!'

"Bethie went home crying; then Melanie let her call me Aunt Dorothy."

Melanie is forty now; Dort recounts this story with animation and affection, as though it happened yesterday.

On her own birthday, which was last week, Dort received twenty-five cards: "beautiful, beautiful cards, oh yes, with little notes and drawings and pictures. I have albums just for all the pictures—my grandnephew just had a baby and sent me pictures—and a *box* to reread on rainy days of all the cards and letters I get."

Last year, Dort's oldest nephew—he's fifty-nine—sent her a birthday card that said, "To the Greatest Aunt That Ever Was." Her oldest niece, who is sixty, sent her the very same card, and they don't even live in the same part of the country. Another card came from two teenage relatives.

Thanks for doing a great job of spoiling us.

"The most adorable card came just today from the five-year-old daughter of a grandnephew. She drew a card with little hearts and things in different crayon colors and a message, 'Happy Birthday.' Her mother added a note to tell me that the little one had asked, 'Do you think Aunt Dort will like this birthday card?'

"I wrote back to her, 'One of the *best*.' "

Dort told me that one of her friends complained when she saw all Dort's birthday mail. "You get so much mail, it's not fair; I don't hear from any of my family."

" 'Do you ever sit down and write a note to them?' I asked.

" 'Well, no,' she says.

" 'I say, You have to give a little of yourself if you want to get love back.' "

Their Roots Are in Your Love

Years ago, I learned an important lesson from my aunt Mary, as I sat in her kitchen drinking orange pekoe tea, balancing the Red Rose tea bag on the edge of the blue willow saucer.

I was worried about marrying a Navy man. Although I looked forward to the adventure of travel and moving around, I was concerned about our future children, that they would have no roots.

"Their roots," said Aunt Mary emphatically, "their roots are in your love for them."

Aunt Mary taught me this truth by example: Love and closeness have nothing to do with geography. No matter how far away you are, roots go with you. The clippings and cartoons, the holiday cards, the birthday notes that Dort sends are little things that say, "I can't be there in person, but you're part of my life. I saw this and thought of you."

When Dort tells about her nieces and nephews, the words pour out of her, telling stories of this little one of three, now thirty, and that niece of ten, now forty-three. She laughs with a soft and musical laugh.

"Oh, my. I could go on and on with stories."

Her contact with them, the mutual love that they share, is so much a part of her life, she hardly thinks it worth mentioning: Oh yes, there was that; she wanted to be helpful, but it is no big deal, really. She dismisses her part.

"It's nothing, really . . . ," and she's right. "It's a simple thing, an easy thing, a bunch of stamps, some notepaper and a birthday book."

A bunch of stamps, some notepaper and a birthday book, and through the mailbox, she has given them love—and roots.

Now You

We all have some youngsters in our family or know a child who would feel special to receive an occasional note. When I travel for business, I have a short list of young ones I send postcards to. Often, I am pressed for time and grab a handful of postcards at the airport newsstand, write a quick message in the boarding area, and hand the stamped cards to the ticketing agent so they get the out-of-town postmark.

Start today. Send a postcard. Then find out when their birthdays are, and mark them on the calendar. Buy some extra cards, or drop a note, at Valentine's and Halloween, and any other excuse Hallmark can think of to advertise. Give the children in your circle of friends or on your family tree a gift—the gift of paying attention to who they are. You will brighten a child's life, and as Dort found, you will also brighten your own.

46
Three-Minute Poems, Three-Day Novels

"All Ages Can Play, and Any Number of Players"

It is hard to find a game that everyone in the family wants to play, one that's easy for all ages yet still challenging enough to be worth doing. *Trivial Pursuit,* for example, is too hard for little ones, and any parent or older child who plays *Chutes and Ladders* or *Candyland* does it out of love. Writing three-minute poems has the necessary qualifications. All ages can play, and any number of players; it's fun, it's fast, and it brings the family together. It is a great leveler—often what the kids come up with is as good as or better than what the adults produce. The game is swift, yet somehow the mood of camaraderie carries over into the rest of the evening.

The rules are simple. Everybody has paper and pencil. Set a salt timer in the middle of the table. The players shout out possible topics until you have four. Flip over the salt timer, and write fast and furiously for three minutes, incorporating all four elements in the one poem. The more mismatched the topics are, the more serendipity in the combinations. The little ones have three minutes to dictate a poem. It does not have to rhyme, but rhyme pops up—especially in the children's offerings. Write until the salt runs out. Then each reads his or her poem out loud to the family, without qualifying it or defending it. Young children write simple verses, but they read them so earnestly and so shyly proud, it warms you. You will feel mellow and amused just hearing them. And you might even get a tinge of pride reciting your own. That's what three-minute poems can do for you and your family.

Once you start on three-minute poems, you will find they are like potato chips. You will want to come back for more. I guarantee it—any member of your family who was reluctant to enter in the first time will beg you to do it again the next night.

At our house, everybody plays, even Grandma when she is visiting, or anybody fortunate or unfortunate enough to have come for dinner that night. In fact, the kids often put me up to it when they have a friend over. They know from their own experience that any initial protestations will give way to howls of laughter.

Why They Work

Fast poems are high-energy because they capture the first thoughts off the top of your head. Your brain does not have time to edit as you write, which is what kills a lot of fine writing to begin with. A side benefit is that they break down resistance to writing—they bombard the barriers of "school writing" and all the baggage that goes with it. They give an experience of writing that is free-flowing and fun.

Something even more important than these practical considerations is going on too, something that makes it worthwhile to do this with your family. A wonderful closeness comes from working on a project together, even if it's only for three minutes. The good bits come, in fact, from that sense of camaraderie. And it's a way to laugh out loud. The hilarity comes from the startle of different interpretations. We are intrigued and delighted to hear how someone else assembled the same blocks.

Writing together so fast, and reading the raucous results, however, gives infinitely more than three minutes of bonding. We go our separate ways, to different parts of the house, to finish homework, or to the kitchen for dishes, or settle down with the evening paper—perhaps even out of the house, off to a meeting, or a rehearsal, or a movie with friends. Wherever we go, we bring each other with us; we have a glow that goes with our evening's occupation. What can I say? A feeling of being loved, a sense of security and happiness, colors and suffuses whatever activity you do for the rest of the night.

Workshop Ice-Breaker

For several years now I have been using three-minute poetry-writing as the first activity in my Planning and Problem-Solving workshop, soliciting the four words from the group. It provides a dramatic, firsthand illustration to workshop participants of what they are capable of doing when they do not have the time to listen to the judgmental side of the brain, the side that says, "You can't do that."

The initial response to this preliminary assignment is predictable. When I first announce that we will write a poem, the interior dialogue, apparent from the looks on their faces, is something like "Write a poem? I thought this was a serious class that was going to help me in my work." Or "I don't do poetry."

Then I advise them not to panic, not to listen to that negative side of their brains. It will all be over quickly, I say. It will only take three minutes. Then I can see the left side of their brains really go nuts. "There is no way I can do justice to a poem in three minutes. I'm out of this task."

At which point I advise waving good-bye.

Because in the meantime the right side of the brain, which is better at poetry anyway, is saying, "Hey, I'm game. What could I do wrong in three minutes?" And that attitude anticipates the built-in buffer: "It's not my best work, but I only had three minutes."

You can write a poem about anything. When I work with the folks at Seafirst Bank, they come up with topics like "interest-bearing accounts." Canadians want to write about the Blue Jays, while Boeing engineers suggest "flight-time navigation." These topics are especially fun when someone else in the group throws a curve ball like "Nike sneakers" or "dandelions."

Because they let go of getting it "right"—they have little choice but to let go, considering the time frame and the topic limitations—what emerges are some remarkable offerings. Nobody has to share unless they want to; there are always several volunteers, though, and their courage inspires others. In one East Coast workshop, participants suggested four disparate topics: "wedding gift," "Saturday," "running," and "friendship." Then we all wrote for three minutes fast. Listen to these delightfully different results.

The first person read:

> *Saturday*
> *Saturday*
> *What a day for running*
> *Running here, running there*
> *Too many tasks, too much to do*
> *Where's an end?*
> *Where's a rest?*
> *Think of all the list of things*
> *Don't forget the weekend wedding*
> *Of your friends*
> *Get a gift, a special gift*
> *Let it tell your friendship.*
> *Saturdays*
> *Saturdays*
> *Where is Sunday's blessing?*
> *Where is peace, where is quiet?*
> *In the vows of the couple*
> *In their bond and their troth*
> *I renew my own life.*

The rushed tone of that poem was a contrast to the hushed beauty of this one, written during the same three minutes:

> *Saturday's early morning light*
> *marks and shines around the reservoir.*
> *Running, marking the pace with the heartbeat and feet,*
> *Matching my pace to my friend's beat, hers to mine,*
> *musing about the many gifts she's given me.*
> *Feeling in my palm the smooth polish*
> *of a stone. A gift for my daughter*
> *on her wedding day.*

Then the whole class roared to hear the brazen beat of this lively combination of the same four themes:

> *My friend Mandy gets married Saturday eve*
> *I'm running to capture a gift to relieve*
> *My frustration and anger and increasing vex*
> *You see, Amanda is wedding my ex.*

Some of the same characteristics that show up when a family writes three-minute poems also appear in the corporate setting. For one thing, these poems are a great equalizer. People seem to take a sense of pride in what others produce, what they have done with the same ingredients; they are glad of a chance to celebrate the uniqueness and creativity of fellow workers and see them in a different light. Often there is a hush or murmur of approval, and even more often peals of laughter at a twisted rhyme or a stunning juxtaposition of the elements. And the mood carries over. It is an instant ice-breaker and sets us up for the day, to work well together.

Three-Day Novel

Think what could happen when you expand the concept from poetry to novel-writing.

The Three-Day Novel-Writing Contest is my kind of contest and my kind of novel-writing.

Started in 1978 by Pulp Press in Canada as an in-house dare among the editors, it had grown to more than seven hundred entries annually by the time they handed it over to Anvil Press, publishers of *Subterranean* magazine, more than a decade later. It has been written up in *The Wall Street Journal, The Times* of London, and *The New York Times,* as well as *The Globe and Mail. The Globe and Mail* called the now-international Three-Day Novel-Writing Contest "Canada's unique contribution to World Literature."

The first prize is publication of the winning manuscript. Brian Lam, one of the early promoters, explains, "It is done on a honor system, but you can tell. I can't explain how, but a piece honestly written during this three-day marathon has a certain frenetic energy. I've read so many of them, I can tell right away."

Held over Labor Day weekend, the contest is based on the popular saying, "If it weren't for the last minute, nothing would ever get done." From the time you start writing, it is already the last minute. There is something more than that urgency at work here: the realization that you are not alone in this insanity.

With six to seven hundred contestants writing simultaneously, you know. While you are down here in Oregon, or Washington, or Florida hacking this out, some poor bloke in British Columbia or Alberta is also sweating it. One year the support was tangible: About twenty-five writers publicly came together at the Canada Pavilion at Expo '86 in Vancouver to write their way to fame. As passersby commented, each contestant kept on writing, corralled in a corner of the fair. The energy was amazing, especially in the wee, wee hours, when the fair attractions closed down and this stalwart crew kept going. They did not banter or kibitz, either among themselves or with the gawkers. They knew their task and kept to it. They supported each other by their presence and their dedication.

Now You

Three minutes to write a poem? Three days to write a novel? Why not? What's to lose?

It's only a game.

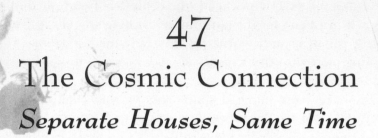

47
The Cosmic Connection
Separate Houses, Same Time

DOUG SMITH, A DISTRICT JUDGE AND MY FRIEND, WAS RUNNING his first marathon. He had been in training for over three months, jogging the Burke-Gilman Trail home every night from his office in Seattle to his home in Lake Forest Park. He felt ready, but he was worried. Would he make it all the way? Fellow marathoners had told him of the physical phenomenon that happens just before completion, the drain of energy, the sense that you cannot take another step. Doug knew in his heart he had the stamina and training to run the twenty-six miles, but he worried about losing steam. Would he have the courage to continue when his feet gave way, when his brain screamed, "No more"?

On the day of the race, a wonderful thing happened. Doug's son Brad, then age fourteen, not himself a runner, came and joined his dad for the last six miles. Together they came triumphantly into the finish line.

Doug got tears in his eyes as he told me this story, and I in turn got a little lump in my throat hearing him recount it. It touched me deeply, and the sense I felt had little to do with running and a lot to do with connectedness.

You can do anything when you know you are not alone.

Morning Writing, Early and en Masse

One thing we want more than anything in this world is to know we are not alone. That is why support groups are so popular, from Weight Watchers to ACOA (Adult Children of Alcoholics). In my seminars, I explain that you can do some extraordinary writing first thing in the morning, before you get up, while you are still half asleep. This approach is particularly helpful if you are writing something difficult or if you have been putting off writing something you need to write. I ask the group to agree to write together at the same time early in the morning, and then, because I know it is easier to be accountable to an individual with a name, I require each to turn to the person next to him or her and say, "(Name), you can count on me to be writing at five-thirty (or whatever time) tomorrow morning." The promise is to write without getting up, before having coffee or going to the bathroom, without speaking to anyone else.

Many people say that the commitment to another is what forced them to keep their word to themselves. There is a sense of belonging, a sense of connectedness, knowing that as you grab your pen and pull your pad of paper into bed with you, across town your partner is grabbing his pen, pulling his pad into bed with him. And while you squeeze your eyes tight and feel the pain of corneal dryness, while you feel hostile and want nothing more than to go back to sleep, your partner across town is having perhaps the same response, fighting the same fights, feeling the same hostility and willing to write in spite of it. You are not alone. And so you write, wrapping that connection around you like a comforter.

When you write with a group in the early morning, separate houses, same time, a hidden force takes over, one that inspires your work in a spectacular way. There is a cosmic bonding, a synergy, and you tap into an energy greater than your own alone, or another person's alone, and greater than the simple sum of your two minds added together.

I started to notice that the people who kept their agreement to write simultaneously at the preordained hour would sense a new community in the room, while those who opted for a few extra zzzzz's felt left out. Often a participant would come into class starry-eyed with excitement at a breakthrough, conscious that she was able to have that breakthrough because she felt the power of the group behind her. A person might share, somewhat sheepishly, that he had written in a different persona or solved a problem for someone else in the class. Or a man would share what he had written, and a woman might exclaim, astonished, that some phrases in his writing echoed her own words from that morning.

In early morning writing, it seems, the ideas are in the air; you may catch the one you need, or someone else may catch it for you. In a good brainstorming session, nobody is directly responsible for the best ideas. The ideas are like butterflies that float from shoulder to shoulder carried on the momentum of the group, held aloft by the agreement to suspend judgment, to withhold criticism. Finally a butterfly rests on a particular shoulder, and that person speaks. All in the group are responsible, are victorious. Alone in a garret, no one would have come out with that.

Okay to Feel Hostile: Write Anyway

When I begin early morning writing, I often feel hostile.

5:30 a.m. Oh man, this is madness. I want nothing more than to stay in bed—well, I'm doing that—to stay asleep with a headache do I have to do this? Okay guys, here I am. Keep on writing.

I persevere because I would not let the group down; I could not face them if I had not kept my word.

7:30 a.m. early morning writing with the group—so I have their support behind me. My eyes are squinted shut, my head is screaming ten more minutes please ten more minutes, but I write because I know that somewhere in this city across the deserted streets, my partner keeps his word and writes also. So I write, knowing I am not alone. I do it for him—and to keep my word.

Sometimes when I write in the morning against all odds, I think of an experience I had in the medieval walled city of Carcassonne, in the south of France. I had promised my friend Nancy Ernst that if I ever made it to this fabled city, I would walk the ramparts, as she had done, at dawn. We rose at five A.M.; it was still dark. I remember yet how reluctant I was to get up, how my whole body screamed, forget it, go back to bed. Deep down, another voice said, do it anyway. Someday you'll be glad you did.

It was an act of supreme will to swing those leaden legs over the side of the bed onto the cold stone floor. One step after another I forced myself to function. I felt like a paraplegic taking painful practice steps. I roused Jim. As we walked through the cold and deserted town, some of the lethargy started to shake off. By the time we got to the jousting grounds, the stupor had lifted somewhat. We climbed a tower and began our march around the ramparts as the sun struggled its way out across the valley below us and began its rise over the battlements. It was a mystical experience. Centuries melted away. I felt one with Charlemagne, and Raymond-Roger Trencavel, and all the simple soldiers who had kept the watch. It was a peak experience of my life.

Never could I have achieved that connectedness with my fellow human beings of six hundred years ago, had I opted to go back to bed, to take a stroll during the day instead.

There are similar elements with early morning writing: the predawn hour, the commitment to another, the sense of protest, with every fiber of my being fighting it. And then finally, the reluctance giving way to an "I'm glad I did this in spite of not wanting to," followed by feeling connected in an almost mystical way. The cosmic connection seems to come because of your willingness to go the extra mile, to push beyond comfort, and to keep your word.

5:30 a.m. I almost forgot and hit the snooze button, then Chuck's earnest face came to haunt me—he looked me straight in the eye and shook my hand so firmly when he gave me his word that he would write at 5:30. I hope that Joel is doing fine and pray Tom has a breakthrough—

The other element of morning writing is a promise to continue writing for a certain specified period of time, usually fifteen minutes. Once again, it is your integrity, your commitment to the group that keeps you going, past the point of wanting to quit. And it is worth the stretch. Often the best, the most usable ideas come at the end.

I have been doing early morning writing for over seven years. The bad news is, at least for me, it does not get any easier. The good news is, as your confidence grows, the quality of what you write in this twilight zone gets better and better, more and more useful.

I am in pain—my eyes hurt my whole body aches—but I just had a fleeting glimpse of all of these workshop participants writing away. I have to admit I don't relish doing this and the thought of writing another book this way makes me wince.

So now you know. Fully one-third of this book was written with my eyes closed.

What's in It for Me?

One early morning I found myself writing not for myself but for someone in the class. This man's name was Jerry. He worked at a bank. He was unhappy in his job, discouraged in his life, skeptical about the workshop. For the first day he kept his arms folded across his chest; his body language said, "Show me." He challenged me on every point.

The whole class promised to write together at six-thirty the following morning, and Jerry reluctantly agreed. That morning I started out writing in the first person, as myself. Writing in an erratic hand with open a's that look like sprung o's and no crosses on t's or dots on i's, I began pretty typically by protesting the early hour, and then rambled on for a while about what I wanted to cover in the class that day. Then came a sudden switch: I became Jerry. It was as if it were Jerry, not me, who was writing, Jerry who was raising and answering questions. Unexpectedly I found myself writing high speed, like a runaway train.

Why bother feeling more confident about writing at the bank? Who cares? Does it matter? What's in it for me? What's in it for everyone around me? if I could write more and better, then what? my boss would be happier, I would be happier I would feel more productive I would be more productive I would like my job more the people I am trying to help would get serviced faster so they would be pleased and my applications would have more results positive results they would work and that would make my world work and the world of people around me work so I would be surrounded by successes and there is a power in that a power of satisfaction and completion a sense of fulfillment and mission and what builds on that is a chance to be more open with others, a chance to relax at work and home, content in the fact that the skids are greased at work, I am free to investigate other projects other adventures and because of that I can spend time with my family without distraction and because of that my wife and children will feel important in my life and because of that they will themselves be empowered to do what they are called to do and because of that they will be able to be nice to the ordinary grocery clerk and the cranky neighbor and because of that our neighborhood will be a better more pleasant place to live set in motion by the pleasantness of one building on the agreeableness of another—and because of that, the people who travel will come in touch with others and be ready to greet them warmly armed with power from their neighborhood and families and because of that people from different countries will smile at one another Pass it on! Pass it on! and because of that the leaders of these countries will sense a new mood in the air among their people and because of that these leaders will be willing to go to the treaty table together and because of that they will have the power of the people behind them and be courageous and be powerful and vulnerable all at once and because of that, Jerry's children will sleep better at night and because of that, Jerry will be able to do his work at the bank more productively content in the knowledge that his children are sleeping soundly at night, content in the knowledge that his work has global implications, content in the knowledge that he makes a difference in the world that he makes a contribution to people's lives—

This run-on writing was itself a mystical experience. It was as though I were not writing it but the words were flowing through me (and I always hated it when authors said that). When I came to class, three other people in that class had written about Jerry, one of them echoing phrases from what Jerry himself had written. That alone was enough to convince Jerry. He uncrossed his arms and opened himself up to the possibility of having a breakthrough. P.S. He had a great workshop.

---

*   *   *

That message to Jerry of global implications was a message to all of us. Our work has ramifications; everything we do extends beyond us. When as a group we agree to write simultaneously at an early hour, it creates an atmosphere, an energy of advocacy. Everyone is rooting for everyone else. We are all on a common wavelength, operating on the same frequency.

"I Thought You Were My Friend"

It was one of the nicest compliments I ever received. At a large convention a young woman intercepted me between sessions. She wanted to tell me that she had read *Writing on Both Sides of the Brain,* and it had been a help to her. She summed it up:

"When I read your book, I thought you were my friend."

I turned my head away quickly; I was embarrassed. I did not want her to see the tears that sprang into my eyes. How did she know that about me? I *was* her friend. My fondest wish, when I wrote that book, was that each reader would know that. An enormous task, to convey caring, and I was not sure how to do it.

When I give a workshop, my body language helps people know I care. I make it a point to know people's names and call them by name. I set up a mental filing system to remember what is important to each of them, the stories they share. I refer to their specific concerns.

I make eye contact, and I lean my body or tilt my head. I am thinking all the time, What do they need? How can I help them? What do I need to say or do to make them glad they came out today?

My goal in my writing is somehow to make each paragraph a conversation with a reader who is my friend. How do you do that? I do not know.

My guess is that the first part of it is a mindset. I do care. I write out of that caring. The other element, equally essential, is that my first book grew out of the commitment of others. If you read there the voice of a friend, it is not the choice of verb or adjective; it is the support of the people behind me. It is Mimi calling me at five o'clock: "Good morning, it's time to write." It is Dorothy minding my then-four-year-old and picking up the twelve-year-old from school so I could write, uninterrupted. It is Richard imploring me to exert myself and bequeathing me courage. It is eight-year-old Emily's hand-lettered sign, when I got half-way through, "You have done more than is left."

And if you know, when you read this book, that I care, it is not just me caring. It is the prayers of people behind me as I wrote: a Buddhist, an atheist, two Catholic nuns (one a cousin), two convicts, an artist who promised to pat my picture every day, to name just a few. They were not just praying for me; they were praying for you, for my readers.

We can do anything when we know that someone who cares is running alongside.

Now You

Be willing to ask for support. Let someone else who believes run alongside you. Doug Smith's son Brad, who was not a runner, ran with him for the last six miles. That got him over the hump.

The cosmic connection works even with only one other person, when you have a promise to write at the same hour. You can set it up as a one-time arrangement, or establish a mutual time for a week or a month of mornings.

Connectedness helps us keep our commitments. You will be amazed at the amount and the quality of the writing you accomplish.

Ask a friend, a co-worker, "Write with me. It is not important what you write, not important to critique or edit, just be with me, pal, okay?"

Separate houses, same time. Early morning. Keep your word. Write.

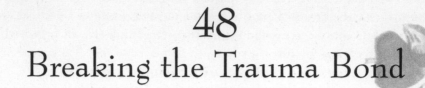

48
Breaking the Trauma Bond

WHEN SOMEBODY HAS WRONGED YOU AND YOU HOLD ON TO IT long past the offense, you are held by what is called a trauma bond. The trauma bond holds victim and offender together in a viselike grip. It is an invisible cord, still binding both, eating up psychic energy, coloring decision making, and interfering with fullness of life.

Breaking the Trauma Bond
Through Correspondence

Sexual abuse is one example of a traumatic event that can bind the victim to the offender even years after. According to Jan Hindman, in *Just Before Dawn,* a victim of sexual abuse can often break the trauma bond through correspondence, even through a letter which is never mailed. In many cases, victims will not be able to locate an abuser; in such cases, writing a letter and burning it can be healing. Where you do know the offender, a clear and direct statement of the facts, without any request for response, is sufficient. Says Hindman, "There can be tremendous satisfaction for the victim [in this approach] and there is little risk involved. The purpose . . . is simple. The victim simply wants the perpetrator to be advised that the abuse was not unnoticed. The patient demands nothing and, in fact, cautions the perpetrator about making any response. The satisfaction of the victim is simply recognizing that the perpetrator was not allowed to continue the secrecy."

Hindman quotes from one such letter, sent by registered mail:

The purpose of this letter was to simply live the rest of my life knowing your eyes had to pass over these words.

Asking for a Response

If, on the other hand, the victim wants a response, it must be on the victim's own terms, within the boundaries he or she proposes.

Hindman warns that a request for a response "can be more precarious, but also more rewarding, if successful. The victim must be careful to close doors from unwanted responses and open only the doors where the victim has control . . . so that further victimization does not occur." This is sometimes best done with the assistance of a therapist as a buffer.

Following are two stories, shared with me, of successfully breaking the trauma bond through correspondence. One was done under the guidance of a therapist, one without. In both cases, I have changed the names.

Mike is an adult who was molested as a child by his stepfather, Jeff. The stepfather is now in a treatment program, so Mike's therapist, with Mike's go-ahead, arranged a meeting with Jeff. When they met in therapy face to face, it was too traumatic for Mike to speak up, to ask the questions he needed answered. He later described the pressure as unbelievable; the only way he could handle it, he said, was by spacing out, almost moving outside of his body. He could not hear; he was in a fog. His therapist suggested he write a letter as a follow-up to the meeting. His letter is not eloquent, but it is direct and to the point. It said the things he could not say in person.

Jeff,

I really appreciate you meeting with me and explaining some things that happened. It lifted guilt and blame off my shoulders, and that was relieving. There are some things that I would like to hear from you. What was I like when I met you? Was I a good person, did I enjoy life, were my goals high? I do have a question. Do you know how this changed my life? When the molesting first started, I loved to get in front of a group of people and speak like drama class, but after being molested I was afraid to get in front of class because I thought people might see what was going on, see right through me. That changed some goals for me.

After a while I didn't know if I was gay or not.

I don't hate you. I just want you to know how this changed my life.

By being in counseling it has changed my life in lots of ways for the good, and I hope your therapy is going well and you are getting things out of it.

Writing a letter, he said, gave him a "space to think." After that, with both therapists acting as what Hindman calls "insulation," Mike was able to get some answers to his questions.

''You Thought I Was Sleeping I Wasn't Sleeping''

Ella, as a child, was molested by her older brother. She held it inside as a dark secret. Then as an adult, she wrote him a letter to break the silence. She told me some of the background.

"My mother was very sick when we were young, and my father began cutting himself off from everyone through the use of alcohol. My brother began furtively touching my sister and me sexually, and we felt helpless to stop him. When my mother became sick, I had uncontrollable crying spells. All of these things were never talked about: my mother's anger at my father's drinking, their sadness over my mother's illness, my own anger at my brother. All were there, and all were hid away."

Ella, her brother, and her sister did well in school, but they were alienated from each other.

"When my brother began touching my sister and me sexually, it cut us off from him emotionally, and what resulted was that none of us knew what was going on for the rest of us. We were emotional strangers to each other.

"The emotional numbness that I experienced from age fourteen to twenty was replaced when I was twenty by a very serious depression lasting three years. Later, when I came out of it, I married and had children. My older brother remained isolated from me and the rest of the family."

In what she calls an "interventive move," Ella decided to reestablish communication with her brother. She wrote him a letter telling him she wished to reconnect with him but at the same time letting him know that she knew the cause of their separation.

I guess we started becoming distant back when you touched me sexually. You thought I was sleeping I wasn't sleeping.

It made me really angry, and then I didn't want to talk to you or be close to you in the day. It made it so that there were a lot of things we never talked about.

Ella was not sure if her brother would answer her letter or ignore it.

"I realized that he might be too fearful to respond openly the first time, so I prepared myself to not take it personally."

He did respond, though. He called her on the phone, and they agreed to meet for dinner at a restaurant of her choice. It was a remarkably pleasant meal; Ella dropped her defensiveness and felt that they were both able to listen to each other for maybe the first time in their lives. He seemed genuinely interested in her work and in what was going on in her life.

After dinner they went to a bar to have a drink before he had to catch his train home. It was then that they got around to the content of her letter.

"He said he knew I wasn't sleeping. He said, he had always, when he was doing it, wished I would make him stop and that back then he didn't know how else to be close to us (my sister and me). I said that we can hug now, but it can never be like that again.

"He invited me and my family over to his wife's parents' house for Thanksgiving dinner. We parted happily—both thrilled.

"I was floored that it turned out so incredibly well—that I could actually say those things and that we could talk.

"I felt like a different person after that."

Because of her willingness to write and mail that letter and to meet with him, the lines of communication that had been long since shut down were reopened. Before, Ella had severed all contact with her brother. Now he was welcomed into her home and met his niece and nephews for the first time. Gradually they were able to heal the breach between them.

From Ashes to Eternal Fruit

The trauma bond exists not only for sex offenders and victims but within any person whose life has been radically, irretrievably altered by the actions of another. With the permission of his client, whose name I have changed, psychotherapist Terry Copeland shared with me a letter that helped break another kind of trauma bond.

When Laurie was fifteen, her father was killed by a drunken driver. This devastating tragedy ruled her life from that point on. For eleven years her rage and hatred against the driver who had taken away her childhood colored her actions, her decisions, her choices in life. Not a day went by that she did not think about, dwell upon, this incident and its consequences, mostly on her anger against the driver, who through his negligence had stolen something precious and irreplaceable from her.

Laurie went into counseling to learn to let go of the rage that was eating her alive, driving her every breath. Dr. Copeland told her to find the name of the driver and write him a letter. Tell him the impact that his actions had on her life.

This was not a mock letter, to be symbolically confined to the flames. Laurie needed to move from the helpless victim state to take action.

Dr. Copeland prepared her for the fact that the driver might not respond; what was important, he told her, was for her to face her fear of confronting him, to unburden herself of her pain and mail the letter.

Now here was a true test of the principles I espouse in Chapter 1: to let go of the outcome, to consider the alternative, to be responsible only for your end of it. Laurie knew she might not get an answer or that whatever answer she got might not be satisfactory.

Writing the letter and mailing the letter was a great relief. For the first time in over a decade, she felt free.

The unexpected answer was a pure gift, a bonus filled with grace, a reward for her courage to do something difficult.

It was written in a careful hand, with a deliberate selection of words. One can only imagine how many times it was written and rewritten, how many agonizing drafts it took.

Somehow the writer knew instinctively to drop the *Dear*; quite appropriately, he began his letter,

Laurie,

As you might imagine, this is not an easy letter to write. First of all, while it was painful to receive your letter, I very much appreciated hearing from you. Not a day goes by that I don't relive the events of that tragic October day.

I see that not only do I need to seek your family's forgiveness for causing your father's death through my negligence, but also for not communicating with you over the past eleven years. While my intent in writing you is not to offer excuses, it was my belief that you would have preferred to have nothing to do with me. I was wrong and can only hope that this letter will help to set that right.

As for causing your father's death, I can offer no excuses, there are none. I was totally at fault, irresponsible, and negligent. My remorse is acute, and if I could alter what happened, I surely would. However, it did happen and I can't change that. I do appeal to you and your family to forgive me for the great loss I inflicted upon you. . . . I am deeply deeply sorry!

I would like to share with you what has transpired as a direct result of the sacrifice of your father and your family. I want you to know that your father's death has resulted in abundance of life for many.

Less than one month after the accident I committed my life to Jesus Christ, as did my wife and many in my family. From that point on my life has been totally transformed . . . from ashes to eternal fruit. Laurie, I have

not consumed alcohol since then, nor had as much as a speeding ticket. I have shared the events of the accident, including a frank confession of my guilt, to many in the past years. Many of those I've shared with are young adults whose lives are heading down the same dead-end path mine was. I believe many lives have been changed, and I know a number of decisions for Christ have resulted.

Not that any of this will change your pain, but I trust it will help to know that much good has resulted from your father's death. I only wish my heart hadn't been so hardened to God back then that it took your father's death to change me. Again, I do seek your forgiveness and repent for the wrong I caused you. If I can be of any assistance to you and your family, financially or otherwise, please let me know.

According to Dr. Copeland, this letter "allowed Laurie to forgive something she was not able to deal with as a kid. Forgiveness is coupled with justice, and the first step of justice is understanding. The driver conveys to Laurie that he understands her pain."

Now she could let go of what ruled her life.

49
Dear John
Saying Good-Bye to Addiction

Everybody knows what a "Dear John" letter is—a farewell to a love affair. Although no one knows who the original jilted John was, the expression started during World War II, when soldiers received letters from the "girl back home" who had found another love. Maybe she tried to break it to him gently, acknowledging the good times, lamenting the particulars forcing her to break up, but at the same time it was a clean cut. It might be painful, but John knew where he stood—out in the cold.

From the Sender's Point of View

We usually think of farewell letters in terms of the poor bloke who receives one. Consider for a moment the sender's point of view. A Dear John is usually written after a great deal of agonizing soul-searching. The circumstances leading to the severance build over time. Making the decision to quit has tied up tremendous mental energy; writing it down releases that hold.

As with any other kind of scary message, there are decided advantages to putting it in writing. A letter can say words that are too hard to say out loud. You might be afraid that if you saw your former love face to face, you would lose your resolve—the emotional impact would be too large. The writer has, perhaps for months, wanted to end the relationship; in most cases, once the letter is delivered, it is truly over. If you are the writer, the Dear John letter is a way of distancing yourself, putting the decision out in front of you so it is no longer in your head.

Dear John to an Addiction

Armin Baier is the clinical director of the Parallax Center in Manhattan. One of his specialties is working with people in therapy for substance abuse.

Through treatment, his clients recognize their unhealthy relationship with drugs. Even then, it is hard for them to let go. Baier found that they needed some kind of an anchor to remind them of their resolve to live a clean life. One technique he finds useful is to guide the recovering addict through writing a letter of departure, saying good-bye to the drugs.

Baier points out certain advantages: "Most addicts are deeply ambiguous about stopping. What happens in a Dear John letter is that the addict is identifying with the part of themselves that wants to be clean.

"The chief advantage of the letter is that it *concretizes the stance.* That is the most valuable aspect of writing it down. It takes the part of him that wants to stop, that knows he must stop, and makes it real, puts it out in black and white, so to speak."

Just exactly like a letter breaking up a romance that has become destructive, it includes some of the traditional elements.

"It is a real Dear John letter, and as such it includes both anger and sentiment," says Baier. "It includes 'Dear John, This is what I hate that you did to me' and also 'These are the good times I hate to give up.' Every addict knows there were good times too. And lastly, 'These are the reasons I know I must give you up.' "

Dear Cocaine

As an example of the form, one of Baier's clients gave permission to publish his Dear John. "If it will help anyone else," he said, "I am glad to share it." I was struck by his generosity and touched by the resiliency and courage his letter reveals between the lines. Here is the letter, in its entirety, with only the names changed.

"Dear Cocaine," he begins, and then he goes back and with a caret amends it to:

Cruel

Dear ∧ Cocaine,

I don't know why I call you dear, so I'll add cruel.

Where are you or where were you when I needed you most?

You know I've never written to you before, so start plotting your next move. Or maybe you shouldn't. You see, I have nothing left. I'm not interesting to you anymore. Save the tears and go on to your next unsuspecting fool.

You know I loved you more than life itself. I thought of suicide when I couldn't have you.

Remember how you came into my life? It was Alice. Who thought I would have to choose between you two? But then you know that no man can love two women or serve two masters. I wanted to, and did for a while.

I cherished you and sacrificed everything I owned for you. My health, my family, Alice, my money, my car, my friends, and my dignity. But you cheated on me unmercifully. Everywhere I looked, you were pleasing another man, cheating on me in broad daylight.

This is how much I loved you: I fantasized about winning Lotto just so I could spend every waking minute with you.

Oh how you hated my friends and my family. You only would allow me into your closed evil society. You did not mind me hanging around with heroin, alcohol, and pills.

But now, despite your strongest wishes, I have friends who will help me stay away from you.

So now it's good-bye forever. Had you not been so cruel and expensive, I'd still be with you.

I warn you for the last time. Stay away from me. I hate you as much as I once loved you. Don't bother with me anymore—you won't like what you see. I'm not the same man you once knew and controlled.

Love <u>no more</u>,
David

Keep It Green

The very act of writing a Dear John letter to an addiction is incredibly freeing, but it also has an ongoing purpose. The letter is meant to be kept and reread. Although a Dear John alone is not enough to release an addict from the powerful pull of drugs, it can be part of the package.

When clients have impulses later to do drugs again, it helps them to reread the letter. In addition Baier tells them to call someone or start writing again:

" 'Make a phone call, talk to someone, or write. If you feel like using, start writing, do anything that concretizes your decision to stay away from drugs, that reminds you of the part of you that wants to stay clean.' "

According to Baier, "What you are doing by writing it down is connecting to the emotional reality."

Baier told me that members of Alcoholics Anonymous and other twelve-step programs sometimes speak of "keeping it green." To "keep it green" means to remember what the addiction was like, maybe by going to meetings and hearing someone new share their struggles.

Writing and rereading a Dear John letter is another way to "keep it green."

Now You

You could write a letter like this to any unhealthy obsession: a farewell to fat, *sayonara* to cigarettes, good-bye to gambling. Acknowledge the "high," the pleasure connected with the habit, and be clear about the pain and the price you pay to continue the relationship even after realizing it is harmful.

Spell it out plainly. You are no longer willing to continue this engagement. The price you are paying is not worth it anymore.

I want you out of my life.

Good-bye.

50
Remembering the Good Times

MY FRIEND SUELLEN AND I MET THROUGH A PROGRAM WE ARE both active in: introducing opera to schoolchildren. Suellen is a fourth-grade teacher, and I often see her at performances with her daughter, Amy, who is thirteen now, and her eager students flocking around her.

It was at a daylong seminar for *Ariadne auf Naxos* that we got to talking about writing and relationship. Suellen told me, "This year Amy and I wrote down all our favorite events that we could remember and who we did them with. We noticed who the people were who meant so much to us, and we wrote to thank them."

This game, combined with a journaling class that she was taking, led Suellen to an idea that was a breakthrough in her relationship with her mom. Their relationship had been strained for some time; rather than cut off communication altogether, Suellen started writing to her about how events of her daughter's day triggered memories of special times when Suellen was a child.

At the time she started this, Suellen and her mother had not talked on the phone for two years. An occasional exchange of cards on birthdays,

Mother's Day, and some holidays was their only contact. Not very deep. Suellen longed to be closer to her mom, but every time they spoke on the phone, it put her stomach in knots.

"Our communication verbally was totally broken down. You see, she never forgave me for moving out here. She expected that when I got divorced, home was where I'd go, back to Cincinnati. Instead, I chose to go far away with her only grandchild, which was completely unforgivable to her. I was drawn to the mountains; she knew that, because my whole life was always coming west, always.

"I said, 'Mom, I need to be my own person, I need to go to where my heart is being called. I feel this is the place for me.' Her spirit understood this, even though her head did not."

Writing and Remembering

Suellen enrolled in a journal-writing class for teachers and decided as her project to write to Amy about some of the memories she and Amy shared as mother and daughter, some of the special times she cherished between them. As she wrote these stories for Amy, she had the idea that maybe something similar could be a link between her and her own mom. When she wrote to Amy about shopping for new school shoes and how much fun she had doing it with her, she wrote a letter to her mom, first telling her about the scene with her and Amy and then tying it in to a similar memory of back-to-school shopping with her own mom.

Suellen calls it "writing and remembering."

"Each time I write to my mother, I tell her the joys of special times that I am sharing now with my own daughter, and then I connect it with some memory of her.

"The essence of it is that so many times you can't tell somebody something that you can write. She didn't realize that through these letters I was reaching for her. I was loving her in the only way I knew how. I couldn't find any other way to connect. I couldn't stay on the phone longer—or it would come, the 'Why don't you come home?' and I would feel miserable. These stories became a bridge, a way to tell her exactly where I am now."

The crucial element was not just the memories but the fact that Suellen related them to something in her present life. She wanted so much for her mom to see her as grown up but still rooted in happy memories of her own childhood.

"How many parents live away from their kids? Those parents often don't know how much they are still there. They are part of their children's lives forever.

"My dad died, but I talk to him all the time: 'Dad, are you glad I am doing this?' or 'Dad, are you mad at me for this?' This is a way of staying connected to him. It helps keep him alive.

"My mom is still alive, and I carry her with me too, even more so. I talk to her in my head, I see things the way she might see them. I appreciate what I learned from her.

"Writing little notes and letters to my mom was a way to say 'You are part of my life now and always will be. This is what I took with me when I moved away from home. I may be geographically distant, but you do not realize how much you are with me every day, as I recreate with my own daughter the traditions and the close times you and I shared.'

"As an example, I am going to the opera with Amy, and I write it up for Amy's book, and then I write to my mom and tell her how going to the opera with my daughter reminds me of the times when she and Dad took me to the opera. That was in the days before supertitles, so I wrote to her how I remember sitting in the back seat and my dad driving us, and her reading the opera to me so I would be prepared and follow the plot. I can see it as if it happened yesterday."

Suellen thinks of her mom while she is gardening. She suddenly has a vision of her on her hands and knees in her own garden, with Suellen as a child playing ball nearby. Now here is Suellen on *her* hands and knees in her garden, with her own daughter nearby. The sudden flash is so real. "I can even recall the conversation going on between the young me and my mom. Then I dig in the earth some more and remember how my mom felt about worms—she said, 'Yuck'; she was squeamish about them, but I always liked worms. So there's another remembrance to write to her."

When Suellen moved to her new house, she saw that the previous owner had planted roses in the front yard. Suellen considered digging them all up and transplanting them into the back yard. Then one day she was standing in her living room when a thought came to mind. She wrote her mom a short note:

I look out my front window and see you in the roses. Just like the roses you put on my cake when I was six.

This year the roses bloomed in time for Amy's birthday, and Suellen put them on her cake.

"My mother didn't like to fuss with icing, and she liked things to be 'natural'; she would cut the roses and put them in a glass of water in the middle of an angel food cake ring. So I did that for Amy this year and then took a picture to send to her."

Suellen decided to keep the roses in the front yard.

When Amy was eleven, Suellen moved to a new neighborhood.

"I was looking out at the woods behind the old house, and I was crying. I started to write in my journal to Amy about the sorrow of moving, and as I wrote, it all came back to me, what it was like to move when I was young. I was fourteen when my family moved to another suburb. I went back into the empty house, and I took a picture of every wall. And I wanted to leave a blessing behind, in every room, for those who would follow us.

"Now I can laugh about it, but I was serious, and it shows how even then it was hard for me to move. Even when I know I am moving on to something better.

"I sat down that evening and wrote to my mom."

It was one more way to make a connection.

"I was telling her, through an event that she had shared with me, what was going on with me now so she could see through my eyes now. Those childhood connections are with me as I do what I do now.

"I want my mom to hear my passion. Because it's what she gave me. It comes from her.

"I want her to see my life as I am. I want her to see how I feel about my daughter. I am trying to say, 'This must be how you felt about me.' All of us want respect from our parents. We want them to respect what we do with our lives. When I write to my mother with this dual vision, it gives her a chance to see me as me instead of as her child. I am a mother myself. She can see me as I feel—grown-up."

Many months after our conversation at the opera seminar, I called Suellen to ask how her campaign to reconnect with her mother was coming along. Suellen's voice was blissful.

"What can I say? All I can say is, 'It's working.' Do you know how long it has been? Put down the phone and cry for me—it's a miracle. After two years of no phone calls, to be able to talk to her! They're not long conversations, they're about ordinary things, they don't delve into emotional things, and she hasn't brought up my past, which is something she used to do."

Suellen had just returned from a conference called Art in Menucha, studying art on the Columbia River Gorge, in Portland, Oregon, surrounded by "the beauty of the scenery, the beauty of the people, the beauty of the art." This event was something she had planned for carefully, "mentally and physically, down to every detail," for a long time.

"Before I left, I had a phone conversation with my mother. I decided to call and tell her I was going, and I told her I was taking with me a sweatshirt that she had given me. I told her the sweatshirt was a symbol of the talent she had, combined with my courage, and it would give me strength to have it with me. She answered, 'You don't need my talent; you have all your own.' "

It stunned Suellen to hear that. It was the most positive thing her mother had ever said to her. She had never known that her mother thought she was talented.

"I took that one sentence with me and wrapped it around me like a cloak. I said it over and over again during the two weeks.

"I am convinced that the letters I have been writing her opened her up to be able to say that to me."

Coming back from Oregon, Suellen decided to call her again.

"You have to understand, I never call her. I dread talking to her on the phone. These two phone calls were the only two times I have spoken to her all year, and both of them were miracles.

"My mother is a fabulous artist, very gifted, wonderful stuff—and all of it is hidden in the basement. All that passion, all that beauty, locked up. She won't let anybody see it.

"I meditated to get the courage to call again, and after describing my experience at the art retreat in glowing terms, I tentatively said, 'Maybe you should do something like this yourself.' And she heard me! She received it openly.

"These breakthroughs are like miracles. I directly attribute them to the writing class where I decided my project would be letters to Amy, and the letters that followed that I wrote to my mom. That was the catalyst."

Pachysandra, Parcel Post

The other day, Suellen called me, animated with excitement. She had just received an unexpected gift in the mail.

"My mother sent me a huge box of pachysandra, with plastic bags and wet paper towels around all of the stems to keep them wet and comfortable, for me to root and put in my garden. Isn't that incredible?"

Pachysandra, Suellen explains, is a ground cover that is about six or eight inches tall; some parts of the country call it spurge.

"This came right after you and I talked, and I was focusing on my gardening and remembering her garden and my talks with her.

"The wonderful part about it is that she is not into packing things up. She had taken it down and had one of those services do it—she made the cuttings and found a way to get them to me. I was overwhelmed with joy, I couldn't believe it. I took the risk of picking up the phone to thank her, and we had an amazing conversation; I giggled the whole time, focusing on the pachysandras and how adorable they were.

"When I was growing up, she was always teasing me because I could never spell *pachysandra,* so I told her, 'I know how to spell it now, so I'm sure it's going to grow great roots.' She laughed! This is the mother who used to send my college letters back to me corrected."

It takes courage to do what Suellen has done, not only her persistence, her refusal to give up, but even more, her willingness to start, to make the first step, to let go of the grudge.

"It's true, you have to get past all your hate, all the words that come pouring in that make you so mad, and also get rid of the old ways of how you 'used to.' You know—you *used to* pick up the phone and call your mom and then get mad and hang up because it was another horrible call. Stop doing that! Find a new way. The new way for me was writing. And you can't just write any old thing: you have to find a new way of writing. It was writing for Amy that helped me remember; I wrote to myself first, and it linked with my past. The writing helped me to remember, and that's the whole point."

Suellen concludes, "It is worthwhile to do this. It sounds dramatic, but I would sum it up by saying, Writing about the good times gave life back to a relationship that was dead."

Farewell

KATHERINE WAS ONLY EIGHT WHEN SHE OVERHEARD ME TALKING with a friend of mine about notes. I was brainstorming some ideas for an article that later became the basis for one of the chapters in this book. That night as I crawled into bed exhausted, I found a small square of paper on my pillow underneath the spread:

Mom, I lov you slep well don't let the bed bugs bight. Love, Katherine.

I slept well indeed, with a feeling of peace and contentment. I felt wrapped in a protective cocoon, as though an angel held me in her wings. Next morning, I opened my drawer—a note from Katherine was in with my stockings, an oval note on blue paper that read,

#1 Author the Best in the World

I checked with the rest of the family; they were all abuzz. An elf had been through as we slept and sprinkled pixie dust on us all.

"Did you get one too?"

"I found this in my hairbrush."

"This was in my laundry basket."

She had written ten little notes, two for each of us, not more than a sentence apiece:

Dad, you look nice in your new clothes.

Peter, thanks for reading to me.

and hidden them, one to find at night, one to uncover in the morning.

have a good day

make someone smile

The whole family felt close that day. That magic powder Katherine sprinkled was like a giant can of MSG tenderizing us all, making us more gentle toward each other and kinder all day to the people we met along our separate ways. An eight-year-old had done that for us, had made our world for a little while a brighter place to be, and because of it the people we came in contact with were made a little bit brighter too.

Katherine is eleven now, and she is still hiding notes. Yesterday I turned over a page in a manuscript section I was editing to find—

> *Mom*
> *Good luck*
> *on your book*
> *you spunky*
> *Lady*
> *Love*
> *Katherine*

In a single stroke my work environment changed. I grinned to myself. See? This stuff works.

I read a day-brightener in a Spokane paper. The reporter was at the bus stop. It was rainy and cold. Everyone was glum or at best preoccupied. Another dreary day. Trudge along. Turn your collar to the cold and damp. A woman came along with a baby bundled up in her arms and stood there in the rain for a moment, as grim as her fellow passengers. Then unexpectedly, the baby let out a little happy sound—"a vowel sound," the reporter called it. People looked up and smiled, smiled at the mom, smiled at each other, and smiled inside. The sound triggered a response that for a moment lifted the gloom. Katherine's notes are like that; they make me smile. Something shifts, feels different, just as being in the room with a high-energy person can charge you up because it charges up the room, changes some say the molecular structure in the air around you.

After a fight between them, Emily wrote Katherine a letter. Emily didn't want me to read it, and Katherine respected that. ("She didn't even want *me* to read it, and it's written to me.") Katherine sat on the front stoop and read it to herself. I could tell she was touched.

She wrote a note back to Emily:

Thanks for the letter. It made me look at myself in a different way.
It also made me
want to hug you!

Love,
Katherine

(The "dot" on the end of the exclamation point was a little heart.)

Now You

Putting your heart on paper can change the molecular structure of the world you live in. If an eight-year-old can do it, so can you.

ABOUT THE AUTHOR

James Arrabito

Henriette Anne Klauser is the president of Writing Resources and author of the best-selling book *Writing on Both Sides of the Brain.* She is a workshop leader on the topics of overcoming writing anxiety, creativity, and relationship-building. She received her doctorate from Fordham University and has taught at the University of Washington, Seattle University, California State University, University of Lethbridge (Canada), and Fordham. Her business clients include Fortune 500 companies like Boeing, Weyerhaeuser, Xerox, Hershey Foods (she had to be restrained from jumping into a vat of chocolate), and Armstrong World Industries. She is a professional member of the National Speakers Association and addresses trade associations, universities, and government agencies. Her workshops have taken her around the world, including to Cairo, Egypt, and the island of Skyros in Greece.

You may contact Henriette by writing to:

Henriette Klauser, Ph.D.
Writing Resources
P.O. Box 1555
Edmonds, WA 98020

or e-mail, henriette @ aol.com.